Religion in the
Contemporary World

For Meryl Aldridge

Religion in the Contemporary World

A Sociological Introduction

ALAN ALDRIDGE

polity

Copyright © Alan Aldridge 2000

The right of Alan Aldridge to be identified as author of this work has been asserted in accordance with the Copyright, Designs and Patents Act 1988.

First published in 2000 by Polity Press in association with Blackwell Publishing Ltd.

Reprinted 2001, 2003

Editorial office:
Polity Press
65 Bridge Street
Cambridge CB2 1UR, UK

Published in the USA by
Blackwell Publishing Inc.
350 Main Street
Malden, MA 02148, USA

Marketing and production:
Blackwell Publishing Ltd
108 Cowley Road
Oxford OX4 1JF, UK

A catalogue record for this book is available from the British Library.

Library of Congress Cataloging-in-Publication Data
Aldridge, Alan (Alan E.).
   Religion in the contemporary world : a sociological
introduction / Alan Aldridge.
       p.   cm.
   Includes bibliographical references and index.
   ISBN 0-7456-2082-5 (alk. paper)
   ISBN 0-7456-2083-3 (alk. paper)
   1. Religion and sociology.   I. Title.
   BL60.A53   2000
   306.6—dc21   99-26047
                                                           CIP

Typeset in 10.5 on 12 pt Times by Ace Filmsetting Ltd, Frome, Somerset
Printed in Great Britain by MPG Books Ltd, Bodmin, Cornwall

This book is printed on acid-free paper

For further information on polity, please visit our website: http//www.polity.co.uk

Contents

Acknowledgements

Every effort has been made to trace the copyright holders but, if any have been inadvertently overlooked, the publishers will be pleased to make the necessary arrangements at the first opportunity.

Although no one apart from myself bears any responsibility for the content of this book, many people have helped by their teaching, research, and acts of kindness and encouragement. My introduction to the sociology of religion was through the work and example of Bryan Wilson; I join many other sociologists in owing him an enormous debt of gratitude. Members of the British Sociological Association's Sociology of Religion Study Group have been helpful in more ways than they know. I should like to thank them all for their support, and in particular Jim Beckford, Grace Davie, Kieran Flanagan, Mike Hornsby-Smith, Peter Jupp, David Martin, Denise Newton and Sarah Potter. My colleague Russell McKinlay taught me about Quakers. Joan Chandler has been most encouraging; she is a discerning reader, so I hope she enjoys the book. I should also like to thank Eileen Barker, a stimulating thinker and a great source of encouragement. I am grateful to Ernest, Elsie and Marjorie Aldridge for their healthy attitude to the subject of this book. I owe more than I can say to Meryl Aldridge, to whom the book is dedicated.

1

Studying Religion Sociologically

Any study of the sociology of contemporary religion needs to address two basic questions. First, is religion worth studying? Second, can sociology add to our knowledge about religion? This book is geared to answering those two questions. It does not assume, but aims to show, that religion is important and that sociology enhances our understanding of it.

Religion – worth our continued attention?

One reason why the study of religion in the modern world is a problem for sociologists is that the sociology of religion has been dominated by a debate about the secularization thesis. Although, as with any key term, there are deep disagreements about the meaning of secularization, for the moment we may adopt Wilson's (1966: xiv) concise definition: 'the process by which religious thinking, practice and institutions lose social significance'.

This definition, and the theories of secularization which lie behind it, are profoundly challenging to the status of religion as an object of study. First, if we accept that religious thinking, practice and institutions have been in decline for centuries, is there anything left? Surely religion is simply withering away, as the Bolshevik revolutionaries, inspired by the work of Karl Marx and Friedrich Engels, believed to be inevitable? Second, the process is often presented as irreversible. Hopes for an uplift in religion's fortunes are said to be misplaced, and the facts are correctly labelled 'statistics of decline'. Third, secularization is seen as a universal phenomenon affecting all advanced societies. Countries of the Third World will find, whether they wish it or not, that modernization will inevitably bring secularization.

Finally, the loss of social significance means the potential loss of everything that is significant. Religion may survive for a while in the recesses of social life, as a source of meaning and comfort to individual believers, but it no longer shapes the social, cultural, economic or political destiny of any modern industrial society. If that is so, it may not be long before religion loses even the role of comforting individuals.

Perhaps it is this last point, above all others, which accounts for the view held by some sociologists that the sociology of religion is a backwater of no interest to those who navigate the main river. 'Religion – where the action isn't?' was one sociologist's memorable query (Eldridge 1980). Religion tends to be seen as an epiphenomenon, that is to say an effect rather than a cause, with no independent impact of its own. On this view the most religion can offer is a gloss of legitimacy to institutions that can increasingly do without it.

Here, then, is a striking paradox: in accepting the secularization thesis, the sociology of religion appears to be cutting the ground from under its own feet. No other field of sociology does this.

However, not all sociologists accept the full-blown secularization thesis, as we shall see in chapter 5. Objections to it include the following.

First, it appears to assume a 'golden age' of religion, or sometimes 'golden ages', located, so far as Christianity is concerned, in the early church, the Middle Ages and the nineteenth century. Arguably, the religiosity of those periods has been greatly overstated in order to point a contrast with an exaggeratedly secular present. In the past many people went to church and obeyed its authority not because they were devout but because they had no choice.

The contrast between the Middle Ages and the modern world has been characterized as a transition from *religious culture* to *religious faith* (Sommerville 1992). In the medieval period, religion was not something to think about, but a mode of thinking as basic as our understanding of time and space. Culture was so steeped in religious conceptions and preoccupations that atheism and agnosticism were scarcely possible. All knowledge was religious knowledge. By the beginning of the eighteenth century, well before the Industrial Revolution, this hegemonic religious culture had dissolved. What had replaced it was religious faith. Religion became a matter of reasoned and self-aware affirmations of personal belief and commitment. This was true not only of Protestantism but also of Counter-Reformation Catholicism.

How should this transformation be interpreted? Does it represent religion's loss of social significance, as some secularization theorists have argued? Or has modernity set religion free to transform the hearts and minds of ordinary people, giving them real choice instead of the chill compulsion of subservience to the authority of the church?

A second objection to the secularization thesis is that it pays too much attention to formal religious organizations. They have indeed lost social functions. But this is differentiation, not secularization. Differentiation does not equate to the decline of religion. Rather, it entails division of labour and specialization of function. Activities which were carried out by one social institution are parcelled out among several. Thus, in the west, the churches have lost much of their influence and responsibility for education and the law. Similarly, economic production and formal education are no longer the sole or prime responsibility of family units. In Talcott Parsons's theory of social change, societies, like biological organisms, evolve from simple to complex forms through the process of differentiation. His account of the evolution of Christianity is one in which society becomes more religious rather than less: its moral standards are higher and it is more in accord with Christian values than any previous society.

'Believing without belonging' is one apt way of characterizing the persistence of the sacred despite the decline of churchgoing (Davie 1994: 93–116). Latent religiosity survives as a resource to be mobilized at times of crisis in the lives of individuals or the history of the society.

Third, nothing is allowed to count against the secularization thesis. All the evidence, it is said, is reinterpreted to fit the theory. Ecumenical co-operation between denominations and faiths is a product of their weakness, and merely accelerates the process of decline. Regeneration movements within faiths, such as charismatic renewal, are shallow and disruptive. Attempts by religious leaders to accommodate faith to the canons of modernity are self-defeating, and simply invite secularism into the sacred sphere. The growth of sects and cults is a doomed protest against the secular world by marginal minority groups. Religious conflicts in Northern Ireland and elsewhere are not really religious at all. The apparent prosperity of Christianity in the United States conceals the fact that it has been secularized from within. The collapse of communism means that religion no longer serves as a symbol of national identity in protest against grim communist regimes and their Soviet backers. The resurgence of Islam is a temporary stage of social development and will be surpassed as modernization proceeds.

Far from showing the truth of the secularization thesis, this treatment of evidence perhaps demonstrates that what we are dealing with is not a testable scientific theory at all, but an anti-religious ideology – one which dogmatically protects itself against the force of any evidence whatsoever.

This allegation of ideologically motivated hostility raises the question of the relationship between social science and the truth claims of religions. We can distinguish four basic ways in which sociologists have approached these truth claims. As ever, the reality is complex, which means that in practice the four approaches are not so sharply distinguished. They are presented below as 'ideal types': intellectual constructs or models which simplify the messiness of empirical reality.

Reductionism: explaining religion away

Contemporary sociology inherited a reductionist legacy from the great thinkers of the nineteenth and early twentieth century who pioneered the development of the discipline. They were not all hostile to religion, as Marx was. Many, like Emile Durkheim, saw it as fulfilling necessary social functions. Nevertheless, the majority were atheists. According to them, religion as a cognitive system for understanding the world would give way to science, including the science of sociology.

The reductionist position explains religion as being 'really' something else: for Marx, an ideology legitimating class oppression; for Freud, an obsessional neurosis; for Durkheim, society worshipping itself. Reductionism is often offensive to the faithful and is sometimes meant to be so.

Comparing the analyses of these three social theorists shows some of the different strands to be found within reductionism. To Marx, religion is an ideological system necessary to the maintenance of class oppression but destined to wither away once the classless society is achieved. Religion is degrading and dehumanizing. Although atheism has been proved true at the level of philosophical argument, that is not sufficient to bring about social change. It is through the revolutionary activity of the secularized proletariat that an atheistic classless society will be attained, liberating the human spirit from the fetters of ideology.

Sigmund Freud's atheism is pessimistic and stoical rather than joyous. For him, religion is an obsessional neurosis in which people regress to an infantile state of dependency on a projected father figure, God. Dispensing with God, however uncomfortable, is necessary to full maturity as a human being. Freud equated religion with empty consolation and science with informed resignation (Rieff 1965: 298). He acted out this stoicism in his own life. It is not just that he did not turn to God. He died in London in 1939, having fled Austria the previous year when Hitler invaded. Freud had suffered for sixteen years from cancer of the palate, and had undergone more than thirty operations. His biographer Ernest Jones described in chilling clinical detail the circumstances of Freud's last days, during which he refused despite excruciating agony to take any painkilling drugs until just before he died.

For Durkheim, religion fulfilled essential functions in society. In his quotable formula, religion is society worshipping itself. Although religious beliefs are invalid, religion is an authentic expression of human sociality. In Durkheim's mind, this meant that religion was not founded on an illusion, as it was for Freud. The reality of religion is not God but Society – and society is all too real. The problem as Durkheim saw it was to devise a viable substitute for religion which would fulfil its social functions on a scientific basis.

Sociography: sociology at the service of religion

One view of the relation between sociology and religion is that sociology should limit itself to examining the social context of belief rather than its content. This is a position adopted by some conservative theologians, for whom the faith cannot be arrived at by human deduction from logic or induction from experience. Instead, the faith is divinely revealed. What religious leaders often expect from sociologists is not sociological analysis but factual data about the social context in which their church finds itself. Theologians are seldom discontented with this division of labour, since it leaves their discipline intact.

To most professional sociologists, however, this is not sociology but sociography. Sociography is at most a preliminary stage in sociological analysis. It involves the collection and correlation of raw data about social life, for example mapping patterns of church attendance by region, age, social class and similar variables. What sociography does *not* do is subject the data to theoretical analysis. In the case of religion, the sociographic approach is careful to respect the boundary around divinely revealed truth. In practice, this entails deferring to the religious authorities.

Probably the leading example of a sociographic approach to the study of religion was the 'religious sociology' of the French sociologist Gabriel le Bras (1891–1970) and his colleagues (Willaime 1995: 40–5). Anglo-Saxon commentators (M. Hill 1973: 9–11; Robertson 1970: 10) have been generally lukewarm about his work, while acknowledging its significance for the development of sociology of religion in France.

Le Bras rejected Durkheim's theories. He did not aim to explain the supernatural or transcendent. For him, the mysteries of the Christian faith were given to humankind by God. Le Bras' work and that of his colleagues turned away from grand theories of religion towards detailed empirical studies of 'the religion of the people'. He concentrated on Roman Catholicism, and on levels of participation in church life. This focus meshed well with the concerns of the Catholic hierarchy in France, who were preoccupied with falling church attendance after the end of the Second World War. Le Bras' emphasis on religious practice as the key variable corresponded to the Catholic emphasis on attendance at mass as a religious obligation.

Names are symbols, and symbols matter; so it is worth saying that the labels 'religious sociology' and 'religious sociologist' are not acceptable to most sociologists of religion as a characterization of our work or ourselves. Unfairly or otherwise, they have come to imply subservience to ecclesiastical authorities and their organizationally driven priorities. In response to these concerns within France itself, le Bras and his colleagues founded an influential research centre in 1954 with the title 'Groupe de Sociologie des Religions', as a clear signal of their intention to 'deconfessionalize' their approach and to encompass all religions within it.

Phenomenology: apprehending religious meaning

Phenomenology has had an important influence on the sociology of religion. The phenomenologist aims to apprehend, describe and analyse the states of consciousness of people in their everyday life, their *Lebenswelt* or life-world. Since we tend to take the life-world for granted, the phenomenologist's task is to bring it to our attention, showing the subtlety and complexity of the human activity that makes it up. To do this, judgements about social forces and social structures are suspended or 'bracketed off'. Instead of seeing humans as the passive carriers or playthings of social forces, the phenomenologist stresses that we are conscious agents who actively, knowingly and skilfully create our life-world. Our actions have meaning, which we produce in the course of interacting with one another. This is a sociological version of the philosophical defence of free will against determinism.

In the sociology of religion, one leading exponent of a phenomenological approach is Peter Berger. For him, 'religion is the human enterprise by which a sacred cosmos is established' (Berger 1967: 34). Following Durkheim, Berger characterizes the sacred as 'a quality of mysterious and awesome power, other than man [*sic*] and yet related to him, which is believed to reside in certain objects of experience' (1967: 34). Anything can be held sacred: a city – Jerusalem; a river – the Ganges; a building – the Golden Temple at Amritsar; a person – Christ; a word – the unutterable name of God; a time – Ramadan; a rock – Uluru, also known as Ayer's Rock. The sacred order confronts us as an immensely powerful reality. Again following Durkheim, the opposite of the sacred is the profane: the mundane, functional material and routines necessary to staying alive and making a living.

The crucial point Berger adds to the Durkheimian approach is that the sacred is opposed not only to the profane but also to chaos. Chaos is a random jumble of events without meaning. Significantly, many religions have creation stories in which a god or the gods create the universe out of chaos. Religion supplies us with ultimate meaning in the face of chaos and its human embodiment in death. Religion for Berger is 'the audacious attempt to conceive of the entire universe as being humanly significant' (1967: 37).

Berger and also his collaborator Thomas Luckmann emphasize the cognitive dimension of religion: it provides us with concepts and categories of thought through which we can find meaning in and therefore understand the existential problems of life, joy, suffering and death. Berger and Luckmann assume that all of us, by virtue of our common humanity, share these existential concerns.

This phenomenologically inspired sociology of religion faces a number of objections. It has been characterized as 'cognitive reductionism' (Turner 1991: 245), since it allegedly places too much emphasis on the subjective meaning of religion. It also posits a common culture shared by all. Turner argues that we should recognize that religious concerns are socially stratified. So, while it may be that existential problems do impinge on us all, they tend to have highest salience for the intellectual strata of society.

In his widely read *A Rumour of Angels*, Berger (1971) advances what appear to be sociological arguments for the existence of God. He claims that within everyday social life we can find 'signals of transcendence'. These phenomena are part of our worldly reality but 'appear to point beyond that reality'. Berger says that we do not need depth psychology to excavate these signals of transcendence from our unconscious mind; they are not Jungian archetypes. Nor is he thinking of mystical religious experiences, cultivated by spiritual virtuosi and not readily accessible to everyone. Signals of transcendence occur in the everyday experience of common humanity, and become apparent when we reflect on that experience.

Berger suggests five signals which point to a transcendent realm.

The argument from ordering asks us to reflect on such actions as a mother reassuring her child that a nightmare is not real and that all is well. The parent, Berger says, is not lying to her child: all is indeed well, and the child is right to trust the mother's assurance about the order of reality. The final truth is not terror. Freud was wrong: religion is not a childish fantasy. 'Thus man's ordering propensity implies a transcendent order, and each ordering gesture is a signal of this transcendence.'

The argument from play is that the joy experienced in play – the suspension of the mundane structures of time which govern our humdrum 'serious' activities – points beyond itself to an eternal timeless order.

The argument from hope is based on the fundamental human rejection of death, our own and that of our loved ones, as the end. Stoical acceptance is not mature and hope is not childish; in Dylan Thomas's words, 'death shall have no dominion'.

The argument from damnation is that monstrous evils such as the Nazis' crimes against humanity cry out to heaven for divine retribution. These are crimes which no human punishment can fit. 'Deeds which cry out to heaven also cry our for hell', and for punishment which passes human understanding. Faced with such horror, we suspend any personal or professional commitment we have to relativism and scientific detachment. A dehumanized variant of scientific detachment was mobilized by the Nazis in perpetrating their abominations. The easygoing relativist ethical principle, when in Rome do as the Romans do, does not extend to: when in Auschwitz do as the SS did. Thus damnation, like hope, is an aspect of the transcendent vindication that human life has meaning and purpose.

The argument from humour is that comedy arises from a discrepancy between human beings and the universe in which we live. Reflecting the imprisonment of our spirit in this world, humour and the comic point to the spirit's liberation in the world to come. The final word lies not with the dogged realism of Cervantes' Sancho Panza, but with the vision of his comic creation Don Quixote.

The fact that Berger produced *five* arguments was no doubt deliberate. Numbers, like names, are symbols. His arguments are a sociological counterpart to the medieval theologian Saint Thomas Aquinas's *Quinque Viae*, the Five Ways of proving the existence of God from the evidence of the natural world. Whereas Aquinas pointed to the natural world, Berger focused on the social. His arguments draw on the everyday experiences of all of us. The book implicitly challenges theologians to ground their work in empirical data taken from everyday life.

But how do these signals of transcendence relate to the practice of sociology? Sociologists rarely see themselves as being in the business of proving or disproving the existence of God. Nor was Berger doing so. His arguments may or may not be persuasive, but they involve a leap of faith and are not proofs. Berger was stepping outside the discipline of sociology to make them. Perhaps his main point is that they are neither more nor less valid than the disproofs of God advanced by the reductionists.

Many contemporary sociologists of religion have a religious faith. Unless they also have a split personality, they may be expected to show some respect for the integrity and authenticity of the religious phenomena they study. In this spirit, the social anthropologist Ernest Evans-Pritchard (1965: 120–1) suggested that in evaluating any theory of religion we should ask whether it helps us to understand our own religious life. If the answer is no, we have a good reason for being sceptical about it; for any theory which 'explains' other people's faith but not our own is a piece of ethnocentric arrogance. Evidently, this test can be applied only by people who have a religious faith. However, some definitions of religion are so inclusive, so general and all-embracing, that they imply that every human being is religious. Although these definitions have been heavily criticized, they have the advantage that Evans-Pritchard's test forces every one of us – atheists, agnostics and believers alike – to apply to other people's faith the same standards we do to our own.

Sociology as a value-neutral science

Sociology may be constituted as a value-neutral social science which has nothing whatever to say either for or against the truth claims of religion. This position, supremely expressed in the work of Max Weber, is the dominant one in the contemporary sociology of religion. It is also the position adopted in this book.

At first glance, a value-neutral sociology may appear less problematic than the positions discussed above. Abstaining from value-judgements may sound more acceptable than explaining religion away or endorsing the perspective of the faithful. Judgements of value are not the province of the sociologist, whose task is to analyse religion dispassionately as a social phenomenon. Even so, it would be a mistake to see value-neutral sociology as a bland middle way between two stimulating extremes. Owing to its profound relativism and universalism, the value-neutral sociology of religion is acutely challenging. The Weberian view of sociology, as Turner points out (1991: 16–17), is at odds with hermeneutical and phenomenological approaches, which seek to understand the human experience of the transcendent. In so doing, they give priority to the believer's frame of reference and definition of reality. What matters in these approaches is to apprehend and convey the believer's experience of such devotional acts as contemplation, prayer and worship.

Sociology aspires to a universal frame of reference. Hence the sociology of religion is the study of all religions. Sociological theories of religion and sociological classifications of religious movements aim to be all-embracing. They are not in accord with the sentiments expressed by Mr Thwackum, a character in Henry Fielding's novel *Tom Jones* (1749): 'When I mention religion, I mean the Christian religion; and not only the

Christian religion, but the Protestant religion; and not only the Protestant religion, but the Church of England.'

In the sociological enterprise, hierarchies of status and prestige between religions are not observed. Anglicans do not take precedence over Christadelphians; the Bible, the Qur'an and the Book of Mormon are all sacred texts; Sun Myung Moon is no less Lord of the Second Advent than Jesus Christ is Son of God. This relativism, though shocking to some, is of the essence of value-neutral sociology. It is comparative religion with a vengeance.

As a scholarly discipline, comparative religion focuses almost exclusively on 'major world religions'. Nowadays this always includes Buddhism, Christianity, Judaism, Hinduism and Islam – which we may note, sociologically, share the common feature that they have the backing of at least one powerful nation state. Analysis may also extend to other world faiths, those which have an established footing within a nation-state, for example the Jain and Sikh faiths, with their long history on the Indian subcontinent. Very little is said about so-called 'sects' and 'cults' such as Christian Science, Jehovah's Witnesses, Scientology and Seventh-day Adventism. Neither their theology nor their spiritual practices nor their worldly commitments are given serious attention.

Theologically, minority religions are not usually accepted as part of the legitimate mainstream. Many of them do not wish to co-operate ecumenically with other religious movements, even the most socially respectable. This is no doubt the main reason for their neglect by comparative religion. They are simply not believed to make a significant contribution to the mainstream of religious thought, practice and experience. As a test of this, we may ask: who, apart from Mormons themselves, reads the Book of Mormon, and who reads *The Divine Principle* apart from Moonies? Yet both these works are claimed to be divine revelations bringing the Christian faith to fruition – rather as Christianity claims to be the fulfilment of the Jewish faith, and Islam the fulfilment of them both.

Minority religious movements are often unpopular and politically controversial. They have few friends in positions of authority and lack the backing of any nation state. They are therefore vulnerable to discrimination and persecution. Unlike comparative religion, the sociology of religion has given close attention to them. Sociologists' value-neutral approach has earned them the reputation of being 'soft' on 'the cults' or even in their pay. What many people are looking for is not value-neutral analysis but condemnation. They point to disasters such as Jonestown and Waco, arguing that the drive to self-destruction is an inherent feature of all cults. People who have left cults often present us with firsthand stories of brainwashing and mind control. Minority religious movements face a wide range of accusations, including preying on vulnerable people, brainwashing them, breaking up families, creating childlike dependence, raising money by false pretences, and tax evasion. Some movements are said to be not really religions at all: their religious claims are a cover for their true purposes, such as economic gain, political influence, or sexual exploitation of their own members. If sociologists cast any doubt on these accusations they are themselves accused of being fellow travellers.

The animosity new religions can arouse, and the anathema pronounced on 'fundamentalism', may be signs that the modern world is not entirely secure in its supposed secularity.

Carrying the sociological tradition forward

'A science that hesitates to forget its founders is lost.' This view, advocated by the philosopher A. N. Whitehead, has some merit. Sociology, like any academic discipline, can mutate into a form of ancestor-worship, a cult in which the same old story is recited over and over again in a litany designed to socialize the young and comfort their elders.

At times the sociology of religion has exactly this quality. Core themes become all too familiar and repetitious: inclusive versus exclusive definitions of religion; the secularization debate; churches, sects, denominations and cults as types of religious movement. If we are not careful, the world and the rest of sociology will pass us by, leaving us preaching sociology of religion to the converted – a dwindling band of true believers stranded on Dover beach like the poet Matthew Arnold, contemplating the 'melancholy, long, withdrawing roar' of the sea of (sociological) faith.

The temptation is to cut through all this and start from scratch, relaunching the sociology of religion as a new movement with a new mission. We discover startling things to study – the body is currently in vogue – and abandon the hard-won understandings generated by careful empirical research, replacing them by dazzling theories concocted by postmodernist literary critics. Some of this 'theorizing' deserves Ernest Gellner's label: 'metatwaddle'.

A cure may be worse than the problem it purports to solve. Far better to build on the past, adapting the discipline to new developments in sociological theory and in the society it seeks to comprehend. In this book the core debates that have characterized the sociology of religion are not ignored but addressed. At the same time, I have tried to place them in a social context, which means in a context of power. So, the question of defining religion is vitally important to social movements themselves, some of which have every reason for desiring the label while others equally strongly oppose it.

The secularization debate is important but not all-important; there are other questions worth asking, and the secularization thesis should not be allowed to blind us to them. Classifying religious movements, if treated as an end in itself, is utterly futile, but becomes meaningful if it enables us to draw important distinctions between movements and their likely trajectory. People are justifiably interested in knowing which movements pose a threat either to their own members or to the wider society.

None of the answers we can offer will ever be definitive. Society changes, and sociology has to change with it. Religion is dynamic, and has the capacity perpetually to surprise us.

2

Defining Religion: Social Conflicts and Sociological Debates

What is religion? How can we distinguish authentic religion from substitutes or imitations? What part does religion play in the lives of individual believers and society as a whole? These questions have been discussed down the centuries by theologians and philosophers, and more recently by social scientists – anthropologists, psychologists and sociologists.

Answers to the questions can have fateful consequences for the believers themselves. Two cases will illustrate this. The first is a movement which has grown rapidly in many countries, but has also been unpopular and controversial: Scientology. The second case – the Baha'i faith – raises no problems in western liberal democracies, where Baha'is are seen, in so far as they are noticed at all, as tolerant, peace-loving people who value education and give equal rights and status to women and men. In parts of the Muslim world, in contrast, the Baha'is are treated as heretics.

Scientology: authentic religion or imposture?

Scientology grew out of the therapeutic system called Dianetics, which was developed by L. Ron Hubbard (Ron to his followers) and canvassed by him in the May 1950 issue of *Astounding Science Fiction*, before publication in book form as *Dianetics: the Modern Science of Mental Health*. Dianetics involves a therapeutic relationship between an *auditor* and the individual – the *preclear* – undergoing the therapy. The auditor asks a series of questions, and the responses given by the preclear are registered on an *E-Meter*, a skin galvanometer similar to a lie-detector. The readings on the E-Meter enable the auditor to identify areas of stress caused by *engrams*, traumatic experiences typically in early childhood which the preclear has repressed into his or her subconscious *reactive mind*. The aim of auditing is to release the preclear from the harmful effect of these accumulated engrams by erasing them from the reactive mind, thus enabling the subject to 'go clear'. A *clear* enjoys enhanced powers, such as higher IQ, better memory, and improved mental and physical health.

Scientology built a complex cosmological and metaphysical system on the basis of Dianetics. Human beings are in essence spiritual entities, *thetans*. Immortal, omniscient and omnipotent, thetans created the universe – made up of *MEST* (Matter, Energy, Space and Time) – but foolishly became trapped in their own creation as they deliberately shed their powers, eventually forgetting their own origins and status as thetans. Thetans have occupied innumerable bodies during the aeons that have elapsed since the creation of MEST. The techniques of Scientology enable the thetan to recover its lost powers by elimination of the reactive mind, so that the thetan can be *at cause*, that is able to determine the course of events.

The development of Scientology from Dianetics had two crucial elements. First, Scientology adopted a centralized authority structure. Dianetics had been relatively free and easy: if a particular technique worked for you, fine – the customer was always right. As a result, a number of practitioners launched independently their own alternative versions of Dianetics, thus threatening the authority of Ron himself. Ron responded to this by developing a bureaucratic hierarchy and an internal system of discipline, designed to prevent the emergence of rival sources of authority within the movement.

Second, Scientology increasingly defined itself as a religion. Greater emphasis was given to ritual, ministry, ethics, creed, and similarities to the philosophical systems of Asian religions. Alternative practitioners and their followers were transformed into *heretics*.

In its short history, Scientology has been caught up in a series of clashes with the authorities in several countries. One of the earliest signs of the conflicts to come was in 1958, when the US Food and Drug Administration seized, analysed and then destroyed supplies of Dianazene, a compound which had been claimed to be effective in preventing and treating radiation sickness.

Publication in Australia in 1965 of the report of a National Board of Inquiry, chaired by Kevin V. Anderson, gave rise to hostile media coverage and government-sponsored investigations into Scientology in many parts of the English-speaking world. Anderson condemned Scientology as an evil system which posed a grave threat to family life and to the mental health of vulnerable people. In the wake of this, the Australian authorities banned the practice of Scientology. In 1968, the UK government decided that foreign nationals would cease to be eligible for admission to the UK to study at or work for Scientology establishments; many were deported.

Throughout these turbulent years, the Church of Scientology has continued to affirm its identity as a religion, and has frequently taken its case to court in an effort to assert its legal rights and to qualify for the tax concessions granted in many countries to recognized religions.

One country, however, in which the Church of Scientology has so far failed is the Federal Republic of Germany (Boyle and Sheen 1997: 312–14). The German authorities regard Scientology as a threat to the democratic principles on which the state was founded after the defeat of Nazism. The Weimar Republic, which collapsed in 1933 when Hitler became Chancellor, is judged to have been suicidal. In particular, Weimar politicians were too relaxed about democratic liberties and too indulgent towards undemocratic elements such as the National Socialists who cynically exploited the very freedoms they would then destroy. The Federal Republic is not about to repeat this self-destruction, but will be robust in its own defence. It takes firm measures to prevent what it sees as attempted Scientological infiltration of public agencies and private industry and commerce. Some German companies have dissociated themselves from Scientology so that their business will not suffer. Scientologists experience widespread discrimination, ostracism and intolerance. Above all, Scientology is denied the status of a religion. The prevailing official view is that Scientology's religious claims are bogus on two counts. First, they are no more than a smokescreen for the movement's lucrative commercial activities. Scientology's therapies are expensive. They are sold to members who are engaged on a never-ending quest for higher states of being, a process aptly described as 'the exchange of wealth for status' (Bainbridge and Stark 1980: 134). Second, Scientology claims to be a religion allegedly in order to secure democratic freedoms it does not merit and would abuse. In response to this accusation, the Church of Scientology has repeatedly appealed to the United Nations to intervene with the German authorities on its behalf.

Scientology has also had a mixed relationship with academic researchers. On the one hand, Roy Wallis gave graphic accounts of attempts by members of the Church of Scientology to discredit him personally and professionally, and to subvert or suppress his research findings. On the other hand, Scientology has also sought scholarly support for its campaigns for recognition. In 1996 I received, unsolicited, free copies of papers written by twenty-two distinguished academics. All of them concluded that, like it or not, the Church of Scientology qualifies as a religion.

Baha'is: world faith or apostasy?

The origins of the Baha'i faith lie in a radical religious movement within Shi'a Islam that began in Iran and Iraq in the 1840s under the leadership of the prophet known as the Bab (in English, the Gate). In some respects the Bab is to Baha'is what John the Baptist is to Christians: John prepared the way for Jesus, the Bab prepared the way for Baha'u'llah (a title meaning Glory of God).

Baha'is believe that God has sent a series of prophets with a divine message for humanity appropriate to each stage of human cultural development. These prophets include Abraham, Krishna, Moses, Zoroaster, Buddha, Jesus Christ, Muhammad, the Bab and Baha'u'llah. The prophet for our age is Baha'u'llah, and the Baha'i faith is destined to become the major worldwide religion, uniting humanity in a shared theocratic system. From the end of the nineteenth century, Baha'is began to spread their faith to the west, gaining converts in the United States, Great Britain, France and Germany. There are now more than five million Baha'is worldwide.

Neither the values nor the activities of Baha'is have caused any problems to western liberal democracies. The faith is peace-loving and law-abiding, opposes superstition and racial prejudice, supports education and science, is committed to environmental protection and sustainable development, upholds family values and promotes equality of women and men.

In many Islamic countries, in contrast, Baha'is have been seen as heretics, apostates and undercover agents for the western powers. Persecution of Baha'is has been severe in the country where the faith had its deepest roots, Iran. The Baha'i faith is doctrinally offensive because it does not recognize Muhammad as the final Seal of the Prophets and the Qur'an as the absolute and definitive word of God that has existed for all eternity. In this perspective Baha'is are apostates, that is, they have wilfully abandoned Islam – the crime of *irtidad* or *ridda*. Although the death penalty for apostasy is not mentioned in the Qur'an it is in the *hadith* (the sayings of the Prophet and his companions) and is recognized by Islamic law.

After the overthrow in 1979 of the regime of Mohammad-Reza Pahlavi, the last Shah of Iran, many Baha'is were arrested, tortured and executed. Their property was confiscated, their institutions closed and their burial grounds desecrated. These actions had popular support. Baha'is were considered to be not only apostates but also unpatriotic and subversive. They were judged to have supported the Shah's programme of modernization on western lines.

Their extensive international contacts, and the location of their administrative headquarters at Haifa in Israel, were held up as proof that they were agents of the west, and not members of a genuine religion at all (Smith 1987: 175–8).

The cases discussed above highlight the fact that the definition of religion, and any attempt to distinguish authentic from bogus religion, is of more than scholarly interest. It can profoundly affect people's lives. It raises issues of church–state relations, the constitutional rights and liberties of religious minorities including intolerant ones, and the prospects for international agreement on human rights.

So, before discussing some of the definitions and conceptualizations of religion proposed by sociologists, it is worth setting out the reasons why some social movements insist that they are a religion while other movements equally emphatically deny it.

Advantages of being recognized as a religion

Gaining legal protection

Religious movements are granted wide protection under the law in many countries. For example, the First Amendment to the American Constitution states: 'Congress shall make no law respecting an establishment of religion, or prohibiting the free exercise thereof; or abridging the freedom of speech, or of the press; or the right of the people peaceably to assemble, and to petition the Government for a redress of grievances.' As the guardian of the Constitution, the Supreme Court has played a crucial role in determining the context in which religious movements operate in the United States.

The unconstitutionality of any establishment of religion in the USA means that no arm of government may pass legislation singling out any particular church or religious belief for special treatment. In Thomas Jefferson's much-quoted phrase, there is 'a wall of separation' between church and state. After a protracted legal campaign – the so-called 'saluting the flag controversy' – a decision of the Supreme Court in 1943 overturned earlier rulings and upheld the Jehovah's Witnesses' constitutional right not to say the Pledge of Allegiance. The constitutional guarantee of free exercise of religion was reaffirmed in 1993 under the Religious Freedom Restoration Act, which restated the principle that the government could interfere with religious practices only if it could show not merely a reasonable but a *compelling* case for doing so.

Reciting the Pledge of Allegiance – *I pledge allegiance to the flag of the United States of America and to the Republic for which it stands, one*

Nation under God, indivisible, with liberty and justice for all – is a regular ritual at school and at civic events. It is a normal, taken-for-granted aspect of being American. To Jehovah's Witnesses, however, it is an idolatrous act. It means worshipping the nation state and its flag instead of Jehovah, much as the Israelites bowed down to the golden calf.

Over and above national legislation, religious movements may appeal to international organizations such as the European Union or the United Nations.

Gaining tax benefits

Many countries grant tax concessions to officially recognized religions. Achieving recognition can therefore be an important goal. For example, the Church of Scientology's long-running campaign against the Internal Revenue Service in the USA finally succeeded in 1993, when it was granted tax-exempt status. This brought with it the additional advantage that anyone giving money to the Church of Scientology could claim tax deductions on their contributions.

In the 1980s, the then Prime Minister Margaret Thatcher urged the UK Charity Commissioners to reopen the case of the Unification Church (the Moonies), to review their qualification as a religion for charitable purposes, with the tax advantages that followed. Despite the clear wishes of Mrs Thatcher and intense public hostility to the Moonies, the Attorney-General dropped the case against them, leaving their status as a religion intact. In the USA, meanwhile, the Reverend Sun Myung Moon was successfully prosecuted and imprisoned on charges of tax evasion.

In the Federal Republic of Germany, religious organizations with public law status enjoy the benefit that the state will collect taxes on their behalf from their members. To achieve public law status, a movement must prove its durability. It is required to show that it is well organized, with a sizeable membership and sound finances. It also must have been in existence for some thirty years at a minimum. The law is designed to exclude short-lived volatile 'cults', particularly those which target young people, such as the Unification Church.

Jehovah's Witnesses have been engaged in a campaign to qualify for public law status in Germany. Like the Church of Scientology, Jehovah's Witnesses are not well regarded by the federal authorities, which see their movement as totalitarian.

Establishing a link to an ethnic community

The position of a minority religious movement may be strengthened if it can demonstrate its ties to an ethnic community and through that to a major world religion. This is the case for the International Society for Krishna Consciousness (the Hare Krishna movement). ISKCON was founded in 1966 by His Divine Grace A. C. Bhaktivedanta Swami Prabhupada. Its devotees became a familiar sight in western cities, processing in their colourful robes, the men with heads shaven to leave only a top-knot remaining, chanting the mantra *Hare Krishna, Hare Krishna, Krishna Krishna, Hare Hare, Hare Rama, Hare Rama, Rama Rama, Hare Hare* – which even became a minor hit record. ISKCON was vulnerable to derogatory classification as a 'cult', with allegations that it targeted vulnerable young people, brainwashed them, used deceptive techniques of fund-raising, broke up families, and moulded members to be dependent on the movement and its semi-monastic life. To counter this image, ISKCON has emphasized the priestly functions it performs for the wider Hindu community (Carey 1987). This role derives from ISKCON's roots in the centuries-old tradition of Vaishnava Hinduism, which cultivates worship of the god Vishnu and his *avatars* (roughly, incarnations), Krishna and Rama. Bhaktivedanta Swami's mission to save the west from its materialism was not simply an end in itself, but also a symbol aimed at India, calling on it to return to the truth path of spirituality. The objective is to position ISKCON not as a 'cult' but as a component of a great world faith that deserves respect.

Achieving respectability

As well as the specific benefits outlined above, religious organizations enjoy a degree of respect as religions. As ever, this varies from society to society. In Great Britain, for example, ministers of religion are generally regarded as men and women of integrity, the charitable work of churches is well thought of, and many people continue to look to churches to provide rites of passage such as baptism, marriage and funeral services. Perhaps all this is in decline – an issue to be examined in chapter 4. Even if decline is under way, the mainstream churches retain a significant degree of public esteem, and minority movements are likely to continue to seek a share of it.

One key element in respectability is to be known to perform good works for the benefit of others. This taps into deep-rooted themes in the major religions of the world. For Jews, giving material help to people in need is a cardinal principle of the faith. Traditionally, Jewish homes have a container, the *pushka*, into which members of the family drop coins for charity, usually just before the lighting of the candles at dusk on Friday, marking the beginning of the Sabbath. The Christian faith inherited this commitment to charitable giving. The third of the Five Pillars of Islam is *zakat*, alms-giving (the other Pillars are *shahada*, profession of faith; *salat*, worship; *saum*, fasting; and *hajj*, pilgrimage).

Minority religious movements may gain respect through their charitable work. A long-standing example of this is the Salvation Army. The Church of Scientology combats drug abuse through an organization known as Narconon, and the Unification Church has had a variety of famine-relief programmes. One reason young people may be attracted to movements like the Moonies is the opportunity to engage in socially worthwhile activities.

On the other hand, minority religious movements' charitable work may be seen as little more than a calculated exercise in public relations. This allegation was directed at the Unification Church when its practice of 'heavenly deception' became widely known. For example, the Moonies do not necessarily disclose their identity as Moonies either to potential recruits or to people from whom they solicit money for charitable purposes (Barker 1984a: 176–88). Their scriptural justification for heavenly deception is the subterfuge by which Jacob passed himself off as his elder brother Esau and stole his birthright (Genesis 27: 1–40). To Moonies, the means justify the ends in heavenly deception, since it carries out the divine purpose. In any case, they argue that it is Satan rather than God who is deceived.

Disadvantages of status as a religion

Legal restrictions

The First Amendment to the American Constitution guarantees free exercise of religion but denies religious movements access to public institutions, restricting their operations to the voluntary sector. Transcendental Meditation fought unsuccessfully in the USA for the right *not* to be recognized as a religion, so that it could be taught in public institutions such as schools and the armed forces (Barker 1995: 146).

Brought to the west in 1958 by the guru Maharishi Mahesh Yogi, Transcendental Meditation was made world-famous through its adoption in 1967 by the Beatles. Although its roots are in Hinduism, to most of its hundreds of thousands of practitioners it is a technique of meditation open to people of any faith or none. TM tends to underline its therapeutic, medical and scientific dimensions, particularly in marketing itself to the staff-training managers of secular business corporations.

Negative images of mainstream religion

A number of religious movements, including many that stand in eastern traditions of faith and practice, distance themselves from religion as it is understood in western countries with a Judaeo-Christian base (Barker 1995: 146–7). Thus the Brahma Kumaris (founded in Karachi in 1937 by Dada Lekh Raj), who practise a form of yoga known as Raja yoga, prefer to be seen as a spiritual or educational movement. Ananda Marga (meaning the Path of Bliss, founded in Bihar in 1955 by Shrii Shrii Anandamurti), whose members meditate and practise yoga as a daily regime, sees itself as a way of life or socio-spiritual organization. Subud (founded in Indonesia in the 1930s by a spiritual leader called Bapak) is not so much a religion as an enlightenment gained through the shared spiritual experience known as *latihan*. In traditions such as these, western religion may be thought of as moralistic, spiritually lifeless and authoritarian.

A very contrasting movement, the Jehovah's Witnesses, do not refer to themselves as a religion, even though they demand status as a religion under the law. Jehovah's Witnesses are literally that: witnesses to God, whose name is Jehovah. Religion is the false teaching of the churches who have led humankind away from obedience to Jehovah. To Jehovah's Witnesses, theirs is not a religion, but the Truth.

Even in the mainstream of western faith, terms such as 'religion' and 'religious' are contentious. Asking people such questions as 'Are you religious?' is not only hopelessly imprecise but also likely to provoke unfavourable reactions and a negative response even from some of the most committed and active churchgoers. Religious discourse is complex and subtle, and the very term 'religion' carries pejorative as well as favourable meanings. According to Towler (1974: 156–7) religion is an emotive topic for the English, for whom it is associated with a mixture of components including 'fanaticism, dishonesty, respectability, controversy or hypocrisy'.

Christian theology, too, can have negative conceptions of religion. An illustration of this is the work of the Swiss theologian Karl Barth (1886–1968). Barth distinguished sharply between divinely revealed faith and humanly constructed religion. To him, liberal theologians had contaminated the Christian gospel (faith) with worldly ideologies (religion). Barth's own 'neo-orthodox' theology rejected the naïvely optimistic approach of what came to be called 'cultural Protestantism' (*Kulturprotestantismus*). Barth's commentary on St Paul's Epistle to the Romans, published in 1919, was a reaction to the fervour with which liberal Protestant theologians in Germany had greeted the outbreak of the First World

War in 1914. Later, when Hitler came to power in Germany in 1933, Barth supported the Confessing Church in opposition to the German Christians, those willing instruments of Nazism who sought to purge Christianity of its Jewish elements, such as the suggestion that Jesus was anything other than an 'Aryan' hero. This dark period in German history shows that supporting modernity is not necessarily the same thing as upholding liberty, equality and fraternity. The Nazis were the modernizers. They were the ones claiming to have a programme relevant to the needs of contemporary society. Barth's conservative neo-orthodox theology asserted the Christian faith in opposition to its corruption by Nazism.

Identification as a cult

Although recognition as a genuine religion can confer respectability, identification as a 'cult' carries extremely negative meanings. In many societies the rights of religious minorities are uncertain and precarious. Anti-cult movements are able to tap into a reservoir of popular hostility, and the mass media have relative freedom to target religious minorities, who do not enjoy the level of protection granted to ethnic or 'racial' minority groups.

Freemasonry provides an illustration of the wish to avoid being labelled as a deviant religion. It emphatically denies that it is a religion at all. The brotherhood says that its rituals are not religious, that it has no sacraments, and that discussion of religion is forbidden within the lodge. Admittedly, in many traditions of Freemasonry members are required to profess belief in a supreme being – the Great Architect or Grand Geometrician. Masons assert that this is entirely compatible with monotheistic faiths such as Judaism, Christianity, Islam and Sikhism, and also with the ultimate reality – *brahman* – revealed in Hinduism despite its apparent polytheism. Masons' self-image is that they are an ecumenical brotherhood of morally serious men whose faith in God inspires them to do good works in the world. They have therefore been embarrassed by repeated accusations that theirs is an occult faith which worships a composite deity called Jahbulon, who is different from the god of the world's great religions. Denial that Freemasonry is a religious cult is a condition of its claim to respectability.

Max Weber: on not defining religion

One of the great founders of sociology, Max Weber (1864–1920), began his major investigation of religion, first published in German in 1922, with this statement:

> To define 'religion', to say what it *is*, is not possible at the start of a presentation such as this. Definition can be attempted, if at all, only at the conclusion of the study. The essence of religion is not even our concern, as we make it our task to study the conditions and effects of a particular type of social behaviour. (Weber 1965: 1)

Weber has been criticized for this refusal to define religion at the outset. How can we know what to include in a study of religion if we have failed to define what religion is (Robertson 1970: 34)? In any case, there is bound to be an implicit definition in operation, and it would be far better to have it out in the open for us to examine (Berger 1967: 175–6; Hamilton 1995: 11–12). Obviously, Weber himself included some things and excluded others, so he had an implicit definition which the reader can work out. The suggestion is that Weber ought to have spared his readers this trouble. For, although he said that a definition of religion might be attempted at the conclusion of a study, in the end he failed to do so.

Although plausible, this critique of Weber can itself be challenged on several grounds.

First, is it true that a formal definition of religion is indispensable? Many sophisticated sociological studies of religious movements – for example, *The Making of a Moonie* (Barker 1984a), or *The Trumpet of Prophecy* (Beckford 1975) – do not include a formal definition of religion. Readers are not troubled by the omission and probably do not even notice it.

Second, any formal definition of religion is bound to contain theoretical assumptions that are contentious. 'Religion' is a contested concept. We cannot expect to agree on a definition and then debate matters of substance, since matters of substance are built into any definition. There is not, and never will be, a universally agreed definition of religion.

Third, sociologists should ask: who is demanding a definition, why, and with what consequences? The cases discussed earlier show that the repercussions of definition can be serious. Defining religion involves an exercise of power. When sociologists are asked by secular authorities or by religious movements to define religion, it is to lend scholarly support to inclusion or exclusion: to have the Moonies deregistered as a charity, or to defend Scientology as an authentic religion, or to protect the children of Exclusive Brethren from being taught computer science in school (to them, computers are a blasphemous attempt to create life).

Fourth, society changes and religion changes with it. Given this, surely the search for a timeless definition of religion is misguided? Looking back over two centuries, it appears unlikely that even the far-sighted framers of the American Constitution envisaged the possibility of Scientologists or Rastafarians. The explosion of new religious movements in the west in the late 1960s came as a surprise to most people including sociologists, who had to revise their conceptualization of religion in consequence. The same might now be said of New Age religiosity. To deny that these phenomena are truly religious shows a failure to comprehend them.

Far more significant than the absence of a formal definition is Weber's statement that it is not the sociologist's task to search for 'the essence of religion'. Instead, sociologists should investigate religion's 'conditions and effects'. Weber's own work involves wide-ranging historical studies of major world religions and the role of religious leadership, discussion of key themes such as magic and taboo, and analyses of social classes and status groups as the carriers of different recipes for salvation. His sociology is clinically detached and value-free, refusing to support or oppose any particular political, moral or religious position (though he did write, most uncharacteristically, that the Book of Mormon was 'a crude swindle').

Emile Durkheim: defining religion sociologically

Weber's great contemporary, Emile Durkheim (1858–1917), insisted on arriving at a clear and distinct definition of religion as a prelude to any further analysis of it. In his last major work, *The Elementary Forms of the Religious Life*, Durkheim produced a definition of religion which is densely packed with contentious elements:

> A religion is a unified system of beliefs and practices relative to sacred things, that is to say, things set apart and forbidden – beliefs and practices which unite into one single moral community called a Church, all those who adhere to them. (Durkheim 1915: 47)

First, and most strikingly, the definition contains no reference to God, or the gods, or spiritual beings, or the transcendent, or another world, or the soul, or a life after death. Durkheim apparently believed that Theravada Buddhism (a more ancient and stricter form than Mahayana Buddhism, and prevalent in Sri Lanka and South-East Asia), although indisputably a religion, lacked any supernatural conceptions. Any definition of religion had to allow for this. It may be that he was wrong about Theravada Buddhism, confusing its elaboration as a sophisticated atheistic philosophy for an intellectual elite with its operative reality as a religion for the vast majority of the faithful, who do indeed believe in the supernatural (Robertson 1970: 36).

Second, the core concept in Durkheim's definition of religion is the sacred, detached from any divine origin. In a Durkheimian perspective, it is not God who has made Lourdes or Jerusalem or Mecca a sacred place of pilgrimage. The sacred is a social construct; sacredness is conferred not by God but by society. There is no qualitative difference between Lourdes, Jerusalem and Mecca on the one hand, and Anne Hathaway's Cottage, Wembley Stadium (the 'home' of Association football) or the Tupelo shack where Elvis Presley was born. Things are not sacred unless we treat them as such. To a believer this can seem a shockingly misguided, even blasphemous position.

Third, and unlike Weber, Durkheim was aiming to capture the essence of religion. To do so, he argued, it is necessary to begin by examining religion in its simplest form, which he assumed was to be found in the simplest society in existence. This led him to focus on the totemic religion of the native people of Central Australia, supplemented by material from North America when it suited him. Having grasped the essence of religion by analysing its most elementary form, we could then progress to study the more complex but essentially similar religions of advanced societies. As Parkin remarks (1992: 42), 'this was not a position guaranteed to win Durkheim many friends among the churchly', who did not relish the attempt to derive their own 'higher' faith from the beliefs and practices of people they saw as savages.

Fourth, Durkheim's definition places beliefs and practices on an equal footing. He deliberately avoided the 'intellectualist' error of assuming that the essence of religion is belief.

In some religious movements, the formal belief-system is indeed central. Jehovah's Witnesses are one example of this. They devote much of their time to studying the Bible through the perspective of the books and magazines produced by the Watchtower Bible and Tract Society. Becoming a Witness involves such study, plus a commitment to go out on 'the work', 'preaching and teaching' from door to door. As students, Witnesses are required to learn the Truth, not to question it. Emotional outbursts are viewed with deep suspicion. This is not a revivalist faith in which people stand up for Jesus, or testify that they have been born again, or hug and kiss one another, or dance, or speak in tongues (*glossolalia*), or raise the roof with rousing hymns. Meetings are low-key and businesslike, and have an instrumental goal: equipping the Witnesses for doorstep proselytizing, by training them in effective presentation of themselves and their Truth.

In contrast, the Religious Society of Friends (Quakers) has consistently rejected the formulation of any doctrine, creed or dogma. Quakers are concerned to acknowledge and cultivate 'the light within', or 'that which is of God in everyone'. Practice takes precedence over belief, and belief has meaning only in so far as it is enacted in practice. The Quaker does not learn an authoritative belief-system but experiences a Quakerly way of doing things and a Quakerly mode of worship.

Fifth, for Durkheim religion is essentially social, uniting its adherents into 'a single moral community'. Individual religiosity is secondary and derivative, and Durkheim characteristically showed little interest in it (just as, in his study of suicide, he concentrated on suicide rates and refused to consider individual motivation). Durkheim similarly treated magic as secondary and derivative: the magician or sorcerer has individual clients who do not interact with one another but only with the sorcerer who provides services to them. The clients of sorcerers do not, in Durkheim's view, form a community.

In assessing Durkheim's definition of religion we need to recognize that it is not neutral. His theory of religion is distilled into it. Putting it another way, Durkheim's definition is a Trojan Horse for his theory of religion. If we accept the gift, we can expect a number of theorems to emerge from inside it. Durkheim's theory of religion will be examined more fully in chapter 4.

Contemporary sociological definitions of religion

Sociological definitions of religion can be classified into two varieties: the broader inclusive and the narrower exclusive types. The balance of sociological opinion appears to be in favour of exclusive definitions, though these are not unproblematic.

Inclusive definitions

we propose that religion be defined as a system of beliefs about the nature of the force(s) shaping man's destiny, and the practices associated therewith, shared by the members of a group. (Lenski 1963: 331)

A *religion* is: (1) a system of symbols which acts to (2) establish powerful, pervasive, and long-lasting moods and motivations in men by (3) formulating conceptions of a general order of existence and (4) clothing these conceptions with such an aura of factuality that (5) the moods and motivations seem uniquely realistic. (Geertz 1968: 4)

It is in keeping with an elementary sense of the concept of religion to call the transcendence of biological nature by the human organism a religious phenomenon. (Luckmann 1967: 49)

religion is a system of beliefs and practices by means of which a group of people struggles with the ultimate problems of human life. (Yinger 1970: 7)

The fundamental criticism of inclusive definitions such as those above is simply that they include far too much. This criticism has been expressed in a number of ways.

First, on some inclusive definitions all human beings are religious even if they are professed atheists and utterly reject religion. To define religion in terms of ultimate problems (Yinger), or the forces shaping human destiny (Lenski), or the human transcendence of biology (Luckmann) is to make all of us religious whether we claim to be or not.

However, sociologists who define religion inclusively may be happy to defend the view that humanity is religious by definition. Thus Luckmann (1967: 49): 'The transcendence of biological nature *is* a universal phenomenon of mankind.' And Lenski (1963: 331–2):

> Given this definition of religion, it quickly becomes apparent that every normal adult member of any human society is religious. . . . There are some people, of course, who profess to be agnostics, but any examination of their patterns of action reveals that all agnostics *act as though* they accepted one or another of the competing systems of belief. Human existence *compels* men to act on unproven and unprovable assumptions, and it makes no exception.

It is clear from Luckmann and Lenski that their sociology is built on a conception of humanity – a philosophical anthropology – according to which human beings are essentially religious. While this may be challenged, it is arguably the case that all sociology depends on some sort of philosophical anthropology, even though it is not usually spelled out. Interestingly, denying that native peoples have a religion has been one way in which their lack of full humanity has been 'proved' by their colonial superiors. 'We' have religion, 'they' have ignorance, fear, superstition and fraud. In his discussion of theories of primitive religion, Evans-Pritchard (1965: 6–7) refers to the distinguished Victorian explorer Sir Samuel Baker, who said in 1866 of the people of the northern Nile: 'Without any exception, they are without a belief in a Supreme Being, neither have they any form of worship or idolatry; nor is the darkness of their minds enlightened by even a ray of superstition. The mind is as stagnant as the morass which forms its puny world.' These are not just nineteenth-century views. Chidester quotes the Afrikaner anthropologist W. M. Eiselen, in whose opinion the native peoples of southern Africa had no religion (*godsdiens*) but only patterns of belief (*geloofsvorme*). This 'categorical denial of their indigenous religious heritage' (Chidester n.d.: 3) was one component of the legitimation of *apartheid*.

A second way of expressing the objection to inclusive definitions of religion is to say that they incorporate all sorts of secular phenomena that should be excluded. Turner (1991: 15) argues that the Durkheimian approach 'drags in a diverse catch of social phenomena from baseball to nationalism, from Celtic hogmanay celebrations to royal weddings'. Ideological systems may be included that are openly materialist and anti-religious, for example communism (Scharf 1970: 33). They may equally well include the beliefs and practices of the devoted supporters of a football team or the fans of a rock group (Hamilton 1995: 17).

Sociologists tend to treat religion as a very serious phenomenon. All the great figures who contributed to the early development of sociology, even the atheists, held religion to be crucially important. Durkheim, himself an austerely unfrivolous man, said that religion belonged to the serious side of life – 'c'est de la vie sérieuse'. This intellectual legacy may be one reason why sociologists of religion usually treat fandom as trivial. Is it not possible, however, that in a consumer-oriented and perhaps 'postmodern' society the once-secure distinctions between fans and worshippers, popular entertainers and charismatic leaders, leisure pursuits and religion, are being eroded? This issue will be addressed in chapter 9. As for the atheistic materialism of communist societies, the former Soviet Union spent countless millions of roubles on the systemic promotion of a ritual system which had many of the hallmarks of a religion. This will be examined in chapter 7.

A third version of the objection to some inclusive definitions is that they prevent us from examining the question: is religion growing, stable or in decline? If virtually everything is religion, than a vital question of fact has been 'solved' only by a trick of definition. Would it not be better to treat football, royal weddings and the like as substitutes for religion rather than the real thing?

A final point about inclusive definitions of religion is that many of them are explicitly functionalist. Religion is defined in terms of the functions it performs for individuals or society, where functions are seen as both beneficial and necessary. Religion gives people a sense of identity, purpose, meaning, hope. Religion expresses and creates shared values and the social bonds which hold society together. Anything which performs these functions is religion. Functionalist definitions of religion are often linked to the view, supremely expressed in the structural-functionalism of Talcott Parsons, that the social glue holding society together is neither coercion nor the everyday necessity of earning a living – what Marx called 'the dull compulsion of economic life' – but shared norms and values.

Exclusive definitions

> An institution consisting of culturally patterned interaction with culturally postulated superhuman beings. (Spiro 1966: 96)

> Religious culture is that set of beliefs and symbols (and values deriving directly therefrom) pertaining to a distinction between an empirical and a super-empirical, transcendent reality; the affairs of the empirical being subordinated in significance to the non-empirical . . . [Religious action is] action shaped by an acknowledgement of the empirical/super-empirical distinction. (Robertson 1970: 47)

> The set of beliefs which postulate and seek to regulate the distinction between an empirical reality and a related and significant supra-empirical segment of reality; the language and symbols which are used in relation to this distinction; and the activities and institutions which are concerned with its regulation. (M. Hill 1973: 42–3)

Exclusive definitions of religion are supposed to be free from the objections to the inclusive type discussed above. They are substantive rather than functional, defining religion by what it is, not by what it does (McGuire 1992: 11–15). They are closer to conventional western understandings of religion, and in particular they do not 'drag in' footballers, rock stars and their fans. Nor do they close down the question of religion's decline or growth.

Even so, there are problems. One striking feature of the definitions given above is their avoidance of key terms and concepts which have normally been thought of as core aspects of religion. Exactly as with Durkheim's much-criticized inclusive definition, there is still no reference to God, or the gods, or spiritual beings, or the transcendent, or another world, or the soul, or a life after death. These supposedly exclusive definitions are actually rather inclusive.

What we have instead of the supernatural is the superhuman (Spiro), the supra-empirical (Hill) and the super-empirical (Robertson). Yet these terms are themselves problematic (Hamilton 1995: 15; Willaime 1995: 120). The concept of the superhuman is not found in all cultures. Nor is it obvious who or what should be included as superhuman. Exceptional people who influenced the course of history for good or ill, such as Napoleon? Great artists such as Shakespeare and great scientists such as Einstein? Fictional super-heroes such as Superman? What about the vision of the Extropians, who reject religious dogma and supernaturalism as irrational, but believe that humanity will evolve into a more advanced life-form? In all of these cases, the superhuman belongs to *this* world rather than any other, and so falls well short of the supernatural in its fullest religious sense.

Unlike the superhuman, the terms supra-empirical and super-empirical do point to another world 'above' or 'over' this one. What is less clear is how these terms are an improvement on the supernatural. Perhaps their purpose is to move discussion away from transcendence of the natural world – by, for example, miraculous interventions overriding the laws of cause and effect – to transcendence of human culture.

The drive to include all religious traditions is the reason why sociological definitions of religion, even ones which claim to be substantive and exclusive, are extremely broad, incorporating abstract terms such as 'super-empirical'. There is a profound paradox here. Sociology aims to be universal in scope, and struggles to avoid parochialism and ethnocentricity. Sociologists therefore seek a definition of religion that would encompass all the religions of the world. Yet this search for a universally applicable definition defeats its own purpose. Cultures are too diverse, and new religious movements continually threaten to break the mould with new modes of belief and practice. Ironically, sociologists who adopt exclusive definitions of religion have often shown themselves staunch allies of conservative theology and traditional practices. Radical theologians and liberal clerics who see the divine as immanent rather than transcendent are ridiculed by atheist sociologists for their foolish betrayal of religion.

Religion and definition in use

Whether they favour inclusive/functional or exclusive/substantive definitions of religion, sociologists have tried to avoid giving priority to any one religion. They do not start from, say, mainstream Protestant Christianity, and then see other faiths in the light of it. Because of this, sociologists have become more and more reluctant to use terms such as 'sect' and 'cult'. These terms are normally used pejoratively to imply that the religious movement in question has broken away from or fallen short of the fullness of the true faith, or even that it is not a genuine religion at all.

Durkheim was famously exercised by the example of Buddhism, as we have seen. An equally problematic case is Hinduism, which does not fit western preconceptions about religion (Knott 1998). Hinduism did not have a founder and does not have prophets. It is not defined by creeds. There is no set of doctrines or practices which are essential to it. It is neither a theological nor an ethical system. Although it has sacred texts not one of them is universally regarded as carrying unique authority. It is not organized into church-type structures. Its brahmins are not priests in the western sense.

So much for what Hinduism is not. What it is also diverges from western preconceptions of religion. It is extremely complex and internally diverse, embracing with relative tolerance a wide range of traditions, including local village cults as well as major religious movements. It is identified specifically with India and the Aryan people who have lived there for thousands of years or, as many Hindus see it, since the beginning of time. It is bound up with an ordering of society – the *jati* or caste system – which is linked to the scriptural division of humanity into four great classes: the *varna* (meaning colour) system, a hierarchy composed of brahmins (very roughly, the priestly class), the kshatriya (the warrior caste), the vaishya (the farmers and merchants) and the shudra (the servants and labourers). Utterly outside the varna system lie the untouchables, a potent source of ritual pollution to the members of the varna classes – even their shadow can pollute.

The term Hinduism is itself problematic. It might be more true to the subject to speak of Hindu *dharma* – a way of life, or even *the* way of life, grounded in the cosmological order.

The example of Hinduism makes the point that we might do well to follow the lead of the philosopher Ludwig Wittgenstein, and abandon the search for a set of common factors that all religions must possess. This would not be as disastrous as it might at first seem. Take as a comparison the concept of 'sports'. There are many different sorts of sports – football, gymnastics, synchronized swimming, billiards, darts, angling – with no one element shared by all. A sport may or may not be competitive, involve the use of a ball, be physically demanding or be a team game. What sports share, says Wittgenstein, is not common elements but 'family resemblances', which enable us to recognize them as sports, just as we can see varying similarities of physique and personality among members of the same family, without there being any one characteristic possessed by them all.

A second point emphasized by Wittgenstein is that definitions are put to use in different contexts for different purposes. If we want to know the meaning of a term we should investigate how it is used. For example, the International Olympics Committee has to decide which sports are appropriate for inclusion in the Olympic Games. There was controversy when synchronized swimming was accepted. What about darts? Although it is not widely recognized as a sport, that may be less to do with its intrinsic characteristics than with prejudice against a working-class pursuit. How do the people who play darts see it themselves? One of the strengths of sociology is that we go and ask them.

Is Scientology a religion? With this question, we are back where the chapter started. When Scientologists themselves are asked what they think they are doing, their replies show that they do see Scientology as a religion. Whether this should be definitive is a matter of debate. In any event, we have seen some of the reasons why the answer is important to a number of interested parties, not least the Church of Scientology itself.

Wittgenstein's emphasis on definition in use reflects the sociologist's concern with practice as a dimension of religion that is at least as important as belief. Not all religious movements emphasize beliefs, doctrines and creeds, as we have seen from the examples of Quakers and Hindus discussed above. Not all traditions have been characterized, as Christianity has been, by schisms involving disputes over true doctrine, such as those between the eastern Orthodox and western Catholics, and between Catholics and Protestants. The divisions between Sunni and Shi'a Muslims, and between Theravada and Mahayana Buddhists, have not given rise to heresy trials or wars of religion. Compared to other world faiths, Christianity has been intolerant of internal diversity of belief.

Even within those religious movements which do have formal creeds, it should not be assumed that most participants are knowledgeable about or concerned with matters of doctrine. Rank-and-file members are not usually would-be theologians. The experience of being a Jew, or a Hindu, or a Mormon is often more about doing things than believing things: about abstaining from pork, or beef, or tea, coffee and cola drinks. Often, too, it is the doing and the not-doing that provoke hostile social reactions: Jehovah's Witnesses rejecting blood transfusions, Quakers refusing to enlist in the armed services, nineteenth-century Mormons practising polygamy.

A Wittgensteinian approach to the definition of religion is well suited to modern circumstances. Whether or not we believe that religion has lost social significance in the west – as it has according to the secularization thesis, examined in chapters 4 and 5 – it seems hard to deny that religion has become a more controversial and less predictable force in society (Beckford 1989: 170–2). It has lost its former anchorage in stable communities of faith, becoming instead a cultural resource on which individuals and interest groups may draw for motivation and legitimacy. In western society, religion as a social institution may have declined, but religion as a cultural resource remains potent. This deregulation of religion means that its definition has become a recurring problem in modern societies, with serious consequences both for believers and for society as a whole.

3

Varieties of Religious Movement

Max Weber on church and sect

Sociological attempts to classify religious movements trace their origin to Max Weber. His distinction between church and sect as forms of social organization centred on the differences in their *membership principle*. The church–sect dichotomy in Christianity has been widely discussed and elaborated in the sociological literature following Weber's classic statement of it.

In Weber's account, the church is *inclusive*. Church membership is socially ascribed at birth, which means that people belong to the church unless they choose to opt out. The church, as Weber says, 'necessarily includes both the just and the unjust'. It is not a select community of the chosen few, but a gathering of repentant sinners in search of forgiveness. The church's unique spiritual assets are the sacraments, defined in the Anglican Book of Common Prayer as 'an outward and visible sign of an inward and spiritual grace'. The Catholic and Orthodox traditions recognize seven sacraments as having been instituted by Christ: baptism, confirmation, the Eucharist, penance, extreme unction, priestly orders and matrimony. Protestant churches generally recognize baptism and the Lord's Supper as the only true sacraments. The church offers the sacraments to everyone within its territory, which may be either a nation state or part of a nation state, as with the Church of England, or the whole world, as with the Roman Catholic Church.

The church's sacraments are transmitted as an inheritance from generation to generation, in what Weber calls 'a sort of trust foundation for supernatural ends'. Given this, it is symbolically appropriate that the church administers sacraments not just to adults but to infants and children as well. Conversely, a principal way in which the church exerts its symbolic power is to withdraw sacraments from people deemed unworthy of them – for example, refusing to conduct marriage ceremonies if one party was divorced, unless their previous marriage had been annulled.

The appeal to tradition as a source of sacred authority is always powerful within the church. So it is that people within Catholic, Orthodox and Anglican churches who argue on grounds of tradition against the ordination of women to the priesthood do not regard themselves as appealing to corporate inertia or unimaginative resistance to change. For them, the enduring tradition of the church is based on divine ordinance: God wills it so for all time.

This does not mean that nothing is allowed to change. For example, the Catholic church believes in progressive revelation; hence the doctrine of the immaculate conception – that the Virgin Mary, uniquely among humans, was kept free of the taint of original sin from her conception onwards – was propounded as dogma only in 1854, just as the bodily assumption – that the Virgin Mary was taken up body and soul into heaven – was officially proclaimed as late as 1950.

The sect, on the other hand, is *exclusive*: membership is not ascribed at birth but achieved in adult life. People can become a member of a sect only by choosing to join it. Sects are voluntary associations, funded through the subscriptions of their members and not subsidized or sponsored by the state, as churches often are. Unlike the church, the sect is a gathered community of people typically describing themselves with such exclusive terms as 'the saints' or 'the elect'.

Sects have strict criteria of entrance, and impose stringent performance norms. They have a strong sense of their own identity and of the distinctiveness of their mission. They are protest movements. In sects whose roots lie in the Protestant Reformation, protest focuses on the alleged laxity, hypocrisy and false teaching of the churches. In many sects, however, protest is much wider, even extending to wholesale rejection of the values and lifestyles of the modern world.

People who fail to live up to the sect's demanding moral codes run a high risk of being thrown out – 'disfellowshipped' or 'disowned' – and ignored, 'shunned'. Since the sect is a community of committed adult believers, the churches' practice of infant baptism makes no sense at all. How can an infant profess a faith? And what sense is there in a parent professing faith on behalf of a child? Infant baptism shows just how deeply the churches are in error. Some sects, such as the Salvation Army and the Religious Society of Friends (Quakers), go further, rejecting the concept of sacraments altogether.

We can see the tension between church and sect expressed in internal conflicts within mainstream Christianity down the centuries. The church frequently confronted rigorist groups, such as the Donatists in the third century AD, who claimed that in order for the church to remain pure its sacraments must be administered by people who were themselves personally holy and uncompromised. Mainstream Christianity repeatedly rejected this sectarian principle. The contrasting churchly approach is embodied in the Church of England in the Thirty-Nine Articles of Religion, the twenty-sixth of which is entitled: 'Of the unworthiness of the ministers, which hinders not the effect of the sacrament'.

From sect to church?

Weber's analysis of church and sect is not confined to a static description. Rather, he discusses the dynamics of social change, examining the processes through which one form mutates into another. On his account, successful sects have a tendency to evolve into churches. This is partly a function of size: sects operate most effectively as small, face-to-face, locally self-policing communities. If they succeed in attracting large numbers of new members they find themselves inevitably pushed towards the churchly mode.

The growth of sects into churches is also linked to the process of *routinization of charisma*. The personal charisma of the movement's founder becomes diffused after his or her death into a more generalized charisma of office. In the Catholic Church, for example, Christ's charisma, derived from his unique personhood, is transmitted to the church as the office charisma of Peter, the popes and the priesthood. Even if an individual is not worthy of the office he or she holds, the office is not thereby undermined.

As a religious movement grows, personal charisma is replaced by charisma of office, which in turn gradually shades into bureaucracy – a defining characteristic of the churchly form of social organization. Bureaucracies are rule-governed impersonal structures in which the separation of person and office is complete.

Weber's ideas on the sect-to-church process were taken up and elaborated by other writers. One influential example of this is H. R. Niebuhr's *The Social Sources of Denominationalism*, first published in 1929 (Niebuhr 1957). Niebuhr argued that sects are 'valid' only for one generation of members. The passage of time brings inevitable changes to the movement which propel it in the direction of the church. Niebuhr singles out four main processes at work:

Generational effects   According to Niebuhr, the second and subsequent generations who are born into the movement cannot share the fervour of the original members, whose commitment was forged 'in the heat of conflict and at the risk of martyrdom'. The rugged faith of the pioneers gives way to 'easily imparted creeds'. The sect is forced to pay more and more attention to the socialization of its children, and less to its external mission in society.

Upward social mobility   The work ethic, analysed so perceptively by Weber, has the unintended consequence of worldly success. Hard work, frugal living and deferred gratification bring the sect and its members economic prosperity, which in turn confers growing social respectability.

Social integration   Upward social mobility therefore makes it harder for the sect to maintain the mechanisms by which it originally insulated its members against contamination by the values, lifestyles and beliefs of the wider society.

Routinization of charisma and bureaucratization   As a sect grows, Niebuhr contends that it will unavoidably develop a professional ministry, that is to say a theologically educated cadre of ritual specialists who will eventually displace the original lay leadership. 'So the sect becomes a church.'

With hindsight, it is clear that something is wrong with the sect-to-church hypothesis, since so many religious movements have retained their sectarian character despite the passage of time. Given this, sociologists have focused on the factors which encourage or hinder the transformation of sects into churches. We can consider these by referring back to the processes discussed by Niebuhr.

Generational effects

Niebuhr was incorrect in his hypothesis that second and subsequent generations are bound to lack the fervour of the early recruits. Childhood socialization can be just as powerful as adult conversion in producing unwavering commitment. Take the case of Jehovah's Witnesses. A conscientious family of Witnesses will do everything they can to guard their children against contamination by the false teachings and ungodly practices of the wider society. Their children will attend state schools, but will not participate in acts of religious worship and assembly. A strict Witness family will discourage close friendships with children born outside the faith. A Witness child will not attend birthday parties, since Witnesses do not celebrate birthdays. Christmas is a pagan festival to be studiously ignored. Strict Witnesses do not exchange gifts at all, but purchase items only when they are needed; hence the rich set of symbols, rituals and interpersonal relations expressed in gift-exchange can be quite alien to Witness children. Witnesses will be wary of allowing their children to stay overnight with their non-Witness acquaintances, for fear of exposure to adolescent 'bedroom culture' with its cult of popular celebrities and its easy access to dubious materials available on television, video and the internet. Witnesses cultivate in their children the traditional virtues of self-controlled 'good behaviour', not least uncomplaining obedience to parental authority. More profoundly, childhood is treated unromantically as an apprenticeship for the adult life of the Jehovah's Witness.

Nor is it true that subsequent generations of adult recruits will necessarily lack the strong commitment of the pioneers. Much depends on the movement's strategy for recruitment and adult socialization. Many movements have rigorous entry requirements and impose high performance standards on all their members.

Upward social mobility

Not all sectarian movements subscribe to a Protestant-style work ethic. Even where hard work and thrift are core values they do not necessarily lead to upward social mobility. Members of farming communities such as the Amish work hard on the land. However, they are aiming at self-sufficiency, not profit maximization. Strict Amish communities preserve traditional methods of farming in which power tools and other modern machinery do not feature.

The Amish are representative of a type of religious sect which Wilson calls *introversionist*. For introversionist sects, salvation is found within the sacred community of the faithful. They are pollution-conscious: religious hygiene requires that members are isolated from contaminating social contact with the world outside. They are communities in a strong sense of the word. A number of ethnic groups migrated to the New World to escape persecution in the Old. As well as the Amish (originally from Switzerland and Alsace), there are also the Hutterites (from Moravia) and the Doukhobors (from Russia). All of these set themselves apart geographically in self-contained communities. Introversionist sects aim to be self-sufficient not just economically but socially and culturally as well. Hence there is no prospect of upward social mobility – except by leaving the movement altogether.

Social integration

Isolation is one way to prevent upward social mobility. Another is *insulation*, meaning social mechanisms which protect group members against contamination when they come into contact with the wider society. Jehovah's Witnesses are an example of effective insulation. Witnesses do not live in spatially separate community enclaves, nor do they have their own schools for their children. Nevertheless, they have kept their character as a sect ever since they emerged as a social movement at the end of the nineteenth century. They have achieved this through strategies of insulation, as discussed above in respect of childhood socialization.

Social integration is, in any case, double-sided. Even if a group aims for greater acceptance by and closer integration into the wider society, it is not necessarily granted. Some of the group's beliefs and practices may seem so bizarre or offensive to outsiders that they act as a barrier to wider acceptance. Jehovah's Witnesses' refusal of blood transfusions for themselves and more problematically for their children stands as a vivid negative symbol of their apparent irrationality. The earlier Mormon practice of polygamy continues to be a barrier to respectability. Grudgingly abandoned in 1890 when the Supreme Court upheld a judgement against it, polygamy remains a symbolic problem for the Mormon church, which is obliged to put some effort into justifying the fact that Mormons ever practised it.

Even in liberal-democratic societies, religious minorities can face persecution – or at least what they experience as persecution. The expectation of persecution is often inculcated in sect members and tends to strengthen their commitment to the movement. Persecution is a sign that they have the truth. For example, the Unification Church has been challenged by the activities of 'deprogrammers' who, in extreme cases, have abducted young Moonies to isolated locations for an intensive deprogramming to liberate them from the effects of brainwashing. The Unification Church holds up to its members the activities of deprogrammers as a sign that it possesses the truth which evil people try to suppress. Thus the threat of persecution through deprogramming is used by the Unification Church to reinforce commitment. As Barker suggests (1984b), with enemies like these who needs friends?

Routinization of charisma and bureaucratization

As part of their protest against the mainstream churches, many sects emphasized their rejection of a priestly caste of religious professionals. The phrase 'priesthood of all believers' expressed this sectarian principle, which lives on in movements that have ceased to be sectarian – such as the Quakers, discussed below. However, it is doubtful that this should be made a defining characteristic of the sect. Not all sects have charismatic leaders. The Jehovah's Witnesses' organization has been bureaucratic for many years. Their founder, Charles Taze Russell, is regarded not as a charismatic prophet but as a scholar whose careful and open-eyed research set out the truth that had always been there for all to see had not the churches blinded people to it. Since 1942, when Russell's successor Joseph Franklin Rutherford died, the Watch Tower Society has presented itself impersonally as a body of faithful Bible students who publish the truth but in no sense create it.

Beyond church and sect: extending the typology

The church–sect dichotomy has been a powerful tool of analysis. It is nevertheless limited in its field of application historically and culturally. The contrast of church and sect is characteristically Christian, with some parallels but no exact equivalents in other traditions.

Weber's pupil and colleague, the theologian Ernst Troeltsch, expressed this cultural specificity in the argument that the principles of church and sect were both contained in the gospel as valid expressions of Christian practice. According to Troeltsch, church and sect have continued their dialectic with each other down the centuries.

The church sees itself as possessing the means of salvation, which it is able to dispense to everyone, even to sinners. Churches are conservative. They are willing to accommodate themselves to the interests of the state, and easily become the instruments of state policy. Sects, in contrast, are voluntary communities which repudiate the compromises made by the church and the alleged hypocrisy of its members. Sects are radical dissenting bodies, typically associated with the lower orders and classes. Sects cannot exist without churches, since the very meaning of the sectarian form of religion lies in its opposition to the church.

The church–sect dialectic is limited to a historically specific period within Christianity (Turner 1991: 172). It applies to an age in which churches embraced the national population and enjoyed wide-ranging privileges granted by the state. In that social context, sects and churches were polar opposites. This has never been the situation in the United States, however, and is less and less the case in European societies. Churches are losing their legal privileges. They no longer have either the capacity or the desire to discriminate against other religious groups. They are more and more willing to take part in co-operative ecumenical ventures with fellow

Christians and with other faiths as well. Minority religious movements are less inclined to define their identity in terms of dissent from the beliefs and practices of a dominant church – to do so has lost its relevance. If sects are persecuted, it is not by churches so much as by secular interest groups and by organs of the state. Although some minority religions are deeply un-popular – for instance the Unification Church, and Scientology – the main-stream churches are seldom in the forefront of crusades against them.

Troeltsch's work has been criticized for its lack of either analytical clarity or parsimony (Robertson 1970: 116). In at least one respect, how-ever, Troeltsch was far-sighted, as Campbell (1978, 1972) has emphasized. As well as the churchly and sectarian forms of religion, Troeltsch recog-nized that the rise of mysticism would be a potent force in the modern world. The key to mysticism is its 'radical religious individualism' (Troeltsch 1931: 377). This individualism is not self-seeking but spiritual, aesthetic and idealistic. It is hostile to the religious formalism and dogmatic rigidity of church and sect alike. It shifts the emphasis away from doctrine and worship toward personal, inward experiences. Although it rejects ma-terialism, rationalism and pragmatism, it remains compatible with other currents in contemporary culture, above all the ascendancy of individual-ism and the collapse of deference to traditional authorities. Mysticism's capacity to absorb cultural elements from traditions other than Christianity gives it an evolutionary advantage over churchly and sectarian religion, which are closed and rigid. For Troeltsch, mysticism flourishes in urban societies, appealing particularly to the educated middle and professional classes. In all this, Campbell argues, Troeltsch accurately foresaw a major dimension of contemporary religious sensibility. We see it today in the growth of mystically oriented cults, the revival of Romanticism and the emergence of New Age spirituality.

The church–sect dichotomy has been eroded by fundamental changes in society and culture. Given this, sociologists have broadened the classifica-tion of religious movements beyond the church–sect dichotomy. One ele-gant and powerful typology was originally proposed by Wallis (1976: 13), and has been taken up by, among others, Bruce (1995: 19–21) and McGuire (1992: 138–46).

Wallis's typology (figure 3.1) is generated by two dimensions. The first is *external conception*, that is to say, the way in which the movement is perceived in the wider society. Specifically, is the movement treated as respectable or deviant? The second is *internal conception*, meaning the way in which the movement sees itself. Specifically, does the movement regard itself as *uniquely legitimate* (as, for example, traditional Catholics see theirs as 'the one true Church founded by Christ'), or *pluralistically legitimate*, that is, one of a variety of paths to salvation, as with Methodists?

	Respectable	Deviant
Uniquely legitimate	**CHURCH**	**SECT**
Pluralistically legitimate	**DENOMINATION**	**CULT**

Figure 3.1 Wallis's typology of religious collectivities
Source: Roy Wallis, *The Road to Total Freedom: a sociological analysis of Scientology* (London: Heinemann, 1976), p. 13.

This typology has a number of significant attractions from a sociological point of view. It is sensitive to the social context in which movements are located. The character of a religious movement is a product of the complex interactions between its self-conception, on the one hand, and its relations with other movements and the state on the other. Respectability is socially conferred, and usually brings social and economic advantages such as charitable status and tax exemptions. Many sects seek social respectability – and in that sense see themselves as denominations or churches, often adopting the vocabulary and organizational structure of the church, for instance the Church of Scientology, the Unification Church (i.e. the Moonies) and the Church of Jesus Christ of Latter-day Saints (i.e. the Mormons).

The 'same' movement therefore takes on different identities according to the social context. The Church of Jesus Christ of Latter-day Saints has a more sectarian character in the UK than it does in the USA. So does Christian Science. These examples illustrate a more general point about the American religious scene. Since the Constitution guarantees that there shall be no establishment of religion, there is a powerful tendency for religious movements to gravitate to the denominational position. There is no church in the sociological sense, even though there are plenty of bodies which call themselves churches. In the American context, the Episcopal Church, the Roman Catholic Church, the Methodist Church and so on are all, in a sociological perspective, denominations. Although they appeal to different constituencies in terms of region, socio-economic status and ethnicity, none of them enjoys special legal privileges or is culturally dominant.

The denominational form is ideally suited to a consumer society. Switching between denominations is very common in the United States; it has been estimated that around 40 per cent of the American population have changed denominations at least once (McGuire 1992: 71). This does not usually reflect a conversion experience in the sense that the person has undergone a fundamental transformation of identity. It is, rather, a change of allegiance often caused by other changes of social status, including geographical mobility, social mobility and marriage. People's religious 'preferences' are similar to their choice of supermarket: a question of taste shaped by socio-economic status. This has often been taken by European commentators to demonstrate that American religiosity is shallow, even 'secularized from within'. This equation of consumerism with superficiality may, however, be nothing other than the cultural snobbery of intellectuals.

Wallis's typology includes the cult as a distinctive form of social organization. Like sects, cults are deviant rather than respectable, but they nevertheless define themselves in a non-exclusive manner. In Wallis's phrase, they are 'epistemologically individualist'. This means that the cult's members enjoy a degree of freedom to work out their own path to salvation on the principle, 'if it works for you . . .' Cults do not necessarily have a strong definition of membership. It is possible to drift into and out of them without crossing any very clear threshold in either direction. It is also possible to be associated with a number of different cults simultaneously. There is a 'cultic milieu' (Campbell 1972), made up of alternative therapies, complementary medicine, techniques of divination, and a wide variety of occult beliefs and practices. Cults are not necessarily 'religious' in the conventionally accepted sense. So, for example, Transcendental Meditation is treated by most of its practitioners as a technique for relaxing and relieving stress, without reference to its origins in Hinduism.

In contrast to the cult, the sect is 'epistemologically authoritarian'. Sects impose their own definition of the situation: they have a fixed dogma, rigid codes of conduct and set rituals. 'Doing your own thing' is not encouraged and usually not permitted. Sects typically have a strong definition of 'membership', drawing very clear boundaries around the people inside. As Weber emphasized, they impose strict entry requirements. Some movements, such as Jehovah's Witnesses, expect their members to show that they understand and accept the fundamentals of the movement's belief-system. It is not possible to become a Jehovah's Witness without extensive study of the Bible as interpreted by the Watch Tower Bible and Tract Society. Other movements emphasize experience over knowledge, as in the charismatic renewal movement's cultivation of pentecostal blessings such as *glossolalia* (speaking in tongues) and the experience of being 'born again'.

Sects have strict performance norms. Mormons are expected to abstain from recreational drugs, including tobacco, tea, coffee and cola drinks containing caffeine. They are required to tithe one-tenth of their income to the church. The Mormon church insists on a strict code of sexual morality, and stigmatizes homosexuality as wilful perversion. In keeping with their strict demands, most sects either require or at least strongly advise endogamy – marriage within the community of faith.

The sensitivity to a movement's social context, already identified as a key element of Wallis's typology, is related to another feature: the analysis of social change. Far from being fixed for all eternity, religious movements can and do move from one quadrant to another. There is not a universal one-way sect-to-church pattern.

Wallis shows how Scientology developed into a sect from the cult known as Dianetics (Wallis 1976). In its origins, Dianetics had been a relatively open-minded therapeutic system. Its practitioners and clients had a degree of freedom to experiment with therapeutic techniques, pragmatically adopting those which seemed to work and discarding any which did not. This led to a number of potentially damaging schisms within the movement, as rival practitioners set up their own variants of Dianetics, challenging the authority of Ron Hubbard himself. Ron responded by a fierce assertion of epistemological authoritarianism. Rival practitioners were ejected as heretics. As part of this process of transition to sectarianism, Scientology adopted more and more the character and trappings of a religion. It was during this period that frequent clashes took place between the Church of Scientology and the state – in the USA, the UK, the Federal Republic of Germany and Australia. Scientology was far more threatening as an authoritarian religious sect than it had been when it was an individualistic therapeutic cult.

A contrasting pattern of development is shown by the Religious Society of Friends (Quakers). The Quaker faith arose in mid-seventeenth-century Britain as a religious protest movement under the leadership of George Fox. The movement rapidly developed in a sectarian direction until the middle of the nineteenth century. Quakers' protest was partly against the established church. They objected to paying tithes – the 10 per cent of earnings which everyone was required to pay for the upkeep of the ministers of the state-sponsored church, the Church of England. Quakers rejected churchly sacramentalism along with any development of a professional ministry distinct from the laity. In the public sphere, not only did Quakers refuse to swear oaths, they also adopted a Peace Testimony which for most members has entailed an unswerving commitment to pacifism.

Quakers worked to preserve their own culture. They adhered to puritanical values of thrift, hard work, deferred gratification and abstinence from extravagant worldly pleasures. They founded their own separate schools through which Quaker culture was transmitted. Quakers were marked out by what they called their 'peculiarities' – their distinctive sober attire and their special dialect with its archaic forms of address ('thees and thous', now thought of as formal, but in origin expressions of intimacy, as in the French *tu* and the German *du*). They upheld a strong membership principle and disowned people who married outside the faith.

The origins of Quaker sectarianism can be interpreted as a response to the threat of persecution. At the time of the English Civil War, Quakers ran the risk of being confused with apocalyptic millenarian groups, such as Ranters, Levellers and Diggers (C. Hill 1975). These groups were prepared to use violent means to bring about religiously inspired ends. Religious dissent and political sedition were closely intertwined. Some millenarian movements expected the Second Coming of Christ in 1666, inspired by the observation that 666 is the cryptic 'number of the beast' referred to in Revelation 13: 18.

The Declaration of the Quaker Peace Testimony, which dates from 1661, the year after the Restoration of the monarchy under King Charles II, was designed to distance Quakers from these more violent dissenters. One such group were the Fifth Monarchy Men, who believed that Oliver Cromwell's Commonwealth would prepare the way for the Fifth Monarchy, which they took to be prophesied in Daniel 7 as the successor to the empires of Assyria, Persia, Greece and Rome. It is estimated (Punshon 1984: 33) that some 4,230 Quakers were arrested and imprisoned in connection with the Fifth Monarchy uprising of 1661. The Quaker Peace Testimony, addressed to the King, declared that 'the spirit of Christ which leads us into all Truth will never move us to fight and war against any man with outward weapons neither for the Kingdom of Christ nor for the kingdoms of this world.' It was a resounding affirmation that Quakers were not political dissenters seeking to overthrow the restored monarchy.

From this period until the middle of the nineteenth century, the sectarian characteristics of the Society of Friends came more and more to the fore. Its membership principle became strictly exclusive. People were frequently disowned for marrying out, and for attending the theatre and other unrighteous entertainments. As with the Peace Testimony there was an element of collective self-protection in this. Not only was the Society exerting tight discipline over its members, it was also able to dissociate itself from the activities of people who could be demonstrated to the authorities not to be Quakers.

In the latter part of the nineteenth century the Society of Friends began to move away from an inward-turned sectarian position. One sign of this was the rise of great Quaker business enterprises such as Cadbury's, Fry's and Rowntree's (all chocolate manufacturers), Quaker Oats, the Friends' Provident insurance company, and Lloyd's and Barclay's banks. The success of these Quaker enterprises can be seen as evidence of the relationship between the Protestant ethic and the spirit of capitalism. Their wealth needed to be justified in religious terms. Hence the concerned paternalism of Quaker enterprises, and their engagement in philanthropic projects, such as George Cadbury's foundation of Bournville village on the outskirts of industrial Birmingham as a clean and healthy environment for Cadbury workers.

In the twentieth century the Society of Friends emerged fully from its earlier inward-turned sectarianism. Elements of Quaker culture remain, but have evolved out of their sectarian setting of Quaker 'peculiarities'. Quakers no longer have a distinctive dress; even so, they typically wear plain clothes dictated by practical considerations. They do not have a tradition of 'dressing up' for meetings for worship, and are not usually fashion victims. In speech, although they have long abandoned 'thees and thous', Quakers are not enthusiasts for worldly titles and honours, preferring informal use of first names and family names unadorned. They will not take formal oaths, and do not engage in 'promises' since these add nothing: if you say you will do something you should do so ('let your yea be yea and your nay be nay'). Most Quakers no longer avoid the theatre as a morally corrupt milieu; however, they are unlikely to be found on ostentatious display in the expensive boxes at the opera or the ballet. Quaker schools have lost their key role as transmitters of Quaker culture; nevertheless, education and self-improvement remain core values for Quakers.

Contemporary Quakerism has been classified by Wilson (1970: 178–81) as a 'reformist sect'. This draws attention to the emphasis within the Society on a divinely inspired mission to reform social evils. Quakers have been prominent in campaigns on homophobia, environmental issues and world peace. The Quaker faith cherishes the 'light within', 'that which is of God in everyone', a personal conscience which expresses itself in commitment to social and political causes.

Although the concept of 'reformism' captures very well the essence of contemporary Quakerism as a social movement, it is less clear that the term 'sect' is as appropriate as it once was. In Wallis's framework, the Society of Friends has evolved into a denomination. In terms of their external conception, Quakers have achieved respectability, reflected in the overwhelmingly middle- and professional class composition of their membership, and the good ecumenical relations the Society enjoys with mainstream Christian churches. As for their internal conception, Quakers do not see themselves as a people with a unique command of the truth. On the contrary, Quakers have consistently refused to develop binding doctrines and dogmas. They are epistemological individualists. Their emphasis is on a Quakerly approach, a Quakerly inflection on how to do things. For example, Quaker decision-making involves a painstaking search for consensus, 'the mind of the meeting', reminiscent of Rousseau's 'the general will'. Quaker deliberations are not adversarial debates followed by democratic voting – what Rousseau called 'the will of the majority'. This Quakerly way presents itself as one approach alongside and working with others – a quintessentially denominational viewpoint.

Varieties of new religious movement

One of the most startling transformations of the religious scene in the west has been the emergence and flourishing of new religious movements, particularly since the late 1960s. They include the most controversial social movements in the modern world. Some have even shown themselves to be life-threatening to the wider society (the Manson Family and Aum Shinrikyo, for instance) and to their own members (the People's Temple and Heaven's Gate). In complete contrast, movements such as Transcendental Meditation have a large clientele of respectable people and business corporations who use TM as a technique to achieve personal and career goals in this world. Clearly, as with long-established religions, new religious movements are not all alike.

An influential classification of new religious movements was proposed by Wallis (1984). His aim was to develop a classification which would be useful in analysing new religions in the west since the Second World War; he was not aiming at a set of universal categories beyond space and time. Instead of this, his classification is rooted in the social, economic and cultural conditions in which new religious movements have emerged, conditions which determined the resources available to them. He distinguished three ideal-types: world-rejecting, world-affirming and world-accommodating.

World-rejecting

Examples of this type are the International Society for Krishna Consciousness (Hare Krishna); the Unification Church (the Moonies); the Children of God (also known as the Family of Love); the People's Temple; the Manson

Family; and Heaven's Gate. This world-rejecting category includes the most controversial new religious movements, many of which have been prime targets of anti-cult pressure groups.

World-rejecting new religious movements are the ones which most closely resemble the epistemologically authoritarian sect. They and they alone have the truth. They impose uncompromising standards of conduct on their followers, standards which they demand in the name of an emotionally remote personal deity – a God more of judgement than of love. Human beings are seen as sinful creatures whose salvation can be achieved only through obedience to God's commandments. The price of membership is high – literally so in cases such as the Children of God and the People's Temple, where followers were encouraged to surrender their assets to the movement. Members must show uncritical obedience to the leadership and enthusiastic commitment to the cause. This entails ascetic self-denying lifestyles, sometimes in the context of communal life in a temple, ashram or other form of religious community. The community holds that there is no salvation outside the faith. Non-members are often branded with derogatory terms – for example 'Karmies', which for devotees of the Hare Krishna movement signals that those outside are locked in the karma–samsara cycle, that is a life of karma (action) followed by death and rebirth with no hope of release.

Stigmatization of outsiders is sometimes used to justify exploiting them, for example by asking for donations to 'charity' while concealing the movement's true identity. To Moonies, this misrepresentation is known as 'heavenly deception'. It is justified by their dualistic conception of the world as a battlefield in the war between God and Satan. The same thinking lay behind the Children of God's 'flirty fishing' – the practice of women members offering sex to powerful outsiders in return for conversion or financial and political support.

In general, apart from the sale of cheap trinkets to raise money, and an occasional show of charitable work, world-rejecting movements do not offer goods and services to the wider society.

An important instance of the world-rejecting type is millenarian movements. These are movements which expect an imminent apocalyptic collapse of the existing world order and its replacement by a perfect new dispensation. In the Christian tradition this involves active belief in the Second Coming of Christ. A Muslim parallel is belief in the Mahdi. In Shi'a Islam, the Mahdi is the 'hidden imam', the religious leader who will reappear and establish a reign of peace and justice according to the will of Allah.

Many contemporary millenarian movements are what Wilson (1970: 93–117) calls revolutionist. That is to say, they are not active revolutionaries participating as political agitators or armed combatants in the war against ungodliness. Instead of this, they are waiting for God to bring about the apocalypse. Jehovah's Witnesses are one example of the revolutionist stance. They are good citizens, not seditionists. It is Jehovah who will wage the war of Armageddon against Satan; the Witnesses' task is to obey Jehovah's commandments and to bring the Truth to as many people as they can before it is too late.

What categories of people have been attracted to world-rejecting movements? Wallis (1984: 120) specifies two factors. First, these movements appeal to people who are marginal to their own society or have been marginalized by it. However, this factor by itself is not decisive. Many disprivileged groups – the poor, old people, ethnic minorities – are repelled by world-rejecting new religions. The latter are not, in Lanternari's phrase, 'the religions of the oppressed' (Lanternari 1963). Instead, their appeal has been mainly to white, middle-class, well-educated young people (though the People's Temple is an interesting exception to this). This is where Wallis's second factor is relevant. They attract people whose values are at odds with those of the wider society, and who find the movement's values more in tune with their own. They offer an invitation to 'drop out'. Because of the rigours of life in world-rejecting movements, for many members their stay is a temporary one. Movements such as the Moonies have always had a very rapid turnover of members, as Barker (1984a: 141–8) clearly demonstrates.

Putting Wallis's two factors together, it becomes clear why world-rejecting movements have attracted young white adults from economically comfortable backgrounds. These are the people for whom 'dropping out' may be not only appealing but also feasible, with good prospects of re-entry back into society after the period of 'time out'. Even here, it is only a minority of young people who are attracted in the first place. For all the public concern, media coverage and political rhetoric, world-rejecting religions have a tiny membership.

World-affirming

At the opposite pole to the world-rejecting movements are those which are world-affirming. Examples here are Transcendental Meditation (TM); Erhard Seminars Training (*est* – invariably italicized and lower case); Scientology; and the Human Potential Movement.

World-affirming movements, as Wallis's term implies, find much to value in the world. People are seen not as sinful but as blinkered, restricted, held back. What they need is liberation, and this is primarily individual rather than collective. Although expressed in all manner of different ways, the mission of world-affirming movements is essentially the same: to enable us to unlock the potential which lies hidden in us all. Implicit in this is an optimistic philosophy of human perfectibility.

The ethos of world-affirming movements is individual self-realization. They offer a set of techniques which virtually anyone can use to improve their mental, spiritual and physical powers. The techniques can be taught painlessly. No special talent is needed to practise TM or Scientology. Practitioners do not cut themselves off from contact with friends and family, withdraw from college or abandon a promising career. On the contrary, personal relationships, educational achievements and career goals are all supposed to benefit. Because of this, world-affirming movements are seldom accused of breaking up families or causing people to drop out.

Bruce (1995: 98–9) points out that there are two varieties of world-affirming movement. On the one hand, there are those which have added a spiritual dimension to western secular psychotherapies. Bruce's example is Insight, a movement which became fashionable in Britain in the late 1970s. Insight's training aimed to liberate people from fear, guilt, anxiety, and the clutter of negative self-images, thereby empowering them to take responsibility for their own lives. On the other hand, there are movements which have taken an eastern religious-philosophical system and adapted it to western sensibilities. Bruce's example here is Transcendental Meditation, which was brought to the west in 1958 by the guru Maharishi Mahesh Yogi, and which shot to fame in 1968 after the passing interest shown in it by the Beatles and the Rolling Stones.

Wallis identifies three related themes in world-affirming movements. First, they claim to help people not only to succeed but also to cope with the stress of individual achievement in a competitive capitalist society. Sometimes people are advised to lower their expectations to a more realistic level – a prominent theme in *est*. Wallis (1984: 30) quotes *est*'s founder, Werner Erhard: 'Happiness is a function of accepting what is.' This means people should abandon any false hopes of greener grass elsewhere. Simply changing your job, your home or your partner is unlikely to deliver what you hoped. As Bruce says (1995: 101), 'movements which promise empowerment often actually deliver acceptance of the status quo.'

Second, world-affirming movements emphasize the 'true' self. People are encouraged to cast off the social constraints of convention and tradition, and the personal shackles of repression and inhibition. 'Authenticity' and 'spontaneity' are valued and cultivated.

Third, world-affirming movements offer strategies for coping with the loneliness of modern life. Their emphasis on self-discovery often goes together with a quest for intimate contact and authentic relationships with other people, usually in the supposedly 'safe' emotional environment of the movement.

Most of the people who use the services of world-affirming movements do so as consumers. The consumer is at the opposite pole from what Weber called a religious *virtuoso*. Religious virtuosity involves rigorous discipline suitable only to a few exceptional individuals. For example, the celibacy of Catholic and Orthodox priests is virtuoso religion. It is not expected of rank-and-file members of the faith; on the contrary, their vocation, traditionally, is to marry and have children. In church-type organizations, religious virtuosity is forbidden to the majority. A graphic example of religious virtuosity in the Christian tradition was the stylites of the fifth to tenth centuries. These were ascetics who spent the whole of their life on the top of a pillar. Food and drink were supplied by their disciples. The stylites devoted most of their time to prayer and contemplation. They also provided services to others, such as reconciling quarrels and adjudicating theological disputes. Their inspiration, St Simeon Stylites, was a renowned champion of orthodoxy against heresy. Even in the warmer regions of Christendom theirs was a harsh existence.

World-affirming movements have a inner core of committed members – devotees or adepts – who practise more advanced techniques. In the case of Transcendental Meditation, these techniques, known as *sidhis*, include levitation. However, the ordinary consumer of TM is not required to participate in the *sidhis* and may not even know about them.

World-affirming movements often have the organizational structure and managerial style of secular multinational corporations. The goods and services they provide are efficiently marketed as commodities. In line with their commercially inspired customer orientation, they arrange their courses and seminars at times convenient to clients. Since the mass market in the west is urban rather than rural, the 'good life' they celebrate is not a back-to-nature rural idyll but a more urban and cosmopolitan success story.

These movements are not overtly 'religious' as religion is conventionally understood in the west. Some of the signs of religion that the state looks for may be lacking: consecrated buildings, collective worship of a deity, an ethical code, a set of divine commandments, or a formal theology with dogmas and creeds. Because of this, their status as religions is often contested.

In contrast to world-rejecting movements, they draw their membership not from the socially marginal but from the socially integrated. These are the very people whose material success and prosperity leaves them caught in the pressures of contemporary capitalism. It is precisely to such a constituency that world-affirming movements pitch their message.

World-accommodating

Examples of world-accommodating religious movement are Subud, the Aetherius Society, western forms of the Japanese movement Soka Gakkai, and neo-pentecostal movements such as charismatic renewal. Wallis has relatively little to say about movements of this type, on the ground that they have been less important than the others (Wallis 1984: 5). Some writers such as Bruce (1995, 1996) omit the world-accommodating type altogether, though this seems an unnecessary loss of conceptual precision.

World-accommodating movements are largely content with or at least indifferent to the world. Instead they are concerned to cultivate their members' interior spiritual life through collective forms of worship or spiritual exercise. This may of course have the benefit that members perform their secular tasks more effectively. But that is not the goal. As Wallis says, such worldly consequences are unintended rather than designed.

Unlike the world-rejecting type, these are not movements of social protest. They do, however, express a different form of protest, one which is less against the world than against religious institutions which are held to be spiritually lifeless. Thus charismatic renewal aims at reinvigorating the spiritual life of Christians, and in particular restoring to contemporary Christianity its long-lost access to charismatic blessings such as *glossolalia*. Christian congregations have found themselves bitterly divided into supporters and opponents of charismatic practices. Dancing, hugging and kissing, speaking in tongues, faith healing, exorcism, using non-traditional forms of worship, abandoning the organ and switching to the guitar and the tambourine: all these have aroused deep passions. They are, however, domestic troubles. Unless an individual is demonstrably harmed (as occasionally with exorcism) the mass media are not interested, and fewer and fewer people outside the churches either know or care about them.

World-accommodating movements typically have a mainly middle-class membership. They do not attract socially marginal groups, and joining them does not involve 'dropping out'. Members are free to decide whether or not to reveal their religious identity to outsiders. Involvement can therefore be unobtrusive, and may have little impact on a member's lifestyle or life-chances. The case of the Aetherius Society shows this (Wallis 1975: 17–34). The society's members take part in esoteric rituals in a cosmic battle on behalf of humanity against the forces of metaphysical evil. Their role as cosmological warriors does not prevent them from returning unremarked to conventional work roles.

The social location of new religious movements

The classification we have been examining is useful in analysing the destinies of the various types of new religious movement.

The least controversial type is undoubtedly the world-accommodating. It is not hard to see why. Their membership is mostly middle-class and respectable. They are not protesting against the world; at worst they are indifferent to it. Their overriding concern is with the spiritual life of their members. This means that they are not engaged in what could be construed as political activity threatening major social institutions or even the state itself. Members are not prevented from carrying out their secular work, nor are intimate relations with family and friends under any obvious threat.

The most controversial movements, again predictably, are those which reject the world. Their revolving membership is made up of socially marginal young people many of whom have 'dropped out' – abandoning education or career, and sometimes breaking contact with their family and friends. Members' conversions are often sudden, coming unexpectedly to shocked parents who struggle to understand what has befallen their son or daughter. Whatever efforts the movements may make to cultivate political support – as the Moonies did in the USA – they are unlikely to receive it for long. These movements are often deeply unpopular with the public, and have few friends in high places. No politician, for example, would make the mistake of thinking that votes could be won by supporting them. Their survival depends on the civil liberties they claim for themselves under the constitutions of western democracies; significantly, they do not flourish in undemocratic societies. The rhetoric of world-rejecting movements, and occasionally their reality, provokes widespread concern about the threat they pose to society and to their own members. Evil purposes are attributed to them, together with sinister techniques of 'brainwashing' or 'mind control'.

On the face of it, world-affirming movements are the ones most in tune with the modern world. They draw into membership not the socially marginal but people who are well integrated into society. They are definitely not inviting people to drop out. They offer self-realization, worldly success, and techniques for coping with the stresses experienced even (or especially) by high achievers. They are optimistic about the human condition. Their members are not devotees but clients. Adopting the model of the commercial organization, they display entrepreneurial flair and efficiency in marketing their services to their clientele. As well as individuals, their clients often include secular corporations seeking to enhance the motivation of their labour force. Unlike the world-rejecting movements, they are unlikely to face allegations that they brainwash their recruits, ruining their careers and disrupting their families.

Even so, world-affirming movements have been controversial. One problem they have is the absence or attenuation of features which are conventionally expected of religions. As we have seen, they may not have consecrated buildings, they may not collectively worship a deity, they may lack ethical principles founded on divine commandments, and they may have no theological system of dogma and creeds. Because of this, they are open to the accusation that they are not 'really' religions at all. Their claims to religious status may be thought to reflect their desire to secure respectability, legal protection and tax advantages. At worst, they may be thought of as no more than fraudulent schemes to raise large amounts of money from gullible people. The fact that Scientological auditing is a never-ending and expensive process is taken by its critics as proof that it is no more than an elaborate swindle.

The second major problem facing world-affirming movements is that their system for releasing human potential may come into conflict with well-established professional groups. Scientology again provides an example. It has campaigned aggressively against ECT (electro-convulsive therapy), psychosurgery and the medical use of psychotropic drugs such as Prozac (Barker 1995: 174). Scientological literature on psychiatry is uncompromisingly hostile. Psychiatry is characterized as a pseudo-science lacking any evidential basis for its pretentious theories and barbaric treatments. It is a massive and dangerous deception perpetrated on vulnerable people by powerful vested interests. Psychiatrists routinely misdiagnose physical ailments as psychiatric conditions. Frail elderly people are particularly at risk of being subjected to electro-convulsive therapy, and the reason, at least in the United States, is financial: Medicare (US government medical insurance) will pay. ECT and psychosurgery are social control in the guise of treatment; their primary effect is not to cure patients but to render them docile.

More profoundly still, the Church of Scientology accuses psychiatry of being not merely a pseudo-science but a crude anti-religious substitute for religion. Psychiatry is, moreover, a conscious conspiracy: it has targeted religion as the enemy, and has sought to infiltrate irreligion into the educational system. Psychiatry has corroded personal morality and social order. No wonder, the church says, there is so much mental illness among psychiatrists themselves. Here is a vivid example of a minority religious movement reflecting back to society the very accusations which are made against the movement itself.

The categories world-affirming, world-accommodating and world-rejecting are put forward as ideal-types. Any given religious movement may well exhibit features of more than one type. This can give rise to significant internal conflicts. One example, discussed by Wallis himself (1984: 81–3; Barker 1995: 176–8), is the Divine Light Mission. The movement was founded in the 1930s and brought to the west in 1971 by the founder's youngest son, the thirteen-year-old guru Maharaji. It oscillated between world-rejection and world-affirmation. At various stages in its development, the movement stressed its world-rejecting, ascetic Hindu origin. It sought to recruit young people disillusioned with the counterculture. Devotees ('premies') were invited into the spartan and celibate communal life of the ashram or 'premie house'. The guru was seen as a saviour, the Satguru or Perfect Master, who would usher in the millennium. At other times, however, the movement adopted a world-affirming position, particularly after the dismal failure of its sparsely attended Millennium 73 festival in the Houston Astrodome. In its world-affirming mode, the movement provided 'the Knowledge' in the form of techniques of meditation to a diverse clientele who were not expected to join an ashram. The trappings of Hinduism were abandoned as the movement became overtly westernized. One symbol of this was that the guru married an American and broke with his Indian family of origin. In the 1980s the name of the movement was changed to Elan Vital, the ashrams were dissolved and the term 'premie' dropped. The movement has adopted a low profile, thereby moving out of the spotlight of adverse publicity (Barker 1995: 178).

Classifying religious movements: aims and prospects

This chapter has reviewed a number of the ways in which religious movements have been classified sociologically. There are many other classifications in the sociological literature – so many that it is quite impossible to examine them all. Many of them are, in any case, variants of the ones discussed above. The proliferation of such classifications has been one of the most striking features of sociological work on religion ever since the classic work of Max Weber.

For sociologists classification is not an end in itself. As with the definition of religion, so with its classification: both are to be judged pragmatically in terms of the results they yield. We should apply the principle known to philosophers as Occam's razor: 'entities should not be multiplied beyond necessity', that is to say, we should seek elegant simplicity in theory construction, dispensing with items that are unnecessary. Classification is designed to aid analysis and explanation by distinguishing things which need to be distinguished. Pointless distinctions are the province of the pettifogging bureaucrat, not the sociologist. This chapter concludes with reflections on the usefulness of classifications of religious movements.

First, some of the categories sociologists have deployed are not value-neutral in everyday speech and other domains of discourse. 'Sect' and 'cult' carry very negative associations. For example, in Britain the term 'sectarian' is routinely applied to characterize religious bigotry and inter-community violence in Northern Ireland. As for 'cult', it has been adopted by the mass media as a pejorative term referring to new religious movements, particularly in the context of allegations of brainwashing and mind control. The Moonies are invariably called a cult, even though sociologists may choose to designate them as a sect on the grounds that they are epistemologically authoritarian. No religious movement calls itself a sect or cult. Many do describe themselves as churches, even if mainstream Christianity refuses to accept them as such. Although sociologists who use these terms aim to do so in value-neutral ways, there is an obvious danger that value-loadings will re-emerge or be read into them. For this reason, many sociologists have abandoned the terms, replacing them by neutral formulations such as 'new religious movements' and 'minority religious movements'.

Second, the categories of church, sect, denomination and cult have deep roots in the Christian tradition. Their transplantation to other faiths and other cultural milieux is problematic. They presuppose a context in which religions are formally organized and the mainstream and the periphery sharply distinguished. They have arguably little relevance to the great Asian faiths.

Third, it is doubtful that we shall ever arrive at a universally agreed classification of religious movements that will stand for all time. The reason for this is exactly the same as the reason why no final definition of religion is possible. Society and culture change, and religion changes with them. Thus the classic church–sect dichotomy was useful in analysing Christian societies when a particular church was closely associated with the nation state. This church–state dichotomy never fitted the American religious scene, and has less and less relevance even in Europe. Hence the emergence of the concept of the denomination. In the late 1960s, however, the church–denomination–sect trichotomy came under increasing strain because of the unpredicted rise of new religious movements, many originating in eastern faiths. This led to a period of theoretical ferment, in which the concept of the 'cult', variously defined, was widely deployed to explain the so-called 'new religious consciousness'. More recently still, New Age religiosity has thrown existing categories of analysis into question.

4

Secularization Triumphant: the Social Insignificance of Religion?

There is a strong case for saying that a concern with religion was at the very heart of classical sociological theory (Wilson 1982: 9). What is problematic is to assess the legacy of classical theorizing to the contemporary sociology of religion. Here a key issue is that the majority of the founders of the discipline of sociology were personally atheists and professionally preoccupied with the *decline* of religion and its eventual replacement by other social institutions and modes of thought (Beckford 1989: 42). Their work laid the foundation for the contemporary secularization thesis, examined below through the work of two of its outstanding exponents, Bryan Wilson and Peter Berger.

The majority of classical theorists were also rationalists, not simply in the weaker sense that they held reason to take precedence over other means of acquiring understanding, but in the strong sense that for them reason was the only path to knowledge. This meant denying that knowledge can come through divine revelation. It also tended to encourage a triumphalist celebration of western scientific progress, together with a judgement that western civilization is superior to all others. The value of the classical legacy to contemporary sociology is therefore not unproblematic.

Auguste Comte and the Law of Three Stages

In his monumental *Cours de philosophie positive* (A Course in Positive Philosophy), published in six volumes between 1830 and 1842, Auguste Comte set out a grand theory of the evolution of society and human understanding. It was formulated as the Law of Three Stages, which he conceived as a necessary and progressive evolutionary sequence.

In the *theological* stage, phenomena are explained as the actions of ficti-tious gods and spirits, supernatural beings who are similar to humans though far more powerful. The theological stage can be subdivided into three phases. First, fetishism, in which each individual object is thought to be inhabited by an indwelling spirit. Second, polytheism, in which the world is peopled by spirits operating in particular spheres – gods of the forest, of the field, of the waters and so on. Third, monotheism, the phase of the great salvation religions of the world. In the theological stage, society is organized hierarchically with power shared between the priesthood and the military.

In the *metaphysical* stage, phenomena are explained in relation to the operation of abstract entities and forces such as Nature. Religion as conven-tionally understood is gradually displaced. Society is governed by church-men and lawyers. This stage is, as Comte said, only a modification of the theological stage and thus merely transitional.

In the *positive* stage, explanations are liberated from religion and meta-physics to become truly scientific. Science rests on observation, and aims to discover the laws governing the operation of the natural and social worlds. Scientists are not encumbered with religious or metaphysical baggage, and do not address unanswerable questions about the purpose of creation or the meaning of life (Comte's legacy to the logical positivists of the twentieth century is evident here). Society is ruled by experts, the latter-day equiva-lent of Plato's philosopher-kings, with sociologists at the top of the scien-tific hierarchy. Their guiding principle is summed up in Comte's formula: *savoir pour prévoir et prévoir pour pouvoir* – knowledge for foreknow-ledge and foreknowledge for action (Thompson 1976: 15).

In Comte's scheme the positive stage is the end point of history. Although science will of course develop, there will be no fourth post-positive stage – for what could such a stage be, other than a regression to irrationality?

Comte's grand three-stage scheme of societal change also applies to the development of scientific disciplines. Each of the sciences undergoes a transition from a theological and therefore fictive beginning, through an abstract metaphysical interlude, to the positive scientific goal. Sciences develop at different rates of growth. Those which have 'simpler' subject matter, such as mathematics, physics and chemistry, develop sooner than more complex sciences such as biology and sociology. Individuals also go through the same three stages. Comte asks us to examine our own biogra-phy: 'Now does not each one of us, when he looks at his own history, recall that he was successively a *theologian* in childhood, for his most important ideas, a *metaphysician* in his youth, and a *physicist* in his maturity?' (Andreski 1974: 20). The history of the individual replicates the history of the species or, in scientific terms, ontogeny repeats phylogeny.

For Comte, religion fails as a system for understanding the world, natural or social. However, the question remains, does religion perform useful functions in society? Here the answer is less clear-cut. Comte expresses a concern which has been echoed by countless successors: that religion distracts human attention away from action in this world and reorients it towards a transcendent order to which this world is supposedly subordinate. Appeasing the non-existent gods becomes more important than altruistic action towards our fellow humans. Religion threatens scientific progress and weakens the social fabric. It is perhaps worth noting that Comte is famous for having invented two words. One was sociology, the other altruism.

Comte argued that religion as conventionally understood would have to be replaced by a positive religion with sociologists as its high priests. We need to love something greater than ourselves, and society needs spiritual power. Religion meets these individual and social needs. Hence Comte's proposed religion of humanity, which drew heavily on medieval symbols and rituals, and celebrated collectivism and humanity in the abstract (Beckford 1989: 26–7).

To those who read Comte today, his proposals for the religion of humanity seem absurd and the role assigned to sociologists at worst vainglorious and at best laughable. His vision is sometimes excused as the product of the mental illness which periodically assailed him. Yet there may be at least one point in its favour – its universalism. Raymond Aron, who was no disciple of Comte, defended him against his sternest critics (Aron 1968: 108). Comte celebrated the best in humanity. He did not select one particular tribal faith and insist it be imposed on everyone else. And at least he did not hold up any existing or imaginary socio-economic order as the object of veneration.

Assessing the enduring significance of Comtean sociology is difficult. One way into it might be to contrast Comte's Law of Three Stages with another threefold scheme which has some similarities but one essential difference. This other scheme has been virtually forgotten by contemporary sociologists, and is seldom referred to in textbooks. It was discussed by Parsons, but only in order to distinguish his own thought from it. Whether or not it deserves to be so utterly disregarded is one matter, but among the reasons for its neglect is one which may cast light on the development of the sociology of religion. The theory in question was advanced by Pitirim Sorokin (1937–41, 1947).

In Sorokin's theory, a society is defined by the values which underpin its culture. There are three basic types of cultural system, which he terms the ideational, the idealistic and the sensate. As with Comte, they follow one another in historical sequence. Each has its own coherence as a cultural system, lasting for hundreds of years before giving way to the next. In Hegelian fashion, Sorokin believed that each of these cultural systems developed to a high point from which no further progress could be made without a fundamental change in the system itself. The culture is played out and ripe for renewal.

The *ideational* pattern gives priority to other-worldly concerns. Ultimate reality is beyond the reach of our senses. Life is to be lived in accordance with the transcendent, which implies mystical other-worldly asceticism, as practised by members of religious orders. The ethical system commends individual acts of self-sacrificing altruistic love.

The *idealistic* pattern is not, as Comte's second stage is, a mere phase of transition. For Sorokin it is a synthesis of elements drawn from the other two stages. A high point of the idealistic synthesis was the Middle Ages.

The *sensate* pattern, like Comte's positive phase, is empirical. There is no ultimate reality beyond sense perception; reality lies in the material world, the here and now. The ethical system is hedonistic, and concerned with worldly success and materialistic gratification.

It can be argued that there is neither more nor less evidence for Sorokin's view than there is for Comte's. Based on scientific evidence alone there may be little to choose between the two grand theories. Comte's own theorizing is in many respects alien to contemporary sociology. As Nisbet (1967: 228) says, 'it is often hard to remember that we are reading the works not of a theologian but of a self-proclaimed scientist.'

One central feature of Sorokin's theory may account for its neglect. The sensate pattern is not the final destiny of human society. On the contrary, we live in degenerate times. Sorokin denounces the excesses of sensate culture, which are manifest in the tide of pornography, obscenity and drug abuse engulfing the west. It is not that sensate values are objectionable in themselves. For example, in the visual arts, in which Sorokin was keenly interested, sensate culture is embodied in the great canvases of the Impressionists, who rejected allegory and religious symbolism and aimed to capture the observable but fleeting moment (they were, incidentally, influenced by Comtean positivism). Sensate art is art for art's sake. It depicts everyday life, including low life – prostitutes and their clients, erotic dancers and their spectators, drinkers of absinthe. Hence its capacity to degenerate into pornography. Carried to excess, sensate values are self-defeating and sensate culture unsustainable.

The key point is that Sorokin saw history as cyclical. The ideational–idealist–sensate sequence repeats itself over and over again. Each of these cultural systems can be judged only in terms of its own values. Whereas Comtean positivists are able to condemn the limitations of the theological and metaphysical stages, no such judgement can be passed by sensate culture on its predecessors. In our own times, sensate culture is on the point of implosion, which will be the dawn of a new idealist era.

The Judaeo-Christian world-view, like the Islamic, treats history as linear. The dominant macro-sociological theories of social change advanced by western sociologists share the Judaeo-Christian perspective. Thus Comtean positivism, Parsonian evolutionism and Marxian dialectical materialism all incorporate a linear philosophy of history. History marches onward to a goal, and we are expected to march optimistically with it. The goal – whether the Kingdom of God or the various secular visions of the good society – is a glorious end state of which we are usually told very little except that it will neither be overthrown nor evolve into something else. Arguably, then, the appeal of these sociological theories is that they resonate with the Jewish and Christian faiths, of which they are secular reworkings. They are convincing because they conform to a template laid down over the centuries. Although they relocate the Kingdom of God from heaven to earth, we can still recognize it as the Kingdom.

Karl Marx and the opium of the people

Karl Marx (1818–83) was born in Trier into a Jewish family living in a Catholic region of Germany. Although both his parents' families had a strong rabbinical tradition, his father Heschel was a cosmopolitan intellectual influenced by Voltaire, Rousseau and other rationalist Enlightenment philosophers. Heschel converted somewhat reluctantly to Protestantism in order to be able to continue practising as a lawyer, changing his name to Heinrich in the process (McLellan 1973: 1–8).

Throughout his adult life Karl Marx was an unswerving atheist. He was a socialist who consistently rejected Christian socialism. Thus, when Hegel died in 1831, Marx aligned with the radical Young Hegelians in opposition to the politically and religiously conservative Old Hegelians. McLellan (1973: 1) begins his study of Marxism and religion with an ironic account of the experiences of a delegation of Young Hegelians, including Marx, who went to Paris in 1843 to join forces with French socialists. The German delegates thought that, since they were now in the land of the French Revolution, they would be mingling with the avant-garde of progressive atheism. They were soon to be disillusioned. Their French counterparts shared Robespierre's hatred for godlessness. To them, Christianity was simply socialism in practice, with Jesus the first communist.

Marx believed that religion had been fully explained once and for all in Ludwig Feuerbach's influential book, *The Essence of Christianity*, which was first published in German in 1841 and translated into English in 1854 by Marian Evans (the novelist George Eliot). Feuerbach argued that God is a projection of humanity, and Christianity a form of wish-fulfilment. An ideal of human perfection – perfection of knowledge, power and love – is projected outside this world on to a fictive being, God. The properties of omniscience, omnipotence and benevolence are attributed to this being. Religion is a delusion not just of the human intellect but of the human will and the human heart, and is therefore something far deeper than an intellectual error or a priestly fraud. In projecting our human qualities outward we impoverish ourselves, creating a God who proceeds to coerce us with his imperious demands. Feuerbach held that religious faith encourages dogmatism, intolerance, arrogance and illiberality, and thereby legitimizes the persecution of unbelievers and heretics. His atheism presents itself as a liberation from this dehumanizing bondage. Humanism implies atheism, since atheism restores to us our true dignity as humans. Atheism will transform us from 'religious and political lackeys of the heavenly and earthly monarchy and aristocracy into free, self-confident citizens of the world'.

Perhaps the greatest twentieth-century exponent of a projection theory of religion was Sigmund Freud (1856–1939), to whom God was a projected and forbidding father-figure. The God postulated by theologians and philosophers is an irrelevance; the God who is truly operative in the human psyche is a jealous, oppressive father. Religious faith belongs therefore to an infantile stage of personality development. In adults it persists only as an obsessional neurosis. Religion has no part to play in the life of a mature adult or an advanced civilization. It is worth noting that this was one of the key issues on which Freud's former pupil, Carl Gustav Jung (1875–1961), departed from Freudian orthodoxy. In Jung's perspective, Freud overemphasized the pathological side of life, generalizing from neurotic states of mind to the whole of human experience. This is the case with Freud's diagnosis of religion as obsessional neurosis. Jung, in contrast, attaches a positive value to all religious traditions. He says that among all his patients in the second half of their lives – by which he means everyone over thirty-five – 'there has not been one whose problem in the last resort was not that of finding a religious outlook on life' (Jung 1961: 264).

Marx regarded Feuerbach's critique of religion as philosophically definitive, and therefore wasted no time in elaborating it. He compared Feuerbach's analysis to the Copernican revolution: 'Religion is only the illusory sun which revolves around man so long as he does not revolve around himself.' Marx would reject inclusive approaches to religion which see it as a core component of culture and even of human nature. However, Feuerbach addressed a public of bourgeois individuals, making an appeal simply to their powers of reason. This was not the way to change the world. Thus Marx wrote in 1845 in his *Theses on Feuerbach*: 'The philosophers have only interpreted the world in various ways, the point however is to change it.' Capitalism carries within itself the seeds of its own destruction.

Although it depends on religion to maintain social order, it is nevertheless an agent of secularization. The proletarian masses would mobilize (or be mobilized) to overthrow the system which oppressed them, after which they would have no further need of religion.

Religion is, then, a distraction from effective political action in this world, offering the spurious consolation of a life to come. Religious movements are measured against the norm of class-based movements, only to be found deficient (Scott 1990: 39). Religious protest is merely pre-political, at best paving the way for class action, at worst siphoning energy from it.

In Marx's famous dictum, religion is 'the opium of the people'. Religion is an opiate not because it causes euphoria but because it is a painkiller. It is not only that the ruling class cynically promote religion in order to keep the masses in check, which is where Lenin placed the emphasis. The masses turn spontaneously to religion to relieve their burden. Religion is not a cultural universal, a necessary component of the human condition, but a product of class society. It is also an epiphenomenon, that is, an effect but not an independent cause. Religion will wither away when the conditions that give rise to it are eliminated. In this respect it is unlike other cultural forms such as the arts and sciences. They suffer under capitalism but will be set free under socialism, whereas religion is irredeemably reactionary.

The Marxian legacy to contemporary sociology is thus double-edged. On the one hand, religion is a this-worldly phenomenon, a cultural product open to sociological investigation. Its claims to a transcendental basis are radically debunked. On the other hand, it is hard to escape the conclusion that religion has little significance, being merely a minor element in the ideological apparatus of the state.

Emile Durkheim and the social functions of religion

Emile Durkheim (1858–1917) was born in Epinal in the Vosges. Like Marx, his family had a rabbinical tradition. Also like Marx, he remained an atheist throughout his adult life. His approach was likewise rationalistic. He too believed that religion as a cognitive system is false, and that we arrive at the truth through the natural and social sciences. Despite this, he insisted that religion cannot be written off as a tissue of illusions or a collective hallucination. There is indeed a reality in and behind religion, though it is not what the faithful imagine it to be. The reality is not God, but Society. Religion fulfils important social and psychological functions. Hence, like Comte before him, Durkheim saw the need for social institutions which would fill the role vacated by religion.

Durkheim's definition of religion was discussed above in chapter 2. For him a religion is 'a unified system of beliefs and practices relative to sacred things, that is to say, things set apart and forbidden – beliefs and practices which unite into one single moral community called a Church, all those who adhere to them' (Durkheim 1915: 47).

Durkheim saw religion as essentially social in character. Religion integrates individuals into 'one single moral community'. An individual's religious faith is ultimately derived from the faith of the community. Religion centres on the sacred, and this is a social construct. The power of religion is generated within the community, as men and women signal to each other through symbols and ritual activity that they hold the same things sacred (Lukes 1973).

Lukes (1973: 462–77) distinguishes three aspects of Durkheim's theory of religion. First, there is the *causal* aspect. Durkheim argued that religious commitment is generated in social situations characterized by 'collective effervescence', when emotions are bubbling over. Symbolically charged acts of collective worship are the settings in which religious beliefs and imagery are produced, reinforced and made vibrant for the believer. Durkheim's thinking here may have been influenced by contemporary theories of crowd psychology, though without the implication that crowd behaviour is inherently pathological or disruptive.

Durkheim's causal approach extended to examining the ways in which social structure shapes the content of religious beliefs and practices. He sought to show that even the fundamental categories of thought – such as our ideas of time, space and causation – are socially determined. It was a sociological rendering of Kant, a bold attempt to give an empirical sociological answer to key problems in philosophy.

Second, Durkheim's theory of religion has an *interpretative* aspect, offering an explanation of the meaning of religious beliefs and practices. Religion is a kind of mythologized sociology. According to Durkheim it provides us with categories of thought through which we understand and interpret social life. Religion expresses, symbolizes and dramatizes social relationships. Here then is the heart of religion: through it, society is represented to itself. As Parkin (1992: 47) points out, this meant for Durkheim that if a society lacked religion it would also lack a proper consciousness of itself. A society without religion would be profoundly pathological.

Durkheim typically ignores the potentially dysfunctional consequences of religion. Surely religion can involve *mis*representation of one's own society and its relationship with others? What else is the terrible history of Christian anti-Semitism? Or consider the European explorers who 'discovered' the native peoples of the Americas. Europeans had a pressing need to explain who these people were, how they got there, and how 'we' should relate to them. Among the resources the explorers and the church drew on was the Bible. The answers to the questions were diverse but, as Leach says (1982: 74), they all implied the superiority of the Christian Europeans to the natives, who were categorized as 'sub-human animals, monsters, degenerate men, damned souls, or the product of a separate creation'. Religious categories provided a warrant for their elimination or subjugation.

Third, Durkheim's theory has a *functional* aspect. Religion promotes social integration by strengthening the bonds between the individual and the society of which he or she is a member. Religion also performs positive functions for the psyche; quite simply, it is good for us – a point diametrically opposed to Marx's view. Durkheim wrote that the believer 'who has communicated with his god is not merely a man who sees new truths of which the unbeliever is ignorant; he is a man who is stronger (*un homme qui peut davantage*)' (Durkheim 1915: 416). Participating in the cult of the faith brings peace and joy, serenity and enthusiasm.

Durkheim maintained that religion could not possibly be founded on an illusion: 'the unanimous sentiment of the believers of all times cannot be purely illusory' (Durkheim 1915: 417). If it were so, the normal processes of evolutionary selection would have put paid to religion long ago. It is on these grounds that Durkheim rejected the animistic theory put forward by Edward Tylor and the naturistic theory advanced by Herbert Spencer. In both of these theories, religion is bound up with a phantasmagorical world dreamed up by the human imagination.

Despite his declared position, most of Durkheim's readers have concluded that his own account makes religion out to be at least partly an illusion. After all, his famous aphorism is that religion is 'society worshipping itself'. That is certainly not what the believers of all times have thought they were doing. Evans-Pritchard (1965: 63–5) pointed to the paradox: 'if Durkheim's theory of religion is true, obviously no one is going to accept religious beliefs any more; and yet, on his own showing, they are generated by the action of social life itself, and are necessary for its persistence.' Worse, as Aron argued, society's self-worship is surely the height of idolatry. Aron (1970: 68) puts the point more strongly than most of Durkheim's critics: 'To suggest that the object of the religious feelings is society transfigured is not to save but to degrade that human reality which sociology seeks to understand.'

Durkheim's position is similar to Jung's. For Durkheim the reality of religion is social, while for Jung it is psychological. Like Durkheim before him, Jung believed that his theory was not reductionist. The psyche is real, hence to say that the truths of religion are psychological is not to rob them of meaning but to endow them with it. It was in this sense that Jung declared, in a famous television interview late in his life, that he did not *believe* in religion but *knew* it to be true.

Durkheim's theory stresses religion's positive impact on the individual and its function in building social cohesion. He offers no account of a dark side of religion for individuals or society. The part religion can play in stimulating social conflict and legitimizing inequality and oppression is ignored. So too is the role of religious leaders – priests, prophets, preachers, sorcerers, mystagogues, shamans and so on. Durkheim pays no attention to the strategies through which religious entrepreneurs mobilize scarce resources. His focus is on the demand side rather than the supply side of religion – a focus replicated in contemporary approaches to secularization.

Unlike many of his contemporaries, Durkheim was searching for a middle way, as Lukes puts it (1973: 482), between 'the facile rationalism of the anti-religious and the explanations or justifications of the religious'. Few of his successors think he succeeded. Although he did not judge it feasible to create an artificial surrogate religion, as Comte had tried to do, Durkheim was preoccupied with the fate of religion in the modern world. Just as religion was not founded on an illusion, so 'there is something eternal in religion which is destined to survive all the particular symbols in which religious thought has successively enveloped itself' (Durkheim 1915: 427). Society will always need religion in the sense of a cult of the faith. Durkheim believed that the religion of the future would celebrate individualism. This would not be individualism as self-indulgence and freedom from social restraint, but an individualism based on human dignity and moral responsibility.

Very few contemporary social scientists share Durkheim's concern to ensure that religion has a future. One exception is Ernest Gellner. Gellner examines two major currents in the modern world, religious fundamentalism and postmodernism, neither of which he is disposed to endorse. Fundamentalism is irrationally dogmatic, postmodernism frivolously irrational. In Durkheimian style, Gellner is searching for a middle way between them which will preserve the sane inheritance of the Enlightenment. His outline proposal is an accommodation between science and religion based on an analogy with the political settlement achieved in constitutional monarchies such as the UK (Gellner 1992: 91–6). Constitutional monarchs retain the rituals and symbols of true monarchies, but have transferred effective political power to secular politicians. Similarly, religion might retain its symbolic role in representing and legitimating the social order, leaving to science the cognitive function of understanding the world.

Although on the face of it this is a Durkheimian approach, Gellner departs from Durkheim in one critical respect, as Beckford (1996: 43) points out. Gellner concedes that his so-called 'constitutional religion' is 'an ironic, non-serious faith, disconnected from genuine conviction about how things truly stand' (Gellner 1992: 93). It is a self-conscious fantasy,

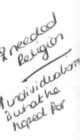

& needed religion

Individualism is what he hoped for

X need to look @ neo-durchemians for Exam ①

rather like adults sentimentally play-acting a belief in Father Christmas. Gellner's solution involves a curious concession to something he despises, the frivolous spirit of postmodernism. It is completely at odds with Durkheim, for whom religion was concerned with serious matters. To divorce symbolism from the serious side of life leaves religion poorly placed to deal with questions of meaning, purpose and evil.

Durkheim's agenda for securing the future of religion reflects his own age rather than ours. The anxieties of contemporary sociology of religion are to be found in the work of Durkheim's great contemporary, Max Weber.

Max Weber and the disenchantment of the world

Max Weber (1864–1920) described himself in a letter he wrote in 1909 as 'religiously unmusical'. Although many commentators gloss over this as if it were a casual or even flippant remark, it may be a profound and perhaps devastating comment on Weber's inner life. Some writers suggest that it prevented him from understanding the nature of religion. What are the limits of a musicology undertaken by an unmusical person? Thus Joachim Wach (1944: 3) said that 'the great scholar's understanding of religion was somewhat impaired by his critical attitude toward it.'

In Weber's perspective, modernity is characterized by rationalization. This is not the same thing as the liberating triumph of enlightened reason. Weber's vision is a long way from Comte's celebration of positivism. Weber's mood is one of resigned and fatalistic pessimism – a mood acutely summarized in Gouldner's phrase, 'metaphysical pathos' (Gouldner 1955). In Weber's view, modernity brings the rule of experts, but these are not benign Comtean scientists. They are bureaucrats. Their outlook on life is summarized by Weber (1930: 182) as follows: 'Specialists without spirit, sensualists without heart, this nullity imagines that it has attained a level of civilization never before achieved.'

Rationalization means the spread of legal-rational systems of domination at the expense both of traditional and of charismatic systems. In *traditional* systems of domination, rulers claim authority on the basis of the sanctity of customs and traditions handed down to a people from time immemorial. Typically, the tradition is seen as God-given, so that the ultimate answer to the question 'why should I obey traditional authority?' is that 'God has willed it so'. Traditional leaders govern by right – for example, the Divine Right of Kings, or the right of the eldest son to succeed his father – and obedience takes the form of loyalty and pious deference to them. Traditional domination involves personal relationships between leaders and their subjects. It is the form of authority exercised by monarchs, sultans, feudal lords, patriarchs and tribal chieftains. Their assistants are not office-holders, still less elected representatives, but dependent subordinates (slaves, family members, vassals, barons, courtiers and the like) whose well-being, advancement and even life itself depend on the leader's favour. Although personal in character, traditional authority is not arbitrary, since the leaders are expected to abide by the canons of the sacred tradition, and risk revolt, usurpation or palace revolution if they are seen to depart too drastically from it.

Charismatic systems of domination also involve personal relations between leaders and led. In popular speech *charisma* is used diffusely, referring to individuals who possess qualities which make them photogenic, or sexually attractive, or persuasive, or generally plausible. Weber meant something much more specific. He borrowed the term *charisma* from the Christian tradition, in which it means a divine 'gift of grace'. Charismatic leaders demand obedience in order to transform their followers' lives. They have the authority to determine things which are normally considered matters of private choice: how you dress, how you do your hair, whom you marry. They can dictate such matters very suddenly and, as Barker remarks (1993: 182–3), without a lot of explanation.

The commands charismatic leaders give often violate the requirements of tradition and the dictates of the law. Charismatic leadership is therefore a source of cultural innovation. Here Weber refers to Jesus's characteristic injunction, 'It is written, but I say unto you'. Charismatic authority implies discipleship, the wholehearted devotion of followers to the charismatic leader. Faith, not critical evaluation, is the appropriate response. The leader and his or her disciples avoid administrative routine and the mundane activity of earning a living through regular employment. They do not have jobs, but depend instead on voluntary donations from the public to whom they minister (Jesus), or sponsorship by wealthy patrons (Krishnamurti), or robbery and extortion (Charles Manson). Charismatic leaders also typically escape the routines of domestic life. Some, like Jesus, are celibate, while others, like Jim Jones, are promiscuous. Avoidance of conventional sex lives and routine ways of earning a living are two of the key ways in which the exceptional qualities of charismatic leaders are symbolized. These people are demonstrably not like the rest of us.

Legal-rational domination is embodied in bureaucratic systems of administration. Authority is impersonal and vested in rules. Commands are obeyed not because of the personal authority of a traditional or charismatic leader, but because they have been issued by the appropriate office-holders acting within their official remit and following approved procedures. Devotion to traditional or charismatic leaders is replaced by meticulous implementation of regulations in conformity to the chain of command within the organization. In contrast to traditional and charismatic systems, legal-rational authority structures separate the person from her or his office. When offices fall vacant, the former incumbent has no say in who should be appointed. A systematic search is undertaken for the person best qualified to fill the post.

In Weber's account of history, the process of modernization makes traditional authority structures obsolete and pushes charismatic systems to the margins of society. Weber's mood in writing of the march of rationalization is not triumphant but resigned. Bureaucracy is described as an 'iron cage' in which we are imprisoned. It stifles human creativity. Legal-rational systems are not necessarily rational in the sense that they involve, in Comtean fashion, the application of scientific expertise for the benefit of humanity. Nor are they necessarily economically efficient. Their rationality is mundane, involving calculation, prediction, measurement and control. If the supreme virtue in a bureaucracy is consistency, the greatest evil is anomaly.

The operation of legal-rational authority structures does not depend on religion for its legitimation. The dominance of bureaucracy is, therefore, at the root of the declining social significance of religion in the modern world. Weber wrote of 'the disenchantment of the world' (*die Entzauberung der Welt*), in the sense that the world has had magic and mystery driven from it. Our forests are managed, not enchanted.

Charismatic leadership and legal-rational systems of domination stand at opposite poles. Charismatic leaders are unpredictable, their lifestyles chaotic, their moods labile and their commands often unfathomable. The authority of charismatic leaders depends entirely on the support of their followers. If the followers lose faith, the leader is left with no power of command. For this reason the charismatic leader's position is precarious (Parkin 1982: 84). In movements with a charismatic leadership, great effort is devoted to what Barker (1993) calls 'charismatization': socializing people to recognize and orient to charismatic authority. Charismatization is achieved through the accumulation of elements, many of them apparently minor but all of them tending in the same direction, to render charismatic claims plausible. Barker points out that the Unification Church has developed an elaborate 'Moonology' similar to Christology, underpinning the belief that Moon is Lord of the Second Advent. References to Reverend Moon pepper Moonie discourse, and in Moonie establishments his photograph is everywhere.

In principle, followers have a duty to acknowledge the leader's charismatic quality, so if they are hesitant or doubtful it is a failing on their part, and one which the leader may come to resent (Bendix and Roth 1971: 175). Lacking the shelter of a bureaucratic office or the sanctity of tradition, the charismatic leader must be ready to perform miracles to satisfy the followers' craving for proof of their leader's charismatic endowment, and to keep them motivated in the face of persecution by the authorities and mockery by unbelievers.

It is therefore a mistake to think that charismatic leaders simply issue commands which followers automatically obey. Leaders may meet resistance, as Muhammad did initially from the people of Mecca, who refused to acknowledge him as the Prophet. Alternatively, leaders may face demands which they are unable or unwilling to satisfy. In the New Testament, Jesus is shown as reluctant to identify himself as Messiah despite being acclaimed as such by the people (Wach 1944: 338).

The tragedy at Jonestown in 1978 (discussed below in chapter 8), where over 900 people lost their lives through suicide or execution, can be seen as an instance of the precariousness of charismatic leadership (Johnson 1979). The charismatic leader of the People's Temple, the Reverend Jim Jones, felt increasingly insecure. He feared persecution by the US authorities and betrayal from within. As the movement developed, members were propelled into a relationship of ever greater dependence on Jones and his entourage. Total commitment was expected, and found its most graphic symbol in the 'white nights', in which members would enact a collective suicide ritual as a test of their faith. The decisive step was Jones's decision to set up a community in virgin territory in Guyana. Members who moved there became utterly dependent on the movement. At the same time, Jones himself was under growing pressure to perform miracles – which he faked. Pressure increased as the community struggled to become self-sufficient, and as the US authorities put increasing pressure on Jones to enable his followers to return to the USA if they wished. In Johnson's account, Jones was caught in a vicious circle. His followers were more and more dependent on him, and he on them. They brought one another down.

If the authority of charismatic leaders is precarious during their own lifetime, the survival of the charismatic movement after the leader dies is also a challenge. In particular, the question of succession is problematic. It is symbolically inappropriate for the movement to advertise a vacancy and interview the applicants, as if they were seeking a new marketing manager. That is not the way charisma is transmitted. Other means are deployed (M. Hill 1973: 170–1). They are typically ritualized and rich in symbolism, involving such elements as consulting oracles, praying for divine guidance and elaborate initiation ceremonies. Weber distinguished three ways in which charisma can be passed on. First, the transmission of charisma can be based on symbolically charged criteria which guarantee the outcome. An example of this is Tibetan Buddhism, which mounts an organized search for the boy child who bears charisma, the new Dalai Lama. Second, the leader may designate his or her successor, sometimes making a surprising choice. Jesus designated Simon (whom he renamed Peter, the rock), a fallible man who would deny him three times. Finally, the leader's close disciples may designate the successor. In essence, this is how the Catholic Church elects a new pope. Cardinals are summoned to Rome, and are secluded in conclave behind locked doors. They are shielded from all communication to or from the outside world, and the whole area is checked for bugging devices. The voting procedure takes place in the Sistine Chapel and is highly ritualized. The world-famous sign that the cardinals' deliberations have reached a conclusion is the emission of white rather than black smoke from the chimney – white being an auspicious colour, and one of the papal colours (the other is yellow). Despite the comparative efficiency of information technology, it can safely be predicted that the traditional convergence on Rome is not about to be replaced by e-mail or tele-conferencing.

Whatever the method of selection, the duty of the faithful is to acclaim the new leader, who governs by right. Over time, charisma may come to be regarded as hereditary, as in monarchies, thus evolving into the traditional mode of domination.

The death of the charismatic leader can unleash a succession crisis. This happened to ISKCON when its founder, His Divine Grace A. C. Bhaktivedanta Swami Prabhupada, died in 1977. He had entrusted the spiritual well-being of the movement to eleven gurus. Within ten years of his death, many of these had either left the movement or been expelled from it (Barker 1995: 185).

The divisions within Islam turn on the question of succession to the Prophet. In the majority Sunni tradition, Muhammad's successors were caliphs, that is to say guardians of the faith, its sacred rites and its traditions. Caliphs were not charismatic leaders. Muhammad is the Seal of the Prophets, so no successor can partake of his divine inspiration. After the first four caliphs, who were held to have known Muhammad personally, the caliphate became dynastic until its eventual abolition by Kemal Ataturk in 1924. In the Shi'a tradition, by contrast, Muhammad is held to have appointed Ali as his successor, the first in a line of exemplary prophets or imams, who through divine inspiration are able to interpret the Qur'an infallibly. Hence the continuing influence of a charismatic element in Shi'a Islam, as shown by the authority wielded in Iran by the ayatollahs. Shi'a also embraces a powerful millenarian expectation. The majority among Shi'ites are Imamis or 'twelvers'. For them the twelfth imam was the Mahdi, the 'hidden imam' who did not die but mysteriously departed, and who will come again to rule according to the will of Allah. Throughout history several charismatic leaders have claimed to be the Mahdi. A minority within the Shi'a tradition are the Isma'ilis or 'seveners', one branch of whom are followers of the Agha Khan. The Isma'ilis believe that after the death of the sixth imam his elder son Isma'il, and not Isma'il's brother, should have been designated the seventh imam. As with other branches of Islam, the Isma'ilis have developed their own distinctive body of religious philosophy and practice. The example of Islam shows that crises over the theology and practicalities of succession can arise and persist long after the death of the charismatic leader.

For Weber, charismatic leadership tends to become routinized. The life of a charismatic band of disciples is hard. As the movement gains new members and spreads geographically, so pressure mounts to institutionalize practices into formal procedures. When the leader dies, something of his or her charisma dies too. The vibrant and innovative personal charisma of the founder mutates into charisma of office – as with the papacy. This, in turn, gradually shades into traditional authority or bureaucracy. Even so, as Hill argues (1973: 172), charisma remains *latent* within the movement as a resource on which revivalists can draw. For example, the claim of charismatic renewal within mainstream Christian denominations is to restore to the faithful the gifts of the spirit – in Christian terms, the *charismata* – which were given to the apostles at the first Pentecost. Speaking in tongues, interpretation of tongues, prophecy, healing – these gifts are available to Christians now. The charismatic foundation of the church is thus a resource on which ginger groups can draw to shake the church out of what they see as its bureaucratic inertia. After all, Weber presented traditional, charismatic and legal-rational forms of domination as ideal-types. Any given empirical situation will normally contain a mixture of elements, and these are resources to be argued over and activated.

Even though Weber's best-known work, *The Protestant Ethic and the Spirit of Capitalism*, proposes a complex link between Calvinism and modern capitalism (Marshall 1982, 1980), it also carries the implication that contemporary societies have moved beyond the stage of dependence on religion.

Weber was specifically concerned with the rational form of capitalism. Other forms of capitalism exist, but they are not the object of his thesis (Parkin 1982: 41). They are *booty capitalism*, in which wealth is acquired through war, plunder and speculation, as with merchant adventurers; *pariah capitalism*, that is economic activities undertaken by socially marginalized groups, for example money-lending by Jews in medieval Europe; and *traditional capitalism*, that is large-scale economic activities which are not however designed for the continuing pursuit of profit. Modern *rational capitalism* involves a formally free market in labour, laws of contract, a money economy and a banking system, double-entry bookkeeping to ensure accurate accounting, and the systematic pursuit of profit over the long term.

Weber believed that most of the world's religions have stood in the way of the development of the spirit of rational capitalism. They give too much scope to magic, mystery, superstition and other-worldly concerns.

Buddhism, Hinduism and Taoism all promote *other-worldly* asceticism: withdrawal from the world rather than engagement in it. Confucianism produces benignly paternalistic societies that give little stimulus to innovation. Islam, to Weber, is essentially a warrior religion, seeking conquest rather than the disciplined pursuit of profit. Judaism lacks ascetic values, and is therefore best adapted to medieval adventure capitalism. Only ascetic Protestantism, particularly in its Calvinist form as developed not by Calvin himself but by the Puritans in the late seventeenth century, was well suited to the spirit of rational capitalism. In part, this was because Protestantism placed few barriers in the way of capitalist development. Weber goes beyond this, arguing controversially that ascetic Protestantism actually *stimulated* rational capitalism – though this was an unintended and paradoxical consequence of Calvinism.

The Calvinist doctrine of predestination, according to Weber, induces 'salvation anxiety'. Our fate is sealed before we are born: we are predestined to be either among the elect who are saved or among the damned. Sacraments administered by a priesthood cannot change this. Nor, according to Calvinism, can we know which category we are in – an intolerable psychological burden, Weber says. People inevitably cast around for signs that they are among the elect, and find these in material prosperity. They draw the theologically invalid but psychologically satisfying conclusion that God will favour with material prosperity those whom he has chosen. As Parkin comments (1982: 45), the doctrine of predestination, which might have encouraged passive acceptance of one's unalterable fate, is transformed into a belief which spurs people to work systematically and single-mindedly in the pursuit of profit, in order to prove to themselves and others that they are among the elect.

Calvinism is characterized by Weber as a form of 'this-worldly asceticism'. Other-worldly retreat into contemplation and mysticism is rejected: God requires us to act in this world to secure the benefits of the next. Our acts must be self-denying, displaying self-control, sobriety, thrift, frugality and deferred gratification. Work is a vocation, a calling from God. Calvinism is not self-indulgent – that is an orientation more suited to booty capitalism. The fruits of one's labour are not squandered but invested.

Weber is clear that modern capitalism no longer depends on religion. Ascetic Protestantism has done its work, and capitalism today is powered by a secular dynamic. Inner-worldly asceticism as a value-system can survive the death of God. It does not matter whether we are Protestants, Catholics, Jews – or atheists. Religious affiliation is no longer relevant. As Weber remarked, in a characteristically bleak diagnosis, 'The Puritan wanted to work in a calling, we are forced to do so' (Weber 1930: 181).

Bryan Wilson on rationalization and societalization

In contemporary sociology, the Weberian approach to religion has deeply influenced the work of Bryan Wilson, a leading exponent of the secularization thesis.

Throughout his writing on religion Wilson has held to a succinct definition of secularization as 'the process whereby religious thinking, practice and institutions lose social significance' (Wilson 1966: 14). As in Weber, the key to secularization is the process of rationalization which inevitably accompanies modernization. Short of a global catastrophe such as thermonuclear war or a cosmic event decimating the human population – possibilities on which Wilson refrains from speculating – secularization appears irreversible. Modernity implies secularization, and there is no reason to believe that any counter-trend could reverse it.

Wilson does not devote much space to defining religion. Even so, it is clear that he rejects inclusive and functional definitions. To him, religion means 'the invocation of the supernatural' (Wilson 1982: 159). Religion without the supernatural or the transcendent is a contradiction in terms. Inclusive definitions simply beg the question. Nothing is gained by adopting a definition so broad that all societies and all people everywhere are equally religious. All this does is to define the secularization thesis out of existence before anyone has taken the trouble to see whether it is true or false. That is a mere definitional trick, and a pseudo-solution to a real problem.

Rationalization, as Weber demonstrated, sweeps aside tradition and marginalizes charisma. Wilson (1975) examines in detail the fate of charisma in the modern world. To him, charisma is quintessentially a property of *pre-modern* societies: there and there alone belief in charisma is widespread and credible. In these societies – Wilson calls them 'simpler' – social relationships and social organization are interpreted in personal terms. This is true of traditional authority as well as charismatic leadership (Wilson 1975: 20–6). In both, power is anthropomorphized, residing in great men and great women. Given this, it makes sense to place faith in a charismatic leader as someone who will transform the world. Jesus Christ did just that. Nowadays, however, charisma survives as little more than a romantic idea from the remote past. It can be reactivated, but only in small social movements operating at the periphery of society and with no capacity to change anything of significance except perhaps the lives of a few followers. Collectively they have never added up to a counterculture; instead, they are 'random anti-cultural assertions' (Wilson 1976: 110), as diverse as they are ineffective.

One symptom of the marginality of charismatic movements in the modern world is the redefinition and even trivialization of the concept of charisma itself. On Shils's (1965) account, *all* leadership has a charismatic quality. This applies not just to religious prophets but to politicians and chief executives of major business corporations. By redefining Weber's concept in this way, Shils turns charisma from a social force opposed to bureaucratic rationalization into its very embodiment. More commonly, the concept is debased into a personality trait manifested by Hollywood stars, rock musicians and other entertainers with a mass public of fans. In the Weberian sense, however, charisma is not a trait of personality but a complex relationship between a leader and a following. Fans are not followers, and entertainers are not leaders seeking to transform society. Except for a hard core of true devotees, fans are in it for fun – and they know it. Fandom is 'time out' from the stresses of modern life, not a radical challenge to it.

Mainstream Christian churches, both Protestant and Catholic, have felt the influence of neo-pentecostal 'charismatic renewal', involving exuberant worship, *glossolalia* and miraculous healing. Here again the concept of charisma is being adulterated. What is missing is the key element of charismatic leaders transforming tradition and legal-rationality (Wilson 1975: 121–4). Paradoxically, the charismatic movement's leaders are not charismatic leaders. Their authority rests not on new revelations but on revitalizing the faith and restoring its blessings. Influential evangelists such as Billy Graham and Oral Roberts are revivalists who preach the word, not prophets who challenge it. They do not say, 'It is written, but I say unto you'. Theirs is a 'derived charisma' (Wilson 1975: 116–19), since everything they do is in the name of Jesus.

Wilson's account of secularization leaves mainstream religion in a straitjacket from which it cannot escape. Any attempt to accommodate to the dictates of secular society is self-defeating. Avant-garde liberal theologians succeed only in making themselves look ridiculous, not least in the eyes of the secular thinkers whose good opinion they so earnestly seek and so rarely receive. Charismatic renewal, although it promises revitalization, is interpreted by Wilson (1976: 85–8) as 'voluntary destructuration' – by which he means the deliberate abandonment of old practices and procedures. Other examples of this are the jettisoning of the Latin mass in the Catholic Church after the reforms unleashed by Vatican II (the so-called *aggiornamento*, the updating of Catholicism), the rejection of hierarchy in favour of lay authority, and ordination of women to the priesthood. None of these changes has the desired effect, Wilson argues. Instead they disrupt and destabilize the organization, occasionally giving rise to schisms which further weaken the parent body. Nor can mainstream denominations renew themselves by merging with their competitors. Ecumenical ventures are a sign of weakness rather than strength, and when denominations unite they invariably wind up even weaker than they were before – as with the union of the various traditions of Methodism in the UK, or the merger of Congregationalists and Presbyterians to form the United Reformed Church (Currie 1968; Wilson 1966: 181–205).

One overlooked aspect of secularization is the long-term decline of the clerical profession (Wilson 1992: 198). Clerical salaries are now sub-professional and falling. For too long, mainstream churches have been living off economic capital accumulated in the past, but this is now dangerously depleted. Hence the burden of financing the profession weighs ever more heavily on dwindling congregations who show themselves reluctant to pay the market price for professional service. The profession struggles to recruit well-qualified people, as indicated by the declining educational levels of the clergy (Towler and Coxon 1979). It is also an ageing profession. As congregations decline so does the pool of people who might come forward with a calling to the ministry. Crisis is averted for a while by drawing on the unpaid services of lay volunteers, particularly women. Under the pressure of financial and demographic exigency, many denominations have opened the profession to women, not without controversy.

Wilson's theory, as Robertson (1993: 2) and Beckford (1989: 109–10) observe, rests on a sharp distinction between *Gemeinschaft* and *Gesellschaft*, community and association. Religion is the culture of community. The latent functions of religion depend upon stable local communities enduring over time. Religion requires particularistic and affective relationships between people who treat one another as whole persons. Priests need close personal relationships with their congregations, gurus with their devotees and charismatic leaders with their followers. Religion and fellowship are inseparable. Wilson made this point succinctly in discussion with colleagues in a forum set up as part of the consultation process involved in Vatican II. He said: 'I interpret religion very largely as necessarily a face-to-face, person-to-person phenomenon; when religion ceases to be that, it loses a great deal of its vigour and of the power it holds over the individual. In our role-articulated world, face-to-face relationships in the community have ceased to be the principal context of people's lives' (Caporale and Grumelli 1971: 177).

The process Wilson calls *societalization* replaces personal ties with rule-governed contractual relations between role-performers – managers and workers, salespeople and customers, bureaucrats and the public. Personal trust gives way to abstract expert systems, and goodwill yields to formally codified rights and duties. People are judged by their performance in achieving secular goals. Morality is replaced by calculation, so that personal virtue counts for very little, often proving to be a liability rather than an asset.

The rise of the nation state spells the end of locality: 'Local crafts, local products, local customs, local dialects have all shown a rapid diminution in our own times' (Wilson 1982: 154). Urbanization and suburbanization leave religion with little to celebrate in terms of community spirit (Wallis and Bruce 1992: 13). Religion has less and less scope to supply an overarching system of transcendentally grounded values.

Once societalization is complete, the social system operates without reference to religious institutions or to the religious orientations of individuals. Religion retreats into the private sphere. People may continue to evince a religious faith, but this is increasingly a matter of personal taste, a private choice which has no impact on the operation of the social system. Religious movements therefore face an unavoidable dilemma. To have any impact in the modern world they must accommodate to the forces of rationalization and societalization, but in doing so they undermine their own *raison d'être*.

Wilson's powerful elaboration of the secularization thesis has not gone unchallenged. In response to his critics, he has repeatedly emphasized a number of fundamental points. First, too much attention is paid to raw statistics of religious activity with little consideration of the social meaning of participation – in short, crude behaviourism. Hence Wilson's interpretation of the situation in the United States (discussed below), where high participation rates cannot compensate for the shallowness of religious commitment and its secularization from within. Attention has focused on church attendance, to the detriment of other relevant measures such as baptisms, confirmations and church weddings. A telling British instance of this is the terminal decline of the rite of passage known as the churching of women (Wilson 1992: 197). Although churching is 'officially' an expression of thanksgiving to God after childbirth, in practice it was treated as removing ritual uncleanness. Women who had given birth were not supposed to go out of doors until they had undergone the rite of churching. The practice had not shed its origins, which lay in the Jewish rite of purification. Churching was a rite integral to pre-industrial community life, and survived until the 1950s in the 'urban villages', the vibrant, close-knit, working-class communities which flourished in all major cities. Thus Young and Willmott's (1957: 39–40) celebrated study of working-class life in Bethnal Green, a community in the East End of London, pointed to churching as a vital ingredient of family and community life. Young and Willmott's respondents in the early 1950s referred to the rite as traditional, old-fashioned and superstitious. Even so, over 90 per cent of the women in their study had been churched after the birth of their last child. It is a measure of how secular we have become that churching has faded to the point where few people have even heard of it.

A second point Wilson makes in response to his critics is to stress the declining economic position of religious organizations. We have already mentioned the clerical profession's drastic loss of status and the implications it has for secularization. That is one sign of the underlying economic reality: an ever dwindling proportion of the Gross National Product of First World nations is allocated to supernatural concerns. If we are looking for a hard indicator of secularization, here it is.

Third, critics of secularization, including the 'new paradigm' and 'rational choice' theorists, discussed in chapter 5, concentrate on the voluntaristic commitment of individuals and the benefits they derive from it. The societal functions of religion – the role it once played in legitimizing secular power, underpinning the law, educating the populace, and interpreting world-historic and cosmic events – are all forgotten. Wilson argues that it is not an accident that critics of the secularization thesis adopt individualistic research methodologies, such as opinion surveys and analysis of aggregate descriptive statistical data, which dissolve culture into the behaviour of atomized individuals. The narrowing of the sociological gaze reflects the social reality of religion: this is indeed what it has shrunk to.

Fourth, Wilson asserts the growing social, cultural, economic and political irrelevance of religion. Even where religious activists gain publicity they rarely achieve their goals – as with the Moral Majority in the United States (Wilson 1992: 203), a point also pushed home by Bruce (1988). Opponents of the secularization thesis often hold up modest revivals experienced by particular denominations over limited periods, as if these were signs of the restoration of religion to the central place it once enjoyed.

Peter Berger on religion and plausibility

The tone of Wilson's work is clinically detached in the Weberian manner. Peter Berger's writing, in contrast, is committed, agonized and confessional. The core problem for Berger is the possibility of authentic religious affirmation in a secular society. Not only is this a cultural problem, it is also a dilemma for Berger himself, who struggles to reconcile professional objectivity as a social scientist with personal commitment to the Christian faith.

Berger draws on a wide range of theory. He takes seriously Marx's contention that religion can legitimize inequality, oppression and alienated social relations. He shares Durkheim's concern for social order and integration. Like Weber, he is preoccupied with the processes through which the world has been rationalized and disenchanted. He draws deeply on existentialist philosophy, in its atheistic as well as Christian form. He also grapples critically with contemporary theology.

For Durkheim, as we have seen, the sacred is opposed to the profane. Berger builds on this, giving it a characteristic twist. For him the sacred is

opposed to chaos. Chaos is meaninglessness, or *absurdity* as French existentialism called it. Religion is 'a shield against terror' (Berger 1967: 22). It
gives meaning to human existence. The meaning it supplies is not proxi-
mate but ultimate, since religion is 'the audacious attempt to conceive of
the entire universe as being humanly significant' (1967: 28). Existentially,
death is the ultimate challenge to meaning. And, as the Victorians tended to
put it, the problem is not only my death but *thy* death.

At the heart of all religious faith is the problem of *theodicy*. This term,
first coined at the turn of the eighteenth century by the philosopher Leibniz,
is a composite made up of the Greek words for god and justice. The challenge of theodicy is to explain evil, suffering and death, and to reconcile
them with the existence of God. The problem is acute for monotheistic
religions. Stendhal expressed this in an epigram: 'The only excuse for God
is that he does not exist.' In the case of mainstream Christianity, God is
characterized as an omniscient, omnipotent and loving creator. Why, then,
is there evil and suffering? Doesn't God know about it? Can't he do anything to stop it? Doesn't he care? These are intricate intellectual puzzles,
and also agonizing questions we all confront (or repress). Berger's starkest
statement of the secularization of the west is that Christian theodicy has lost
its plausibility (1967: 125).

Although Berger refuses to adopt an inclusive definition of religion – on
this point he differs markedly from Luckmann (1967), with whom he collaborated on one of his major works (Berger and Luckmann 1966) – he
nevertheless assigns a crucial role to religion as integral to the human condition. If we can succeed in living without religion it is only with enormous
difficulty. Secular ideologies – Marxism, for example, or scientific humanism – provide some elements of hope, and a role for the individual in building
the future. But how well do they cope with death, mine or thine? Arguably,
secularism boils down to a form of either heroic despair (as in atheistic
existentialism), or psychopathological denial (as in consumerism), or ideological bombast (as in Marxism-Leninism). Secularization is therefore a
profound problem for Berger, personally as well as scientifically.

Berger's conceptualization of secularization is similar to Wilson's. He
defines it as 'the process by which sectors of society and culture are re-
moved from the domination of religious institutions and symbols' (Berger
1967: 107). It has three dimensions. One is *social-structural*: in the west,
Christian churches have lost functions which are now performed by secular
agencies. Equally important for Berger is the *cultural* aspect. The religious
content of western art, music, literature and philosophy has drastically
declined. Meanwhile the triumphant natural and social sciences have promoted a secular perspective on the world. Finally, secularization of society
and culture is accompanied by a secularization of *individual consciousness*.

Fewer and fewer people think in a religious mode. The faithful are a cognitive minority.

Berger rejects monocausal explanations of secularization. To him it is a many-sided process with a set of familiar root causes: industrialization, urbanization, rationalization and the rise of science. Echoing earlier social thinkers including Hegel, Schopenhauer, Nietzsche and Weber, Berger also argues that religion itself has been, paradoxically, an unintentional carrier of secularization (Berger 1967: 110–25). Just as, for Marx, the capitalist system nurtures the seeds of its own destruction through its reliance on an industrial proletariat, so for Weber and Berger the Judaeo-Christian tradition contains elements which lead to secularization.

Weber argued that the origins of the disenchantment of the western world lie in ancient Judaism (Weber 1952; Zeitlin 1984). Like Protestantism but unlike the great Asian faiths, the religion of Israel was this-worldly. Theologically, its key feature was the utter rejection of any form of polytheism, a refusal which had profound social and cultural consequences.

Dictionary definitions of polytheism as the belief in and worship of more than one god, though apparently straightforward, conceal the full implications of polytheism as a cultural system, according to Weber. Polytheistic deities are fundamentally limited:

- they do not reign supreme, but are subject to impersonal forces – the Latin fates, the Greek *moira*
- none of them is omniscient or omnipotent, not even Zeus or Jupiter
- they did not create the universe, but were themselves born out of it
- they can be manipulated and coerced by human magic
- they are dependent on worship and sacrifices
- they are the victims of their own urges, lusting for one another and for humans
- they war among themselves
- humans can become demi-gods, sometimes even gods

The strict monotheism of Israel had no truck with any of this. God is a creator who proclaims a unique covenant with his people. Israel's duty is unswerving obedience to God's commandments. In return, God promises a strikingly this-worldly salvation: wealth, fertility, conquest, deliverance from bondage to Egypt and dominion over Canaan. This is not a god who can be manipulated by mortals: no sorcery or magic can bend God's will. Nor are there any other entities who can influence him: he stands alone. The crucial point which emerges about other gods, such as Baal or Dagon, is that they do not exist.

Magical coercion of the gods, a foolish expression of human arrogance, is replaced by the duty of obedience to the creator. Miracles can be performed only in the name of God, and only if God wills them. Evil is transferred from the realm of mythology to that of ethics.

Monotheism, in Weber's opinion, had powerful consequences. It liberated humanity from dependence on mythology and magic, while at the same time forcing us to confront ethical choices. The natural world had the spirits driven from it, and became an arena for human endeavour in the service of God.

For Berger as for Weber, disenchantment of the world begins in the religion of ancient Israel. Exodus from Egypt was more than a political emancipation. It marked Israel's break with an entire universe of meaning. The religion of Israel repudiated the cosmological world-view of Mesopotamian civilizations. In this world-view, the empirical and the super-empirical are continuous with one another. The human world is embedded in a cosmic order, so that everything that happens in society has its analogue on the level of the gods. To illustrate his point Berger gives two examples. First, he cites disobedience to the God-King of Egypt. As well as political and ethical implications, disobedience upsets the cosmic order. It may jeopardize the annual flooding of the Nile or national security against foreign aggression. Punishing the individual offender is not just a matter of appeasing a wrathful king; it is crucial to restoring a right relationship between Egyptian society and the cosmic order on which it rests.

Berger's second example of the cosmological world-view of Mesopotamian cultures is their practice of sacred prostitution. This is not just the satisfaction of lust by the world's oldest profession, though that was doubtless part of it. Sacred or temple prostitution was *sacramental*. Through an ecstatic act it put human beings in touch with the divinely suffused cosmos. That is why it was rejected by the religion of Israel. To Israel, the world was not divine but a divine creation.

On Berger's analysis, Israel's rejection of the cosmological world-view had three motifs: transcendentalization, historization, and the rationalization of ethics.

Transcendentalization   The God of the Christian Old Testament stands outside the cosmos which he has created. He is radically transcendent, totally other, and not to be identified with any element in nature or culture. Strict monotheism means that he is alone and self-sufficient, lacking parents, companions or offspring. He is not a tribal divinity naturally tied to Israel. Nor does he need Israel's support. He cannot be manipulated by magic. Even when he demands sacrifices he does not depend on them. He is the universal God who has chosen Israel as his people and who makes demands on them.

Historization   The Hebrew Scriptures are rooted in history, more so than any other sacred writings of a world religion, even including the Christian New Testament. All of the books of the Old Testament (except Ecclesiastes and Job, which are among the later texts) have a historical orientation. The world is not populated by mythologized divine entities and forces. Instead it is the arena of the actions of human beings and of the mighty acts of God.

Rationalization of ethics   The God of Israel is not like the gods of Greece and Rome, a capricious deity whose erratic behaviour may be influenced by human flattery or deceit. God's commandments are self-consistent ethical laws that have to be obeyed. Both the priestly and the prophetic elements in the religion of Israel had ethical rationalization as a dominant motif. The priestly ethic entailed a formalization of religious law governing everyday life, and the elimination of magical and orgiastic rites. The prophetic strand insisted that life be devoted to the service of God, which again entailed a rationalized ethical structure guiding all human activity.

In its origins, and in its western development in Catholicism, Christianity reversed two aspects of the secularizing thrust of the religion of Israel while retaining its emphasis on history. First, the doctrine of Incarnation and its theological elaboration into the doctrine of the Trinity significantly modified Judaism's radical monotheism and the transcendentalization it expressed. To the offence of monotheistic Judaism and Islam, God has a Son. Catholicism proliferated a host of angels and saints, culminating in the celebration of the Virgin Mary as mediator and even co-redeemer. The world was re-enchanted, and repopulated with semi-divine entities mediating between God and humanity.

Catholicism also put ethical rationalization into reverse. Unlike Judaism, whose numerous ethical laws apply to all the faithful, Catholicism institutionalized virtuoso religion in monastic orders – a calling not suitable for ordinary people. The piety of the Catholic laity did not depend on a rationalization of ethics but rather on their acceptance of the authority of the priesthood as stewards of the mysteries of God.

The Protestant Reformation reasserted the secularizing dynamic which had been temporarily halted by medieval Catholicism. Protestantism divested itself of mystery, miracles and magic, which meant 'an immense shrinkage in the scope of the sacred' (Berger 1967: 111). Sacraments were pruned. Western Catholicism and eastern Orthodoxy recognize seven sacraments instituted by Christ. They are baptism, confirmation, the eucharist, penance, extreme unction, holy orders and matrimony. Protestant Churches stripped much of this sacramentalism away. Some – Quakers and the Salvation Army, for instance – have no sacraments at all. Others place the emphasis on baptism and the eucharist, redefining them so that they lose much of their supernatural and magical associations. Guardian angels no longer watch over us. Saints and the Virgin Mary do not intercede for us. The Virgin ceases to be an object of veneration. Protestants do not pray for the dead, who are left to face the Almighty without intercession. There are no sacred places of pilgrimage where miraculous cures may be expected. Reality is polarized between a radically other deity and a fallen world of rather lonely men and women. In Weber's phrase, the world is disenchanted.

For Berger, the Protestant Reformation put religion at risk. It reduced the relationship between humanity and the divine to one narrow channel: the Word of God, the uniquely redemptive action of God's grace. As long as this connection remained plausible, religion continued to flourish. But as soon as it was severed secularization proceeded unchecked. That is the modern condition, and Protestantism played an unintended but decisive part in bringing it about.

The key feature of contemporary western societies is their pluralism. Modernity involves a move from fate to choice, including choice of religion. Religious movements operate now in a competitive market-place. One theme in Berger's writing is that this can generate a shallow consumerist approach to religion, in which religious firms, like the manufacturers of detergents, market their products to consumers who are fastidious and fickle. The market is a meeting-place for self-interested consumers and manipulative producers.

Berger's critique of modernity goes much deeper than an intellectual's denunciation of consumerism. Pluralism undermines objectivity. Not only do we make choices, we know that we are doing so. Relativism is a fact of society and of our consciousness. In religion, this is a guilty secret. The Israelite covenant has been reversed: God has not chosen us, we have chosen a god, or even no god at all. According to Berger modernity brings a widespread loss of innocence. Even conservative forms of faith, so-called old-time religion, are self-conscious strident revivals lacking the pristine vitality of the originals. They too are an option. We cannot escape modernity by opting into protest against it, since such protests are themselves thoroughly modern phenomena.

All belief-systems are grounded in what Berger calls a *plausibility structure*, by which he means a set of social institutions and social networks whose functioning and day-to-day reality render belief plausible. It is a Durkheimian insight: religion depends on a practising community, and there is no such thing as a literally private religion. The mistake Durkheim made was to presume that religions and plausibility structures are necessarily society-wide.

In the medieval period, according to Berger (1967: 46–52), the Christian world had four imperatives:

- to socialize successive generations into the faith – hence the church's monopolies in education, scholarship and the law
- to protect the nation state's frontiers against invasion
- to extend the nation state's frontiers – hence the Crusades and other wars of religion
- to deal with religious deviants through either repression (as with the Inquisition) or segregation (as with the ghettoization of Jews).

In the modern world, most nation states embrace a plurality of sub-societal religions and plausibility structures. Claims to absolute authority in this competitive situation are hard to enforce and, worse, hard to credit. Put another way, when religion no longer holds a monopoly it faces a far more difficult problem of social engineering. Religion can no longer construct a sacred canopy over everybody, a common culture in which we all share. The problem of 'other religions' breaks free from its confines in theology and poses a set of practical problems for nation states and their citizens. There is also a pressing problem for religious institutions themselves, in that modernity forces them increasingly into the sectarian defence of a cognitive minority.

In Wilson's analysis it is hard to see what, other than a global cataclysm, could reverse the tide of secularization. Berger's approach, in contrast, does leave religious revival as at least a possibility. Berger is, after all, quite explicit that scientific and secular belief-systems cannot provide satisfying answers to questions of ultimate meaning. No amount of formal rationality can fill the void. Modern men and women are no more enlightened than their forebears. Religion has not been exposed as a fallacy, nor disproved as if it were like the phlogiston theory of combustion. Secular substitutes for religion, including those devised by Comte and others, have not fared well. Originally presented as ultra-modern, they soon come to seem pathetically old-fashioned, so much so that hardly any sociologists nowadays can bear to read about them. Yet dispensing with religion altogether leaves us exposed to the terror of meaninglessness. The prospect opens up of a religious revival.

Turner's (1991: 245–6) critique of Berger accuses him of 'cognitive reductionism'. He means by this that Berger puts too much emphasis on the problem of meaning and its resolution, reducing all religion to these cognitive issues much as Marxism reduced religion to material self-interest. Heavily influenced by existential philosophy, Berger apparently sees meaning as a universal problem for all people everywhere, irrespective of their social class, ethnicity and gender. Berger's concentration on cognition also betrays a Protestant assumption that belief is more important than ritual. Turner articulates a concern of many critics, that existential problems of meaning are a specific preoccupation of intellectuals. 'For other classes', Turner argues (1991: 245), 'religion may be tied to mundane ends – success, health, security'. Significantly, though, Turner accepts that these too are 'existential issues', even though they are 'formulated at the level of practical actions'.

Berger's position may be more robust than is sometimes thought. As a sociologist, he recognizes that religion, like all cultural phenomena, is structured on class, ethnic and gender lines. Perhaps he might have explored this structuring in greater detail. Even so, do we really want to say that meaning is an issue only for intellectuals?

American exceptionalism

The case of religion in the United States presents a much-discussed challenge to the secularization thesis. In the most advanced nation on earth religious belief, practices and institutions appear to be buoyant. Where does this leave the secularization thesis?

One way in which secularization theorists have attempted to account for the American 'exceptional case' is through the experience of successive waves of mass immigration. The classic exposition of this is Herberg's *Protestant – Catholic – Jew*, which was first published in 1956.

Herberg's aim is to address the paradox of the American religious scene, which he says is characterized by a unique combination of 'pervasive secularism amid mounting religiosity' (Herberg 1983: 3). Although American religion has been drained of its doctrinal content, this does not mean that people who participate in religious affairs are fools or hypocrites. Their religiosity is authentic, at least in the sense that it is serving a real function for them.

Herberg quotes what has come to known as 'Hansen's law', named after the social historian Marcus Lee Hansen: 'What the son wishes to forget, the grandson wishes to remember.' On this analysis the immigrant experience undergoes three phases. First-generation migrants cling to their ethnic identity. They hark back nostalgically to the culture of the old country and seek to transplant it to the new. They socialize within their ethnic group, speaking the language of their birth and keeping the faith of their childhood. The trauma of migration increases their sense of nationhood: status distinctions which would have been crucial in the old country lose their salience. The church is a haven in which ethnic identity can be reaffirmed; elsewhere – at school, in employment, in leisure pursuits – American folkways have to be adopted. Significantly, as Bruce (1996: 110) notes, ethnic groups from the same denomination – such as German, Swedish, Norwegian and Finnish Lutherans – each created their own language-group congregations. Even the Roman Catholic Church, with its principle of universalism, could not prevent the growth of churches with an ethnic flavour.

The majority among the second generation typically rebels against this inward-turned ethnicity and the symbols through which it is expressed. They seek thoroughgoing assimilation. The third generation, however, tends to return to its origins in a search for heritage, identity and roots (Herberg 1983: 6–65). Since mass migration to the United States was halted from 1924, the world-view of the third generation came to be the dominant one.

With the passage of time and in the new social context – the 'melting pot' or, as Herberg prefers to call it, the 'transmuting pot' – many aspects of the third-generation migrant's roots are beyond reach. Peasant life is irretrievable, the Jewish *shtetl* (the isolated rural villages of Russia, Poland and the Baltic states) cannot be recreated, and the mother tongue has fallen into disuse. Typically, however, religion is still available as a focus of meaning, identity and belonging. Grandchildren can selectively retrieve elements of their grandparents' world, with religion the most prominent element in the process.

For Herberg, a migrant's ethnic identity is submerged in his or her religious identity. The reason for this is that self-identification on an ethnic basis would imply incomplete integration into the American way of life. Not only is religious identity compatible with integration, Americans are expected to have a religious affiliation. Atheism and agnosticism are culturally deviant options espoused by a minority even among intellectuals. Religion is not socially divisive, since America conceives itself to be 'one great community divided into three big sub-communities religiously defined, all equally American in their identification with the "American Way of Life"' (Herberg 1983: 38). These three communities are the Protestant–Catholic–Jew of Herberg's title.

Herberg's account of religion in America emphasizes its role as a source of identity, meaning and belonging. Religion is important not for its content but for its secondary functions. He sees this as congruent with Riesman's thesis that American culture is moving from inner- to other-direction (Riesman 1969). It involves a profound character-shift. Other-directed people long for conformity and the approval of their peer group. The growing turn to religion is related to the increasing other-directedness of middle-class culture.

Wilson (1966) places Herberg's analysis squarely in the framework of the secularization thesis. He echoes the argument that religious affiliation is a means by which migrants affirmed an American identity, while harking back nostalgically to their origins in the rural communities of Europe. However, the crucial point for Wilson is that religious values in America are not independent and autonomous. Instead they are derived from national secular values and subservient to them. Going to church is part of the American way of life, requiring only a superficial commitment and making few demands on those who do go. The churches – Herberg's 'religious communities' – offer 'synthetic' community life (Wilson 1966: 115), not the 'natural' communities of the old country. As a condition of their acceptance by the secular state, religious denominations have virtually abandoned any distinctive commitments of their own. The apparent vitality of religious institutions in the USA does not, therefore, refute the secularization thesis, but on the contrary provides evidence for it.

Contemporary challenges to the secularization thesis

Although the secularization thesis arguably maintains its position as the dominant paradigm in the sociology of religion it has always had critics. Some writers argue that the thesis has reached a crisis point and is on the verge of collapse. Their argument has a number of interwoven strands.

The ideology of secularism

The equation of secularization theory with militant secularism was made by David Martin in a much-quoted essay (Martin 1965). He suggested that the secularization thesis was a tool of counter-religious ideology and ought to be erased from the sociological dictionary. His article was intentionally provocative, and is better read as an attempt to open up a debate rather than banish a word (Martin 1978: viii).

The charge of secularism can certainly be sustained against Comte and Marx. However, they can scarcely be said to have concealed their mission to oppose religion in the name of science. As an accusation levelled against Wilson and Berger it is wildly implausible, as Bruce (1992: 1–3) has pointed out. Both these authors have been influenced by Weber's pessimistic account of the modern world. Berger's work testifies to his lifelong struggle to reconcile his calling as a Lutheran with his profession as a sociologist. As for Wilson, there is evidence throughout his work of a distaste for many aspects of secular society, and a profound sense of loss of the religious values which underpinned community life. Their work cannot sensibly be read as a joyous celebration of secularity.

Historicist pseudo-science

Secularization is often presented as a law of historical development, a universal accompaniment of modernization and an inescapable destiny. Many critics have been uneasy with this. Their concerns are the same as those expressed by Popper (1957), who objected to pseudo-scientific laws of history such as those put forward by Marx. These laws could not be challenged – not because they were true, but because they were shielded against contrary evidence. Historicist laws in Popper's perspective are not science but dogma.

Among the evidence which they are said to ignore are data on popular religiosity. Secularization theorists exaggerate the religiosity of earlier eras, such as the Middle Ages, while seriously underestimating the extent of religious faith today. Some of the roots of this alleged failure may lie in Weber's work. As Parkin argues (1982), Weber's writing on religion is full of bold speculation unencumbered by evidence. He tended to assume, contrary to his own methodological principles, that obedience to authority is willingly given rather than a pragmatic acceptance of the facts of power. This led him to overestimate the religious commitment found in the traditional and charismatic authority systems of the past. In some ways he can be counted as an exponent of the dominant ideology thesis, a one-sided interpretation of Marx based on his dictum that the prevailing ideas in any society are those of its ruling class. The dominant ideology thesis holds that subordinate groups are successfully indoctrinated by the ruling class, whereas critics of the thesis have pointed out that this apparent endorsement can conceal covert and passive resistance (Abercrombie et al. 1980). Similarly, Weber concluded too readily that dominant legitimations equate to legitimate domination (Parkin 1982: 78), as if people always gladly swallow the ideology of their rulers. As for his interpretation of the psychological impact of the Calvinist theology of predestination, it is pure conjecture. It may be viewed kindly as a subtle act of empathetic understanding (*Verstehen*), or more critically as an instance of the kind of misguided reasoning which Evans-Pritchard (1965) memorably labelled the 'If I were a horse' fallacy.

Patterns of religious change

Some writers have objected to the secularization thesis on the grounds that it grossly underestimates the diversity of patterns of religious change in the modern world. This was one of the points Martin made (1965) in his critique of the secularization thesis. Subsequently he wrote an influential and wide-ranging book entitled *A General Theory of Secularization* (Martin 1978). This has been seen as a recantation, and is thought to mean that Martin has joined Wilson as a proponent of secularization. Thus, in Bruce's defence of secularization theorists against the unwarranted accusation that they are militant secularists, Martin is supported on the ground that he is not just a sociologist but an Anglican priest who has written works of theology as well as sociology.

Martin's 'general theory of secularization' is decidedly double-edged. The whole purpose of the book is to explore the diversity of religion in the modern world. The wealth of detail in Martin's study should undermine any simple faith in a unidirectional and irreversible process of secularization. His view is that secularization theory was devised in Europe and applies mainly to Europe. Even there, the disintegration of communism and the decay of secular republicanism have opened up a space for religious revival (Martin 1991: 473). If this is indeed the secularization thesis it is a shadow of what it was.

The revenge of God

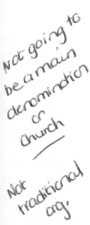

Opponents of the secularization thesis have emphasized the growth of conservative religious movements. Some of these are minority religions such as Jehovah's Witnesses and the Church of Jesus Christ of Latter-day Saints. If they continue at their present rate of growth they will soon cease to be minorities. Even so, secularization theorists may argue that these movements lack the potential to transform the world economically, politically or culturally. Their impact is on individuals rather than on society.

What, then, of the resurgence of conservative forms of Christianity, Judaism and Islam? Within each of these faiths, the 'fundamentalist' traditions appear to be undergoing a renaissance. The crucial difference between these traditions and the Witnesses and Latter-day Saints is in their relation to the nation state. Perhaps there never will be a Witness or Mormon nation, but there are Islamic republics, a Moral Majority in the USA and Orthodox Jewish movements in Israel. It is not so easy to discount their potential to transform their host societies and even the world order.

5

Secularization in Retreat: the Revival of Religion?

The new voluntarism: an emerging paradigm?

At the point where the secularization thesis appeared to have established itself as the orthodoxy among sociologists of religion, it has become the target of a growing challenge that may threaten to overturn it. There have always been objectors, but now, according to R. Stephen Warner (1993), we are witnessing the birth of a new paradigm in the sociological interpretation of contemporary religion. This paradigm is emerging in the work of a few leading scholars who have drawn on a variety of theoretical approaches including economic analysis and rational choice theory. Dissenting from sociological orthodoxy, they have declared the secularization thesis ethnocentric, empirically unsafe and intellectually bankrupt.

The new paradigm is rooted in the social reality of American religion, which has two key features distinguishing it from religion in Europe: disestablishment and institutional vitality. Curiously, European sociologists have treated the United States as if it were deviant from the European norm. On this view, religion stands out as the one field of social life in which Europe shows America its future rather than the other way round. Hence the charge of ethnocentricity.

If one is looking for a classic source of the new paradigm it must surely be Alexis de Tocqueville's *Democracy in America*, published in two volumes in 1835 and 1840 and based on the young Frenchman's extensive travels in the new republic. The significance of religion in de Tocqueville's analysis cannot easily be exaggerated. The condition of religion in America was, he said, the first thing that struck him. He could hardly fail to notice the separation of church and state, and the citizens' freedom of conscience, worship and assembly. The democratic politics of the American republic were paralleled by the democratic plurality of religious sects and denominations. Underlying these parallel institutional forms is something more profound: a vital link between the spirit of religion and the spirit of liberty. Contrary to militant secular thought, a republic needs religion even more than a monarchy does. Or, more sharply, 'Despotism may govern without faith, but liberty cannot.' In a purple passage cited by Aron (1968: 199), de Tocqueville celebrates the affinity of religion and liberty. On the one hand, since religious organizations do not aspire to political power they are all the more socially significant: 'religion never more surely establishes its empire than when it reigns in the hearts of men unsupported by aught beside its native strength.' Liberty, in reply, 'considers religion as the safeguard of morality, and morality as the best security of law and the surest pledge of the duration of freedom'.

Religion is therefore necessary to maintain social integration in societies where citizens have been set free from subservience to an authoritarian state. In the French republic, by contrast, an *intégriste* Catholic church (one seeking to fuse church and nation) is opposed by a secular anti-clerical Left – a cultural rift with profound consequences for the social order, manifest today in the tensions over France's Muslim community.

Critics of de Tocqueville contend that his analysis of the European scene applies only to Catholic countries such as Italy, Spain and his native France. This has misled American commentators into exaggerating the extent of religious persecution in the Protestant nations of Europe. Thus Bruce (1996: 132–5) says that dissenters in Britain were free to leave the established church and join sects and denominations. Religious persecution of British dissenters has been greatly exaggerated by Americans who idolize the Pilgrim Fathers. Perhaps it has – though not all 'dissenters' or 'nonconformists' would have agreed. Bruce adds that de Tocqueville's intellectual descendants have also exaggerated the extent of religious choice actually available in America. Parts of the United States are dominated by one or a few denominations; thus 'Utah is as Mormon as Spain is Catholic' (1996: 134). Choice is further restricted by the fact that many local churches are in practice ethnic churches.

The new paradigm treats American religiosity as authentic. Notions that religion in America is 'secularized from within', infected by shallow consumerism, and a vehicle of ethnic identity rather than genuine spirituality – all these are rejected as unfounded and condescending. As R. Stephen Warner pointedly remarks (1993: 1068): 'Since the new paradigm recognizes the historic popularity of American religion, it is more generous than the old paradigm in crediting such forms as genuinely religious.'

A basic shift of focus is involved in the transition to the new paradigm.

Instead of seeing religious movements as engaged in an embattled effort to shore up plausibility structures, attention switches to the strategies by which religious institutions are built and resources mobilized to help them grow. The emphasis is on the rise of successful religious movements (e.g. Mormons) rather than the decline of old movements (e.g. Methodism) or the marginality of the feeble new ones (almost all of the cults). Alongside this is a concentration on the entrepreneurial activities of individuals – preachers, televangelists, wealthy sponsors, aspiring politicians and rank-and-file members – rather than on the decline of the clerical profession as manifested in the state-subsidized churches of Europe.

This emerging paradigm has been labelled 'the new voluntarism'. People have choices: they can reject their old allegiances outright, convert to a new identity, or return assertively to the faith of their parents. Religious affiliation is typically chosen rather than ascribed for all time at birth.

Choice is valued positively: people ought to arrive at their own beliefs for themselves. That is, after all, one of the core values of Protestantism. Historically, it accounts for the Protestant suspicion of infant baptism. Choosing a faith is increasingly a self-conscious reflexive process – which does not mean, as Berger believes, that religious allegiance is precarious. Choosing one's religion is the privilege not of selfish materialistic consumers but of mature citizens acting as autonomous individuals. People who switch their allegiance do so for serious reasons. Here is a positive affirmation of consumer society – an issue examined later in chapter 9.

Voluntarism according to Talcott Parsons

The new voluntarism is a development of the 'old' voluntarism of Talcott Parsons, which has remained unfashionable since the 1960s. Parsons mounts a fullblooded challenge to the secularization thesis. For Parsons, religion provides a transcendental grounding for a society's ultimate values. All our rules of conduct, folkways, mores and social norms are derived in the final analysis from these ultimate values.

In a sweeping overview of the history of western Christianity, Parsons (1967) argues that religion has gained social significance, not lost it. He rejects the bleak Weberian vision of a disenchanted world governed by utilitarian individualism and imprisoned in the iron cage of meaningless bureaucracy (Robertson 1991: 147–8). Parsons's argument is almost the exact opposite of Berger's account of the secularizing principle inherent in Christianity. In the normal course of social evolution, Parsons says, religion has become differentiated from other social institutions. It has lost functions it once had – in education, the legal system, the political order and economic production. In this it resembles the kinship system, which has also conceded functions to other agencies. The shedding of secondary functions, however, does not mean that religion, or kinship, has declined. Rather, they have been liberated. Religion's primary function is to address the problems of meaning in adult life, answering the core questions of the human condition. 'The cognitive meaning of existence, the meaning of happiness and suffering, of goodness and evil, are the central problems of religion' (Parsons 1960: 303) – a view which is exactly the same as Berger's.

Religion's answer to these questions is far more than a neat solution to an intellectual puzzle. In a similar vein to Berger, Parsons (1991: 163) observes that 'death cannot be treated with indifference'. Parsons, like Durkheim before him, sees a powerful motivational outcome of religion. The religious actor is *un homme qui peut davantage*, a man (or woman) who is empowered to contribute more than he (or she) otherwise would to the functioning of society. This is what is implied in Parsons's somewhat opaque statement that religion's core function is 'the regulation of the balance of the motivational commitment of the individual to the values of his society' (Parsons 1960: 302). Religion is a compensatory mechanism which keeps us motivated in the face of evil. No social system is so well integrated that *all* legitimate expectations are fulfilled. Virtue is not always rewarded, vice often goes unpunished, and innocent people suffer. As Parsons says (1991: 164), 'The moral economy of a human society never has perfectly balanced books.' We are back with the theodicy problem. Religion provides a transcendental *Ausgleich*, that is to say, an ultimate balancing of the moral books.

Parsons's account of the rise of Christianity is a story of the progressive differentiation of religion from other social institutions, the emancipation of the autonomous individual, and the suffusion of religious values throughout society. The process was set in train when the early Christian church made its decisive break with Judaism. Christianity constituted itself as a religious system, whereas Judaism was the culture of a people. The religion of Israel was the whole of culture, not a differentiated part of it. Christ's formula in respect of the Roman Empire – 'Render unto Caesar the things that are Caesar's' – epitomized Christianity's refusal to claim jurisdiction over secular society (unlike Ayatollah Khomeini's Islamic Republic). The church was not the whole of society but a distinct voluntary community concerned to order its own affairs in accordance with God's will and to spread its message throughout the world. Christianity is individualistic at its very core: Christian churches recruit individuals, not necessarily families, tribes or nations. Individualism does not however imply anarchy. Christian churches are normally tightly disciplined, at times fiercely so, as demonstrated by the persecution of heretics.

What, though, of the Holy Roman Empire? Surely the coronation of Charlemagne by Pope Leo III on Christmas Day AD 800 marked the subordination of the secular powers to the authority of the western church? Not according to Parsons, who interprets the coronation both as a religious legitimation of the differentiation between the secular and the sacred, and as signalling their common commitment to shared norms and values. Western Christianity, in Parsons's evolutionary framework, has been more effective than its eastern counterpart. The eastern Orthodox church emphasizes monasticism and other-worldly spirituality, and the subordination of the church to secular authority (Robertson 1991: 155). This may be at the root of eastern Orthodoxy's inability in our own times to profit from the collapse of communism. In Russia, the eastern Orthodox church has been forced to call upon the post-communist state to erect protectionist barriers against the evangelical missionary endeavours of western denominations.

Throughout the medieval period the church struggled to avoid being absorbed into the secular state. Religious orders played an important role in resisting this. They were dedicated to cultivating personal piety, preserving the integrity of religion as an institution differentiated from the rest of society. Priestly celibacy was a symbol of this differentiation. Religious orders were powerhouses of scholarship, first in the monasteries and later in the universities of medieval Europe. Although the medieval church was capable of setting its face against science – as in the censure of Galileo – it allowed far more room for the development of an independent intellectual culture than any other religion did in its medieval period. The contrast with the medieval Islamic stranglehold over intellectual life is striking.

For Parsons, unlike most secularization theorists, the Middle Ages were not the high point from which religion has lost social significance, but simply one phase in the evolution of religion. He rejected Troeltsch's view that medieval Catholicism was the last truly Christian form of society (Robertson 1991: 147). Instead Parsons insists that the Protestant Reformation carried further the principles embedded in Christianity's break with Judaism. Protestant reformers challenged the tutelage of the Catholic church and the high authority of the priesthood as guardian of the sacraments. The individual was enfranchised and placed in a more direct relationship with God. Structures of mediation between the profane and the sacred – priests, saints, the Virgin Mary – were demoted, or had their functions redefined, or were swept aside. Protestantism gave to individuals the responsibility for their own salvation through faith. This is not secularization, but an opening up of the secular world as a field of Christian endeavour and opportunity.

America's denominational pluralism is seen by Parsons as a further extension of the process unleashed by the emergence of Christianity and carried forward by medieval Catholicism and the Protestant Reformation. People are not born into churches. Instead they choose their denominational affiliation as autonomous adults. They decide what to believe and which denomination to join. Implicit in the voluntary principle is religious tolerance. Against secularization theorists, many of whom see tolerance as a sign that religion means very little, Parsons interprets it as an authentic unfolding of the Christian faith.

Underlying the diversity of denominational pluralism is a shared commitment to society's ultimate values. Parsons speaks, controversially, of 'the societal community' (Parsons 1977) – a phrase which for many sociologists is a contradiction in terms, since communities are inherently local and cannot be society-wide. In the United States, the core value-system centres on mainstream Protestantism but extends to encompass Catholicism and Judaism. Religious values are highly generalized – but this does not mean that they are empty of meaning. Despite conflict, consensus is real. Parsons asserts that 'To deny that this underlying consensus exists would be to claim that American society stood in a state of latent religious war' (1967: 414) – which would be absurd. While acknowledging that he risks the charge of complacency, he goes on to say that 'in a whole variety of ways modern society is more in accord with Christian values than its forebears have been' (1967: 417).

Rational choice theory and religion

The new voluntarism shares with Parsonian 'old' voluntarism a positive evaluation of the voluntary principle in religious affairs. However, it departs from the Parsonian framework in a number of important ways. First, it is not committed to a macrosociological theory of evolutionary social change through differentiation. Its focus switches to microsociological analysis, as in Rodney Stark and William Sims Bainbridge's rational choice theory. Stark himself is caustic about Parsonian structural-functionalism, judging it to be pseudo-scientific (Stark 1997: 5). Second, the Parsonian concept of human agency, with its heavy emphasis on the internalization of norms and values, is rejected for failing to take sufficient account of rational choice. Here again Stark is cutting, referring favourably to George Homans's celebrated onslaught on structural-functionalism in his presidential address to the American Sociological Association in 1964 under the provocative title, 'Bringing Men Back In'. Third, the Parsonian thesis of overarching consensus on core values is replaced by a greater attention to social conflict. Parsons's rosy account of the triumph of Christian values in the west gives way to a more sceptical analysis of social conflict within and between religious groups.

The strongest and most controversial expression of the new paradigm in the sociology of religion is the rational choice theory developed by Stark and Bainbridge. It involves a new mode of discourse about religion and a total reconceptualization of sociological theory. It marks a complete break with Parsonian voluntarism, embracing as it does a style of economic analysis which the whole of Parsons's sociology was designed to refute. A crucial message of Warner's seminal article was that sociologists could work within the new paradigm without needing to buy into Stark's rational choice theory (R. S. Warner 1993).

Stark has not concealed the radical nature of his programme for the sociology of religion (Stark 1997). He champions a Popperian approach to theory. Theories begin with axioms, that is abstract general statements about the world. From these are derived a set of hypotheses which can be tested empirically. Theory produces predictions which are either confirmed or falsified by empirical evidence. Science advances by a process of what Popper (1963) called 'conjecture and refutation'. Theories are not proved true, since all theories are corrigible in the light of new evidence; rather, old theories are shown to be false, and are replaced by new theories whose propositions conform more closely to the evidence.

For Stark, most sociological theory is not theory at all, but a set of definitions, tautologies and inductive generalizations which sociologists dignify with the equivocal phrase, 'an approach'. Approaches never arrive at a destination. Sociologists affect to despise prediction as a vulgar activity unworthy of the humane scholar. Sociological theorizing is a form of an-cestor-worship, a cult whose catechism ritually recounts the opinions, insights and prejudices of dead founders, especially the sacred Marx–Durkheim–Weber trinity (gods who, significantly, virtually ignored one another). The so-called theories of sociology are no such thing; they have more in common with astrology than astronomy. They lack any explana-tory power. Instead of yielding empirically falsifiable predictions, as genu-ine theory does, they protect themselves against the possibility of falsification. As Popper emphasized, what is taken for a strength is actually a fatal flaw. These pseudo-theories cannot be proved wrong – not because they are correct, but because they fail to say anything of scientific worth. Stark's aim is not only to develop a theory of religion but to bring theory back into sociology.

The Stark–Bainbridge theory of religion presents a radical challenge to the substance of the secularization thesis. Far from being the irreversible outcome of modernization, secularization is a short-term self-limiting pro-cess. People will always seek the meaning of life and long for immortality, and will therefore need to adopt a supernatural belief-system. Religious organizations which water down their supernatural beliefs will inevitably decline. Their place will be taken by old-time religion and by new faiths such as Mormonism. Contrary to received wisdom, the vigorously competitive religious scene of modern pluralistic societies is more religious than Europe's pre-industrial 'age of faith', which was in reality an age of apathy.

Two fundamental concepts in the Stark–Bainbridge theory of religion are *rewards* and *compensators*. Rewards are anything which people desire. They may be specific or general, easy or difficult to obtain, real objects or imaginary ones. Rewards typically carry costs – that is, anything that people seek to avoid. People will pursue a reward only if they expect that the benefit they derive from it will exceed the cost they incur in doing so. Rewards and costs are covariant. If a reward is forgone, that counts as a cost; conversely, avoiding a cost is counted as a reward.

Some rewards which people seek are scarce or unavailable. Faced with this, people are willing to accept *compensators* instead. A compensator is a substitute for the reward. It may involve the promise of a future reward if gratification is deferred, and an explanation of how the reward can eventually be obtained. People accept compensators only if rewards are not available. However, compensators are typically treated by human beings as though they were rewards.

Among the rewards people desire are some which are so great and so general that only a religion, that is to say a supernatural belief-system, can produce credible compensators for them. Examples are immortality, enlightenment and the meaning of life. Religion offers a set of compensators to deal with the unattainability of these rewards in the immediate future or even in this life. Stark and Bainbridge define religions as *systems of general compensators based on supernaturalist assumptions*. Naturalistic belief-systems, however well grounded in science, simply cannot compete with supernaturalist religion when it comes to the provision of credible compensators for such rewards. Hence the failure of belief-systems such as scientific humanism and Marxism-Leninism to appeal to more than a few intellectuals.

Humans are axiomatically reward-seeking beings. Therefore, people will always prefer rewards to compensators – in that sense, compensators are invariably a second best. In some instances, powerful people and groups may be able to secure rewards while the less powerful will have to make do with compensators. Nevertheless, some rewards – the Christian concept of immortality is a paradigm case – are not obtainable in this life by anyone. We all die, and so doctrines of an afterlife appeal to us all. Given this, everyone has a strong motive for being religious. It is a modern version of Pascal's famous wager, in which the rational calculation is that belief in God is a sensible bet (or a prudent investment). If God exists, the investment made by the faithful yields them an infinite profit, while the unfaithful bear heavy losses – in purgatory or hell, for example. Conversely, if God does not exist the faithful have lost very little and the unfaithful still gained nothing. The unfaithful always lose whereas the faithful stand at least a chance of winning.

It follows for Stark and Bainbridge that the secularization thesis is false. In their conception of human nature and the human condition, people will always seek immortality, enlightenment and the meaning of life, and so will have to accept supernaturalistic compensators. Religious organizations which abandon supernaturalism and thereby allow themselves to become secularized from within, for example liberal Protestant denominations, will no longer be able to supply credible compensators and will inevitably decline (and, like most failing enterprises, will thoroughly deserve to do so). Although denominations which accommodate to the values and beliefs of the wider society will decay, their place will be taken by faiths which revive the old compensators (sects) or create new ones (cults). Secularization is a self-limiting process, and the supply of religion remains fairly constant since there is a stable demand for it.

It also follows that any organization which seeks such rewards as immortality, enlightenment or the meaning of life will gravitate towards supernaturalist beliefs, since only supernaturalism can supply sufficiently powerful compensators. Scientology is a case in point: originally a therapeutic system, its religious dimension has become so pronounced that it now campaigns vigorously to be recognized as a religion.

A fundamental axiom of rational choice theory, as formulated by Iannaccone (1997: 26), is this: 'Individuals act rationally, weighing the costs and benefits of potential actions, and choosing those actions that maximize their net benefits.' This applies to religion as to any other human activity. People choose their religious faith and their level of commitment to it in the light of cost–benefit calculations. Beliefs and commitments change as circumstances change, causing people to recalculate the balance of advantage. Hence, for example, the tendency for citizens of liberal-pluralist societies such as the USA to switch denomination if they experience upward social mobility. Doing so is perfectly rational.

This model of religious consumers as people who act self-interestedly on the basis of calculations of individual costs and benefits points to a crucial issue for social movements: the problem of public goods and free riders. A public good is one which has to be made available to all potential beneficiaries irrespective of whether they have contributed to it. Clean air is an example: the individual driving an environmentally polluting vehicle breathes the same air as the ecologically minded cyclist. Why should a rational person contribute to the costs of an enterprise if he or she can gain the benefits anyway? For example, why bother to pay union dues if everybody, not just union members, receives the pay rises? Or why put money in the church's collection-box? If a sufficient number of other people are prepared to bear the cost – whether through a moral commitment, or through stupidity, or because they are coerced into doing so – the rational individual can enjoy a free ride on their efforts.

One way in which organizations can try to solve the free rider problem is by offering selective incentives (Olson 1965), that is benefits which only members can receive. In the case of religious movements, the most basic use of selective benefits is the claim that theirs is the only path to salvation, and that only faithful members can be certain of it. This is the principle expressed in St Augustine's formula, *extra ecclesiam nulla salus* – there is no salvation outside the church.

This answer goes only part of the way towards addressing the free rider problem. Simply joining a movement is not enough, since a passive member is still taking if not a free ride then certainly a very cheap one, benefiting disproportionately from the efforts of active members. Successful religious movements are not satisfied with passive members who do the bare minimum to get by; they want their members to be actively engaged in promoting the movement through a mix of time, effort and money. According to Iannaccone (1997: 35–6), successful religious movements address the problem by raising the stakes, imposing costly demands on their members. This works in two ways. First, the demands act as tests to screen out the half-hearted. For example, Jehovah's Witnesses require all baptized members to refuse blood transfusions, and all able-bodied members to take part in doorstep proselytizing. The Witnesses' Kingdom Halls are businesslike places where members are prepared for the challenge of spreading a demanding faith to a frequently hostile public. They are not drop-in centres for casual visitors looking for a meal or a chat. Second, successful movements incentivize participation by raising the cost of engaging in activities outside the group. In some cases this involves outright bans on attending places of entertainment such as cinemas, theatres and dance halls, or forbidding members to marry outside the faith and excommunicating them if they do so. Alternatively, the barriers to socializing with outsiders may be indirect, though no less effective. The Mormons' distinctive dietary rules are a case of this, since they introduce an awkwardness into everyday socializing. A more acute problem for Mormons is that if they marry outside the faith they will be divorced at death and remain single for evermore, spending eternity in the terrestrial kingdom rather than the frankly superior celestial kingdom. This prospect is a strong disincentive to exogamy.

On the face of it, there appears to be a contradiction in Iannaccone's analysis. He claims that religious movements prosper by offering people what they want, yet he also says that they raise the cost of membership. Does this mean that people actually want higher costs? If so, it contradicts rational choice theory, which defines costs as things that people seek to avoid.

The answer to this problem lies in the advantages gained by eliminating free riders. Raising the cost of membership has two beneficial consequences. First, a congregation without the debilitating effect of free riders is a more lively place to be (Stark 1998: 48). Everything about it – worship, sociability, evangelism – gains from the absence of people who contribute less than they consume. Second, the belief-system of a group with no free riders is more credible to its members (Stark 1998: 47; Iannaccone 1997: 34). On the Stark–Bainbridge theory, religion has a problem of credibility because it offers compensators, not tangible rewards. Compensators are not jam today, but metaphysical substitutes for jam with the promise of jam tomorrow. It is in the nature of compensators that doubts about them are a persistent, insidious threat. Is there really a life after death? Will the wicked get away with their sins? Shall I be saved, and shall I see my loved ones again? A high level of consensus and commitment among the faithful is necessary, so the reasoning runs, if religious answers to questions like these are to retain their plausibility.

Iannaccone is very clear that the costs of membership must not be pushed too high. If they are, they will outweigh the benefits. Equally important, the costs must be seen to be appropriate, not arbitrary, and the movement must be able to provide acceptable substitutes for the things forgone. So, for example, if members are prevented from interacting with outsiders they must be able to enjoy satisfying personal relationships within the movement. Or again, an introversionist movement which aims at self-sufficiency must succeed in growing crops, clothing its people and educating its children.

To sum up Iannaccone's argument: religious movements which achieve an optimum level of strictness will tend to prosper. This is because they deal effectively with the free rider problem, requiring people to participate either fully or not at all.

The Stark–Bainbridge theory is based on the principle of methodological individualism, a prescriptive doctrine which holds that all sociological explanations are reducible to facts about individuals and individual behaviour (Lukes 1973: 110–22). This principle, rooted in the philosophy of the Enlightenment, has been embodied in a variety of subsequent theories, including utilitarianism, neo-classical economics, and the sociological work of Homans – who was a direct influence on Stark himself (Stark 1997:

5–6). Although it was endorsed by Weber, in principle if not always in practice, methodological individualism runs counter to the mainstream of classical and contemporary sociological thought. Opponents of it included Saint-Simon, Comte, Marx and Durkheim, all of whom gave priority to the social and the collective over the individual. As Lukes remarks (1973: 111), Durkheim founded his sociology on the rejection of methodological individualism. Durkheim insisted that social facts were objective, external and constraining. For Durkheim the religiosity of individual believers is of secondary importance: it is derived from and dependent on the social fact of religion as a collective force. Similarly, Marx was wholly uninterested in individual religiosity; what mattered to him was the social function of religion as a support of class oppression.

Stark and like-minded sociologists use methodological individualism to challenge the basic tenets of the secularization thesis. They do not see religious culture as anything more than the sum of the religiosity of individuals. They therefore reject the notion that pre-industrial Europe was an 'age of faith' which reached its zenith in the thirteenth and fourteenth centuries. Ordinary people went to church and took part in religious observances not willingly but because they had little alternative. In any case, the evidence shows that patterns of observance in pre-industrial societies have been grossly exaggerated. Iannaccone (1997: 41) puts the case forcefully: 'Europe's so-called "age of faith" was in fact an era of widespread religious apathy.' The modern era is the true age of faith, where people participate in religion because they freely choose to do so.

The language of rational choice theory is undoubtedly iconoclastic. Its attack is, however, perhaps best seen as directed less at religion than at received sociological wisdom about religion. Above all, the secularization thesis is declared bankrupt. The Stark–Bainbridge theory is explicitly agnostic about the truth claims of religion. Unlike some of its sociological rivals it is not put forward as a reductionist theory which explains religions as being 'really' something else. On the contrary, it claims to be entirely consistent with religion. For example, the theory predicts that, as societies evolve into more advanced and complex forms, a number of fundamental changes will take place in religious thought. First, people will worship fewer gods who have greater power: minor deities with limited powers are retired from the pantheon. Second, a progressively clearer distinction is drawn between good gods, who benignly intend that humans will benefit from transactions with them (God rewards us immeasurably more than we deserve), and evil gods who seek to coerce or deceive us into unprofitable exchanges (Mephistopheles' contract with Faust is utterly fraudulent). The gods become more rational: the dangerously capricious and morally volatile gods of ancient Greece and Rome are replaced by gods who are consistently benevolent (such as Allah, the Compassionate, the Merciful) or consistently malign (such as Satan). Third, good gods are believed to be more powerful than evil gods – ensuring that it is worthwhile for us to exchange with them, since they will be victorious and we shall be on the winning side.

Stark (1997: 16) argues that, although these propositions may superficially seem shocking, that is merely because of the economistic vocabulary in which they are couched. Careful reflection will reveal that they are entirely compatible with Jewish, Christian and Muslim theology. They are therefore consistent with the mature faiths of the modern world. More than that, social science can comprehend religion precisely because God is rational, just as natural science is possible because creation is law-like.

The supply side: religious firms and resource mobilization

Resource mobilization theory, and rational choice theories of religion, aim to rectify the neglect of the supply side in sociological analysis of religion. The resource mobilization approach underlines the truth that favourable conditions for the growth of a social movement do not guarantee that it will succeed. It is a necessary corrective to deprivation theories which see the connections between grievance, protest and the formation of a social movement as virtually automatic. There are many more deprivations than grievances, and many more grievances than social movements. Social movements are an accomplishment, not a response triggered automatically by a grievance. Social movements are not easy to organize, and behind every enduring movement lie a host of failures. In the field of religion, for every successful religious movement there are countless others which either imploded or, far more frequently, fizzled out without ever being noticed except by a handful of adherents and the people close to them.

Resource mobilization theory draws attention to the work of religious leaders and activists in mobilizing resources – money, people, publicity, other organizations – in establishing a movement and pursuing its goals. It analyses the constraints within which they work, and the causes of their success or failure in resource mobilization. The theory is not new, nor is it the whole story; even so, it has been an important counterbalance to theories of religious movements which neglect the organizational dimension.

For example, Shupe and Bromley's (1980) study of the anti-cult movement in the United States, *The New Vigilantes*, shows its failures in resource mobilization despite general public antipathy towards 'cults'. These failures were fivefold (Shupe and Bromley 1980: 119):

- it failed to expand its membership beyond the families of young people who had joined a 'cult'; despite media coverage of the 'cult' problem, this was not a large pool of people
- it could not prevent many of its members from leaving the anti-cult movement once their own children had returned to them
- it failed to elicit funding from people other than the families affected
- it could not agree whether its national organization should be centralized or decentralized
- it did not achieve a consensus on the definition of 'cult'; it therefore lacked a legally operationalizable distinction between the 'cults' which were to be curbed and the authentic religious movements which were to be left free to exercise their constitutional rights

The anti-cult movement suffered from a chronic shortage of money and members, hampering its effectiveness as a political lobby at the federal level. It had some success in persuading local officials to take measures restricting 'cult' activities in their area, but what this amounted to was 'occasional harassment rather than systematic repression' (Shupe and Bromley 1980: 244). Although the movement did contribute to a general anti-cult ethos in the United States, it failed to mobilize resources in pursuit of its more specific anti-cult objectives.

In their parallel study, *'Moonies' in America*, Bromley and Shupe (1979) examine the rapid growth of the Unification Church in the 1970s after a period during which it was struggling to make any impact at all. Crucial to the movement's take-off were the charismatic leadership, organizational flair and personal wealth of Sun Myung Moon himself. In the 1960s, the Moonies had been an ill-organized, faction-ridden group operating ineffectually on the fringes of the youth culture. They probably had no more than 500 American members at the very most (Bromley and Shupe 1979: 113) – and their commitment was only on a part-time basis. By the standards of commercial consumerism their self-presentation was abysmal. They were uncertain about the tactics to use in seeking recruits: how to approach them – whether face-to-face or impersonally through newspaper and radio advertisements; where to approach people – in a religious or secular context and, if the former, whether in a mainstream church or a culturally deviant setting such as a seance; whether to disclose their own identity as Moonies at first contact, or to conceal it until the prospect was interested; whether to concentrate on young people or not; and whether to target influential people or to prioritize building a rank-and-file membership. This phase of the movement's development was vividly captured in Lofland's (1966) classic study, *Doomsday Cult*. It was, in part, a story of repeated failures in resource mobilization.

Ironically, as Barker (1984a: 47) points out, this unsuccessful period of trial and error may have unintentionally laid the foundation for future success, since the movement was able to learn vital lessons from its catalogue of failed experiments. When Moon arrived in the USA in 1971, he immediately overhauled the movement's organization. The One World Crusade was launched, in which teams of young full-time evangelists dedicated themselves to active recruitment and fund-raising targeted at people aged under thirty. He also made shrewd acquisitions of real estate. The Unification Church publicly espoused a version of American civil religion, endorsing the role of the United States as leader of the free world in the global fight against godless communism, campaigning in defence of President Nixon during the Watergate crisis of 1972–4, and inaugurating its own God Bless America Campaign as part of the bicentennial celebrations.

The significance of the wider social context is emphasized in Bromley and Shupe's (1979) study. They point out that the movement was able to draw on a growing population of young people who were relatively unattached, in full- or part-time education, and concentrated in urban centres. This constituency had expanded significantly during the 1960s. Its growth coincided with cultural shifts including the attraction of experimenting with alternative lifestyles and belief-systems. As disillusionment set in with psychotropic drugs and with secular politicized opposition to American institutions and American civil religion, young people became more receptive to spiritual paths to salvation. They turned, however, less to the liberal mainstream Christian denominations than to fundamentalist Christianity on the one hand and to new and imported minority religious movements on the other. Having been unsuccessful in the United States during the 1960s, the Unification Church's fortunes rapidly improved in the more favourable cultural climate of the 1970s.

Rational choice theorists have built on the insights of the resource mobilization approach. If consumers of religion are profit-maximizers, so too are religious producers. The religious market-place has suppliers and consumers, as any market does. Secularization theory typically concentrates on the consumer, who supposedly is less and less inclined to demand religious goods and services. In contrast to this, rational choice theorists of religion draw attention to the capacity of religious suppliers to stimulate and satisfy demand for their product. The basic proposition is that free competition is highly desirable. Conditions of monopoly or oligopoly, typically with state subsidies and barriers to entry, breed lazy religious institutions which lack the incentive to market their services effectively. In a competitive market, in contrast, religious firms seek to maximize their profits by increasing their membership and other material resources. If there is no state regulation or state subsidy – both of which distort the market – the success of religious firms will depend on their ability to satisfy their customers. Inefficient firms will eventually be driven out of business. As Iannaccone (1997: 27) bluntly puts it: 'In a highly competitive environment, religions have little choice but to abandon inefficient modes of production and unpopular products in favour of more attractive and profitable alternatives.'

Rational choice theory aims to redress the imbalance of the secularization thesis, which in concentrating on changes in demand has neglected the supply side. For example, Finke and Stark (1992: 22–108) put forward a supply-side explanation of two periods of religious revival in American history. The First Great Awakening which began in the late 1730s saw tens of thousands of people flock to hear the preaching of an Englishman, the 'Calvinist Methodist' George Whitefield, just as the Second Great Awakening from the 1790s saw popular enthusiasm for the revivalism of the American-born Charles Finney, a Presbyterian turned Congregationalist, in the Burned-Over District of Western New York and Ohio, together with a rapid growth of Baptism and Methodism. The standard explanation of these Great Awakenings is that they were a response to an explosion of demand. Against this, Finke and Stark argue that the root cause was an increase in the supply of religion made possible because the colonial establishment was gradually losing its grip on the regulation of the religious market-place. Nostalgic and patriotic images of universal piety during the colonial period are untrue to history. The churching of colonial America faced two major impediments. On the demand side, the American frontier presented all the social problems of a transient population. There were indeed virtuous Puritans, as depicted in American iconography, but there were also apathetic people and irreligious scoundrels. On the supply side stood the mainline established churches of the Old World, the Congregationalists, Episcopalians and Presbyterians. The Congregationalists were legally established in New England, and the Episcopalians in New York, Virginia, Maryland, North and South Carolina, and Georgia. These churches made a poor fist of evangelism. Their genteel ministers, schooled in theological intricacies at Harvard and Yale, were out of touch with the grassroots, unlike their Baptist and Methodist competitors.

The two Great Awakenings are the story of failure of anaemic established churches to compete in the emerging free market in religion. Deregulation unleashed competitive energy. The new religious entrepreneurs sold their product hard: the crowds who came to hear George Whitefield did not just materialize or drift in, but had been stimulated by a well-organized advance publicity campaign. In this respect Whitefield was a precursor of Billy Graham.

Finke (1997) also explains late twentieth-century religious revivals in terms of supply-side factors, for example the flowering of religious activity in Japan since 1945. Before the Second World War, the imperial Japanese state exercised tight control over religious practice. It subsidized Shinto, associating it with the identity and destiny of the nation, and repressed alternative religions. Post-war reconstruction of Japan as a modern democratic nation brought with it deregulation of religion, including disestablishment of Shinto. It is in this favourable deregulated market-place that successful movements like Soka Gakkai have flourished. All of this stands in contrast to Germany, also defeated in the war, but which has retained a strong state regulation of religion in order to defend democracy against the threat of authoritarian movements. Unlike Japan, Germany predictably presents us with the familiar picture of apparently irreversible secularization.

Recent American experience provides another telling example of the significance of the supply side. One much-discussed element in 1960s counterculture was the impact of Asian faiths, including Hare Krishna, Transcendental Meditation, the Divine Light Mission, the Unification Church, the Happy-Healthy-Holy Movement, Meher Baba, and numerous others. This apparent turn to the east was interpreted by many commentators as a rejection of western consumer culture. The western version of modernity was thought to be in deep crisis. Against this, Finke and Stark (1992: 239–44) make three main points. *First*, the phenomenon was scarcely new, since eastern faiths and philosophies had attracted interest in America for over a century. For example, the influential Theosophical Society (Wilson 1970: 157–60) was founded in New York in 1875. Its founder, Madame Petrovna Blavatsky, had received her teaching in Tibet from spiritual masters who revealed to her the hidden secrets of the cosmos and the human condition. In its heyday Theosophy became fashionable, and influenced other metaphysically oriented belief-systems. *Second*, for all the debate surrounding them in the 1960s, the Asian faiths in America have always had tiny memberships – typically a few hundred members each. The controversy they provoked is out of all proportion to their membership. If we are looking for growth religions, we should turn not to the east but closer to home – to the Mormons, Jehovah's Witnesses, Seventh-day Adventists and Christian Scientists. *Third* and most important of all is the history of American immigration laws. After the First World War, Congress enacted restrictive legislation which effectively excluded Asians. Eastern religious teachers and gurus were admitted for only brief visits on tourist visas. The crucial turning-point came in 1965, when President Lyndon Johnson rescinded the exclusionary rules against Asian immigration. As Melton (1992: 10) puts it, 'For the first time Asian faiths became a genuine option for religious seekers in the West.' Religious entrepreneurs responded quickly. Before the year was out His Divine Grace A. C.

Bhaktivedanta Swami Prabhupada, founder of the International Society for Krishna Consciousness, had taken up residence in New York. He then shrewdly moved the headquarters of his operation to the symbolic capital of the counterculture, San Francisco.

Levels of rank-and-file participation in religious organizations are high if and only if the market is competitive. This is shown by the striking contrast between the high participation rate of the USA and the low rates in European countries such as Sweden, with its state-subsidized liberal Protestant churches. It is also shown by the revival of religious participation in America. On Finke's evidence, whereas in 1850 only one-third of Americans belonged to a church, by 1980 the figure had increased to almost two-thirds. High rates of religious participation in the USA are not some irrational survival of ethnic identity, but the result of a free market. Over the past century America has witnessed a process of 'churching'. In contrast to the secularization thesis, a similar revival of religious participation would happen in Europe if the state withdrew its subsidies, forcing religious organizations into competition for customers.

The Mormons: a new world faith?

The new paradigm invites sociologists to concentrate their attention on the socially significant growth religions rather than, in Stark and Iannaconne's (1997: 155) cutting phrase, 'the rites of a coven of thirteen Dutch witches'. In periods of extreme secularization an opportunity opens up for new religions to enter the market. They begin as cult movements, a few of which may eventually achieve the status of a world religion. Many movements which were once heralded as carrying global significance have now faded from view (Argyle and Beit-Hallahmi 1997: 134). Moral Rearmament (the Oxford Group) appeared to be the most dynamic new religious movement of the 1930s in the USA and the UK, but is now a minor footnote in the history of Christianity. The Jesus Movement appeared to be sweeping across America in the 1970s, but has now disappeared. These two examples show the perils of predicting religious growth rates without the support of a robust theory. We should also be less impressed with the outlandish antics of successful self-publicists, concentrating instead on hard membership data.

One growth movement Stark identifies is the Church of Jesus Christ of Latter-day Saints (the Mormons). The LDS Church claimed 9,700,000 members in 160 countries as at 1 January 1997; 49 per cent of these members were in the United States and 22 per cent in South America. The Book of Mormon, a sacred text standing alongside the Bible, has sold 78 million copies and is currently available in ninety languages.

The church's rate of growth has been impressive. At its foundation in 1830 it had a few hundred members. After a turbulent period, thousands of Mormons made the great trek to Salt Lake City in Utah from 1846 onwards. When Utah became a state in 1896, the Mormon church already had a quarter of a million members. Since the end of the Second World War it has doubled its membership roughly every fifteen years, which implies an average annual growth rate of about 5 per cent. It had one million members in 1947, two million in 1963, three million in 1971, four million in 1978, and stands at approximately ten million at the time of writing in 1998. As Stark (1990: 205) points out, its highest rates of growth are now not in its most mature market (the USA) but elsewhere, particularly South America, Central America and Mexico. It is worth adding that one feature of the LDS church is its diligence in assembling accurate statistics – an indication of its efficiency as a thoroughly modern organization.

How can this success be explained? According to Stark's original model, there are eight factors which contribute to the success of new religious movements. Let us examine each in turn, seeing how they apply to the LDS church.

Effective mobilization of resources

The resource mobilization approach to social movements, discussed above, highlights the crucial role played by a movement's leadership in mobilizing resources – members, supporters, money, publicity and so on – to further the cause. However favourable its environment may be, no movement can succeed unless it has dynamic leaders who mobilize resources effectively.

There is little doubt that the Mormon church is well organized. Strong leadership has been highly valued from the time of its founder Joseph Smith and his successor Brigham Young. The church encourages all members to participate actively in its affairs, and requires them to tithe a tenth of their income to the church. It is constituted as a hierarchy similar in many ways to the Roman Catholic Church, with wards (i.e. churches) headed by bishops (equivalent to priests) and organized into stakes (dioceses). At the apex of the movement is a quorum of twelve apostles, two counsellors and the president, currently Gordon B. Hinckley, who is endowed with prophetic powers and open to new revelations from God. Obedience to authority is expected. As in Catholicism, women are excluded from leadership roles in the Mormon church's chain of command.

A crucial difference from the Catholic church is that Mormons have a lay priesthood. Not only does this imply active lay involvement, it has also meant that the LDS church escaped one of the critical problems facing

Catholicism and liberal Protestantism: the serious decline in men coming forward with a vocation to the priesthood.

Effective socialization of young members

Movements which fail to retain their own children in active membership will inevitably decline, since they will not be able to recruit enough committed new people to replace those they lose through the normal processes of attrition. An extreme example are the Shakers (Wilson 1970: 203–7), who live on through their artefacts and above all their furniture, which have become collectors' items. The movement of people who came to be known as Shakers originated in mid-eighteenth-century England. Under the leadership of Ann Lee, they fled to America in 1774 to escape persecution. Having experienced the trauma of four stillborn children, Lee became convinced that sex was the principal source of evil. She preached that the saved must lead a life of total celibacy. Predictably, this movement has virtually died out.

In complete contrast, Mormons are fertile people who devote time and effort to effective socialization of their children. Mormon priesthood is divided into two separate orders, the lower Aaronic and the higher Melchizedek priesthood, each of which is subdivided into three grades. The result is an objective career structure through which all Mormon males are expected to advance (O'Dea 1957: 174–85). Children are baptized when they are eight years old. Boys are admitted to the Aaronic priesthood at the age of twelve, when they are ordained deacon. During their adolescence they progress to the status of teacher, and then to priest between the ages of eighteen and twenty. When a young man enters the Melchizedek priesthood, at or around the age of twenty, he is made an elder. The next grade is called seventy, often attained when they go out on missionary work. The final grade of the Melchizedek priesthood is high priest, which is usually attained during middle age.

Mormon children are involved at an early age in the organizational structures of the faith – boys through their incorporation into the priesthood, girls through their role as helpers and facilitators of their menfolk. The retention of distinctive Mormon practices and beliefs has enabled them to combine respectability with a continuing status as a 'peculiar people'.

A normal age and sex structure

Without this, a movement cannot form a community which will reproduce itself. The Moonies and similar movements whose membership is heavily skewed towards young people are too dependent on recruiting new members to replace the constant outflow of people leaving. They also need to keep in tune with youth culture, which is highly volatile. Conversely, many mainstream Christian churches face the problem of a greying membership past the age of reproduction and potentially off-putting to young people.

The family occupies a central place in Mormon belief and practice. Mormon views on family life are conventional and conservative, with the man securely installed as head of the household. His wife is subject to his authority, and is charged with the immediate responsibility for the upbringing of the children, who are expected to be well behaved and obedient. Procreation is valued since it enables a new spirit to enter this life; hence neither celibacy nor voluntary childlessness are valid options. The family is at the heart of human life in this world and the next. Sacred ordinances which Mormons perform in the temple enable them to seal their marriages for all eternity. They also perform baptisms on behalf of their ancestors, so that they can be reunited with their forebears after death. Consistent with this, Mormon proselytizing is oriented towards recruiting families rather than individuals. Exogamy – marrying outside the faith – carries a heavy spiritual penalty. Only couples whose marriage is sealed in a Mormon temple will enjoy eternal marital bliss in the next life. Mormons who marry outside the faith will be divorced at death, and will not be able to attain the celestial kingdom.

Adultery and pre-marital sex are held to be grievous sins. So too is homosexuality. The LDS church sees homosexuality as a perversion which can be corrected through prayer, self-discipline, counselling and therapy. People are not ontologically gays and lesbians – these are not valid nouns – though they may be tempted by homoerotic impulses. The official view appears to be that people will not be excommunicated from the church for a homosexual orientation as long as they do not engage in same-sex acts. On the other hand, it is clear that homosexual attraction is itself contrary to God's will. On this issue the Mormon church – like mainstream Christian churches – denies the charge that it is homophobic.

A favourable ecology

A new religious movement can prosper only if the time and place are propitious. Specifically, it needs three things. First, it requires a deregulated religious economy giving basic freedoms of worship and assembly. Societies which suppress religious activity, such as China and the former communist countries, inhibit the growth of religious movements – though when these regimes collapse we see an outpouring of pent-up religious fervour. Second, it develops from a situation in which the mainstream faiths have been undermined by internal secularization, since this opens up a market opportunity. Third, it needs an environment in which it is feasible to achieve local success within a generation. This enables a movement to establish a secure foundation on which it can base its future expansion.

The United States has been a favourable soil in which new religious movements can grow. The prime reason for this is the constitutional guarantee of freedom of religious worship and assembly, and the absence of state support for religion. Taken together, these two factors make it possible for religions to flourish in free and fair competition with one another. The LDS church has capitalized on the decline of mainstream liberal churches. Having emerged intact from a period of intense persecution, it established a secure base in Salt Lake City from which it has launched its programme of worldwide evangelism.

A dense but not isolated social network

Members' commitment is reinforced if they belong to a close-knit community. However, if this produces an introversionist outlook it will make attracting new members more problematic. Ethnic religious communities such as the Amish, the Hutterites and the Doukhobors have grown and prospered without converting outsiders. Even so, in cultural terms they are 'living fossils' with 'no significant role to play in the making of future religious history' (Stark and Bainbridge 1987: 253) – a challenge which confronts contemporary Judaism outside of Israel.

From the outset Mormonism was a missionary faith, one not content to turn inwards on itself. As the true church of Christ, it has a duty to bring all of humanity into the restored Christian faith. The church's mission extends backwards as well as forward in time. Mormons devote time and effort to genealogical research, so that their ancestors may be offered the opportunity of salvation through sacred ordinances performed in the temple on their behalf.

Resistance to secularization

If a movement allows itself to become secularized from within by accommodating too much to secular culture it will not be able to attract new members or even retain those it already has. In marketing terms, it will have thrown away its USP – its unique selling proposition. This has been the fate of mainstream liberal Protestantism in the west.

For all its drive toward respectability, Mormonism has retained a firm commitment to divinely ordained beliefs and practices which have served as a bulwark against secularization from within. Similarly, it combines a bureaucratic hierarchy with a leadership open to divine revelations which can change the course of Mormon history, as with the abandonment of polygamy and the opening of the priesthood to African-Caribbean men. Although the Mormon church espouses some liberal causes (such as opposing corporal punishment of children, or supporting the rights of Native American peoples), it remains fundamentally conservative and opposed to permissiveness and moral relativism.

As Bainbridge comments, some of the factors considered so far – especially those concerned with leadership, governance and internal organization – are widely recognized as vital to the growth of any social movement. The most original factors in Stark's analysis are the last two – cultural continuity and a medium level of tension with the socio-cultural environment.

Cultural continuity

Successful new religions maintain a significant degree of continuity with the prevailing religious culture. They retain some of the concepts, beliefs, values, mores, symbols and rituals of the dominant religious tradition of the host society. Thus Buddhism drew on Hinduism, the Sikh faith synthesized elements of Hinduism and Islam, Christianity retained parts of Judaism, and Islam incorporated Christian and Jewish components. By contrast to these successful world faiths, movements which depart too radically from the prevailing religious culture are unlikely to succeed, because it is hard to market a totally unfamiliar product.

From the standpoint of individual converts, cultural continuity means that they can retain most of their cultural capital, which they simply transfer to their new faith – they are not starting totally from scratch (Stark 1998: 39–40). Christians who convert to Mormonism do not have to recast most of what they once believed and practised – which they would have to do if they joined, say, Hare Krishna. Mormons read the Christian Old and New Testaments, adding to them new revelations in the Book of Mormon, the *Doctrine and Covenants* and the *Pearl of Great Price*. From the LDS church's perspective, Mormons *are* Christians. The Mormon faith fills out Christianity, answering all kinds of questions which other Christians do not even raise – such as the origins of God himself. Obscurantism and mystery are not features of Mormonism. As O'Dea saw, the Book of Mormon is straightforward, clear and consistent, speaking to its readers 'with a democratic comprehensibility' (1957: 30).

The LDS church regards itself as a restoration of the early church as it was in the time of the apostles in the first century AD. As traditional Catholics see the Catholic church, so Mormons see the Church of Jesus Christ of Latter-day Saints: the one true church founded by Christ. Although many Mormon beliefs are the same as or similar to the teachings of mainstream Christian churches there are some striking departures which mark Mormon belief and practice as 'deviant'. An obvious instance is the status of the Book of Mormon as a sacred text alongside the Bible. Only Mormons and Mormon splinter groups treat it as sacred; other faiths either ignore or dismiss it. Baptism performed vicariously for deceased ancestors is a distinctive Mormon rite, and even more offensive to Protestant Christianity than the Catholic practice of praying for the dead. A further departure from the Christian mainstream is the teaching that God is not an immaterial spirit but a being with a physical body of flesh and bone. One consequence is the belief that Jesus was conceived in a physical union between God and Mary. There is also a widespread belief among Mormons – though it appears to fall short of an official doctrine – that we have a 'Mother in Heaven', implying that God is married (Heeren et al. 1984). Mormons also believe – and there are parallels in this with eastern Orthodox spirituality – that righteous human beings can attain the status of godhead in the celestial kingdom, though without ever becoming equal with God himself.

Significantly, church members do not draw attention to these more deviant beliefs and practices in their initial contacts with potential converts. Unlike mainstream Christian churches, the Church of Jesus Christ of Latter-day Saints is reticent about various details of its doctrine and temple worship, reserving their disclosure to people who are already members. In this respect it resembles Freemasonry: the secrets of the craft are revealed gradually, and only after a man has been initiated into the brotherhood. Joseph Smith based Mormon ritual on Masonry, which he saw as a degenerate version of the early church rites which he was restoring (O'Dea 1957: 57).

The question of cultural continuity can be broadened to consider not just a movement's connection with the prevailing religion but its relationships with the host culture more generally. Viewed in this broader perspective, Mormonism has much in common with core values of conservative Christianity in America. Mormons uphold family life, a conventional gender division of labour, obedience of children to parents and marital fidelity. They oppose abortion, gambling, pornography and homosexuality. They require members to dress 'modestly'. They advocate the virtues of the Puritan ethic, including hard work, thrift and deferred gratification. They virtuously extend the Puritan prohibition of alcohol and tobacco to all beverages containing caffeine, including tea, coffee and cola drinks – an apparently trivial proscription, but one with a deep cultural significance (Davies 1996). Like the Jewish dietary laws it has a boundary-maintenance function, setting Mormons apart as a peculiar people and making commensality with 'Gentiles' more difficult – a factor which is especially important in the socialization of Mormon children. Unlike the Jewish case it is also an aid to proselytism: it signals that Mormons are even more clean-living than conservative Protestants, and it resonates with contemporary preoccupations with a healthy diet.

In other respects Mormons are aligned with the broad centre-liberal consensus. Unlike other forms of Christian conservatism the Mormon church is not part of a rural southern backlash against liberalism. One symbol of this is repeated Mormon opposition to corporal punishment of children. To many conservative evangelical Christians in the United States, corporal punishment – its advocates call it spanking – is not merely an allowable weapon of last resort. In their view the Bible clearly teaches that regular spanking is a divinely required element in the correction by parents of their children's behaviour. Mormonism, in contrast, takes a fundamentally optimistic view of humanity, rejecting the doctrine of original sin. The church agrees with the respectable liberal mainstream that corporal punishment of children is unnecessary, ineffective, and a counter-productive endorsement of violence as a solution to life's problems.

As Wilson says (1970: 200), their adherence to the Puritan work ethic is 'dissociated from the tensions of Puritan asceticism'. Worldly achievement is not a problem to them. On the contrary, Mormonism is an expression of the success ethic and the American dream. Upward social mobility is symbolized in the structure, discussed above, in which male members move through the stages of the Aaronic and Melchizedek priesthoods. Social mobility does not end with death but continues in the afterlife. The Mormon church teaches that there are three heavenly kingdoms, characteristically arranged in a hierarchy. The *celestial kingdom* is reserved for the righteous, who will dwell with God. They will live with their spouse and their children, with whom they have been sealed for eternity, and in the company of ancestors who have accepted the baptism performed for them by their descendants. Couples in the celestial state will continue to propagate children (these will be spirits). Second in the heavenly hierarchy is the *terrestrial kingdom*, which is visited by Jesus but not by God, and in which people will be single rather than married. Mormons who have married outside the faith will reside here, separated from their former partner. Below this stands the *telestial kingdom*, reserved for people who have led unclean lives. They will receive the Holy Spirit and be ministered to by members of the terrestrial kingdom, but are for ever banned from the presence of God and Christ. Although transfer from one kingdom to another is not available, it is possible to improve one's position within a kingdom by good works. Achievement is therefore operative for all time.

A medium level of tension with their environment

This is closely linked to the issue of cultural continuity. As Bainbridge says (1997: 411), successful religious movements are 'deviant but not too deviant'. If they are offering nothing new, why should anyone incur the cost of transferring allegiance to them? On the other hand, if they are too deviant most people will judge the cost of conversion to be simply too high.

In the early years of its history the LDS church existed in a high state of tension with the wider society. Mormons made no fewer than four failed attempts to build their own city. In a recurrent effort to escape persecution, their headquarters moved from New York to Ohio, then Missouri, and then Illinois, where a community was established at Nauvoo in swampland bordering the Mississippi. Violent clashes were frequent, culminating in the murder of Joseph Smith and his brother Hyrum by an armed mob in 1844. The great Mormon trek began two years later under the leadership of Smith's successor, Brigham Young. In a supreme expression of the pioneering spirit, they struggled across Iowa and into Nebraska, before embarking on an arduous 1,300-mile trek to the Valley of the Great Salt Lake. They saw themselves as re-enacting the exodus of the people of Israel from captivity, and their experiences stamped them with a profound sense of ethnic identity as a 'people' (O'Dea 1966: 70).

The violent confrontations between Mormons and the wider society had complex causes. Mormon political activity and block voting aroused opposition (Joseph Smith even declared himself a candidate for the American Presidency). The authoritarian theocratic organization of the Mormon church under the leadership of a charismatic prophet clashed with the spirit of Jeffersonian democracy. Above all, the practice of polygamy (more precisely polygyny – plural wives) was a symbolic affront to Christian and humanistic values. As the century drew on, the federal authorities passed increasingly punitive legislation outlawing plural marriage. Repeated requests that Utah be granted statehood were flatly rejected; polygamy was the chief obstacle. Finally, under mounting pressure, the church's new president, Wilford Woodruff, issued an official statement in 1890 formally abandoning polygamy. This signalled the end of Mormon 'separatism'. Six years later, Utah became the forty-fifth state of the Union. Ever since its drastic about-turn on polygamy, the church has totally repudiated fundamentalist splinter groups – 'hold-outs' – which continue to recognize plural marriages. Within contemporary Mormon thought, polygamy 'has retreated to the limbo of theological relics' (O'Dea 1966: 140).

For most of its history the LDS church excluded men 'of African lineage' from the priesthood. The theological justification given for this was the argument that Noah's son Ham and his descendants had been cursed by God with a black skin, just as the North American 'Indians' had been. This argument, widely used by anti-abolitionists to justify slavery, was absorbed into Mormon theology. With the growth of the civil rights movement in the 1960s the Mormon church stood accused of overt racism. Protests were directed at key symbols of Mormon achievement and respectability including the Mormon Tabernacle Choir and sports teams representing Brigham Young University. Mormon missionary efforts in Africa were hampered by the closure of the priesthood to black Africans. The church faced further problems in Brazil, a 'racially' mixed society in which 'racial' lineage is hard even for a racist to determine; Brazilian Mormons faced the challenge of determining precisely which of their ancestors were eligible for proxy ordination to the priesthood (Embry 1994: 27). In this cultural climate the Mormon church began to retreat from a doctrinaire position on priesthood. The reason for the ban on African-Caribbeans was argued to be a divine mystery; Mormons hoped that God would act soon to lift the ban once the time was ripe. Some Mormons even argued that the exclusion of black men from the priesthood was more a matter of cultural practice than of revealed faith, a practice shaped moreover by the church's unfortunate exposure to racist ideology in the antebellum south. In 1978, the church received a revelation from God that the ban on blacks entering the priesthood had been lifted. As in its abandonment of polygamy, openness to divine revelation provided the Mormon church with a theological basis for a timely reversal of doctrine and practice.

Throughout the first half of the twentieth century the LDS church adopted an accommodationist position, abandoning or playing down Mormon peculiarities. It swung from high to low tension with the wider society. However, since the end of the Second World War a process of retrenchment (Mauss 1994, 1996) has seen moves to reassert a distinctive Mormon identity, implying a medium state of tension with the wider society, as prescribed in Stark's model of successful growth.

One feature of Mormonism that is highly relevant to its prospects for growth is its quintessentially American character. Theologically, Mormonism provides a place for the New World and for Native American peoples in God's scheme of salvation. (These peoples are descendants of the Lamanites, an Israelite tribe who crossed the sea to America. They were a rebellious people, who had been handsome until God cursed them with a dark skin to punish them for their disobedience. They are therefore lapsed Christians, and Mormons have a special duty to reconvert them into the true church.) America is literally the new Zion and Salt Lake City the New Jerusalem. Until the outbreak of war in Europe in 1914, Mormon missionary endeavour was devoted to persuading converts to emigrate to America. Mormonism is an expression of the American dream. The Book of Mormon is full of accounts of heroic triumph over adversity, epitomized in Mormon history by the great trek west, in which the Latter-day Saints re-enacted Israel's exodus from Egypt. Mormonism embraces American civil religion generally and specifically; thus the American Constitution is held to be divinely inspired.

Mormonism's American identity has brought problems. Mormon missionaries and Mormon temples have been targeted in South America and in Africa as agencies of American cultural imperialism. On the other hand, globalization is often synonymous with Americanization. The LDS church is adaptable, not least because it has at its apex a prophet who receives divine revelations. Provided it does not tie itself too parochially to American folkways, Mormonism's American character can be turned to advantage. After all, although ironically Mormons do not drink them, Coke and Pepsi have found their American provenance to be a marketing asset.

Jehovah's Witnesses: a model for growth?

Like the Mormons, Jehovah's Witnesses have enjoyed an exceptionally high rate of growth, and for much the same reasons. As with the Mormons, their net rate of growth is around 5 per cent annually, which means they double their membership about every fifteen years. In 1995 there were around five million Jehovah's Witnesses worldwide. In some ways, their growth is even more spectacular than the Mormons'. Witnesses only count active 'publishers' as members, which means that they exclude from their statistics almost everyone under the age of sixteen.

Although Mormons and Jehovah's Witnesses have little in common theologically, there are profound structural similarities between the two movements. Like Mormons, Witnesses are extremely well organized. Viewed as a business corporation, the Watch Tower Bible and Tract Society is authoritarian and patriarchal, but extremely efficient in achieving its goals. It mobilizes the services of millions of unpaid, dedicated lay volunteers who, despite all the insults they endure, persist in knocking on strangers' doors to bring them the good news and a chance to come into the truth. One particular way in which the society mobilizes its members is to build their places for worship and assembly, the Kingdom Halls. A 'rapid-building crew' of Witness volunteers can erect a functional but well-built Kingdom Hall in a weekend. This is one of the many ways in which the society efficiently substitutes labour for capital (Stark and Iannaccone 1997: 148).

Despite their innumerable differences theologically, Witnesses' belief-system, like the Mormons', is rationalistic and devoid of mystery (Beckford 1975: 201–4). The movement's founder, Charles Taze Russell, asserted that the criteria of absolute truth were in conformity with Scripture and with human reason – in this Russell was far more rationalistic than most of his conservative evangelical contemporaries (Beckford 1975: 103–5). Jehovah is supremely rational, and so, with guidance, reasoning human beings can come to accept the truth. Watch Tower literature is full of proofs that Jehovah's plan is reasonable. The society does not attack reason itself but the perversion of reason by the ungodly and by the churches. Hence the society's dependence on the written word, and the fact that from the earliest days Witnesses have seen themselves as Bible *students*. Jehovah has a rational plan for humankind, as clearly set out in the Bible and confirmed by the unfolding of history. Although the movement is doctrinally authoritarian its beliefs are democratically accessible to everybody. Hence all Witnesses, not just a cadre of theological specialists, are able to preach the truth from door to door.

A common feature of the two movements is the absence of a professional priesthood. All Jehovah's Witnesses are expected to be active 'publishers', spreading the word through calling from door to door. Every Jehovah's Witness is therefore a missionary, and there is no role for anyone who wishes simply to tag along as a free rider. The ethos of the Kingdom Hall is goal-oriented. Sociability is not valued as an end in itself. Beckford (1975: 86) pointed out in his in-depth study of Witnesses in Britain that the Watch Tower Society has not wanted congregations to become social clubs.

As with all forms of 'cold calling' the strike rate of doorstep proselytizing is inevitably low. Nevertheless, the Witnesses' negative image has led many people to underestimate their effectiveness as proselytizers. Consider Smart's treatment of Jehovah's Witnesses in his study *The Religious Experience of Mankind*. The Witnesses are dispatched in one paragraph. We are told that Witnesses are

> peaceful, but fanatical; they know their Bible backward and forward, but they are rarely well educated. Such a movement appeals to those of modest education – clerks and landladies in England, for instance, are well represented in the movement; these are people who know something of what education is through schooling and contact with students, but they have not got higher education. The secret hope of the Millennium and the marvellous

way they can interpret the Bible are compensations for their deprivation. (Smart 1971: 632–3)

The tone of this passage echoes that of Victorian anthropologists speculating on the mentality of savages. Jehovah's Witnesses may not live in darkest England, but Smart clearly does not deem them to inhabit the same cultural world as we, the readers, do. Perhaps the Witnesses' university-educated critics might consider how effective they would be themselves if required to undertake a doorstep ministry? The target to beat is a consistent net annual growth rate of at least 5 per cent a year.

Like the Mormon church, the Watch Tower Society gathers detailed statistics about its own membership. There is no reason to doubt that these are accurate. They are in line with estimates produced by government agencies and independent scholars. The society reports poor results as well as good ones, which may well be a sign of honesty. Equally convincing is that fact that the Witnesses' sharpest critics, the splinter groups which have left the parent body, accept the society's figures as accurate (Stark and Iannaccone 1997: 138). Gathering accurate information is not an incidental feature of these two movements, nor is it obsessive-compulsive behaviour. Any successful business needs to monitor its activities so as to identify strengths and weaknesses, limitations and opportunities. Who would invest in a company which had no idea how many employees it had on the payroll? Investors would be right to interpret that as a sign of gross corporate incompetence. Why should it be any different for religious organizations?

As discussed in the section on Mormons above, a key element in Stark's model of religious growth is a *medium level of tension with the wider society.* This is not an easy accomplishment. In the case of Jehovah's Witnesses, tension has periodically been extremely high. Witnesses were sent to concentration camps in Nazi Germany. They were severely persecuted under communism. In Muslim societies they are in a precarious situation, given that it is a crime to persuade anyone to apostatize from Islam. In some Catholic countries, such as Spain and Italy, it has been illegal until quite recently for Witnesses to function. In the United States, the Watch Tower Society fought a long battle to enable its members to opt out of flag-saluting and the Pledge of Allegiance. Their constitutional rights were eventually upheld by a Supreme Court ruling in 1943. During the Second World War, Witnesses throughout the west were imprisoned for refusal to enlist in the war effort. Their treatment by the authorities was typically harsher than that experienced by more respectable conscientious objectors such as Quakers – which is not to minimize the hardship Quakers suffered.

For Jehovah's Witnesses, then, the problem has been to keep tension with the wider society in check. That said, it is also probably true, as Stark and Iannaccone comment (1997: 145–6), that in their everyday life most Witnesses are not too uncomfortable with the wider culture. Above all, they are not a 'peculiar people' who display oddities which set them apart. They drink alcohol (though not to excess), they do not eat a special diet, they use cosmetics to look smart, they do not wear unusual dress or any uniform, they have no obvious peculiarities of speech, and they take part in popular social activities such as spectating at sports events, going to the theatre and cinema, and watching television (though they are careful to avoid sex and violence). Except when they are on the doorsteps, they are not visible as Witnesses. Stark and Iannaccone (1997: 146) suggest the hypothesis that 'visibility may, in fact, be the crucial factor for identifying when groups impose too much tension or strictness'.

In some respects Jehovah's Witnesses have better prospects for continued growth than the LDS church does. The movement is more universal in the sense that it is less distinctively American even though its origins are in the United States. It was one of many adventist movements whose roots lay in the 'Great Disappointment' – the failure of William Miller's prediction that the world would end in 1843 or 1844 (Bainbridge 1997: 89–96). Its headquarters are in Brooklyn, and its top leadership has always been overwhelmingly American. Even so, it is far less tied to American culture and customs than the Mormon church. Whereas nearly half of all Mormons live in the United States, for Jehovah's Witnesses the corresponding figure is 19 per cent (Stark and Iannaccone 1997: 140). Mormons hold the American Constitution sacred, but Jehovah's Witnesses do not regard any human government as divinely legitimate. American Mormons celebrate the popular festivals of American culture such as Thanksgiving, Memorial Day and Christmas, while the only calendrical rite observed by Witnesses is the annual Memorial commemorating Christ's death. Mormons espouse western-style democracy, but Witnesses reject democracy in favour of theocracy, the rule of God. Historically, Mormons have been encouraged to look to America as the new Zion, and even to migrate to the United States, whereas Jehovah's Witnesses hold no territory sacred but are oriented globally to life on Paradise Earth after the War of Armageddon.

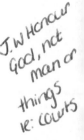

J.W. Honour God, not man or things re: courts

One particular advantage enjoyed by Jehovah's Witnesses is that, unlike the LDS church, the movement has not been tainted with racism. Watch Tower publications take a strongly anti-racist stance, and the movement has a wide range of ethnic groups in membership. Accusations of racism are therefore unlikely to threaten the Witnesses' worldwide evangelical mission.

In the course of its history the Watch Tower Society has had to overcome many problems. One of these was of its own making. The society has frequently issued dramatic prophecies about world events. The most recent of these was that the present world order would come to an end in 1975. Although the movement now denies that it was officially predicted by the society, there is no doubt that the vast majority of Witnesses were expecting momentous events before 1975 was out. Yet nothing happened. How then did the movement survive? *FALSE PROPHECIES !*

did it strengthen them ?

A classic study by Festinger, Riecken and Schachter (1956), *When Prophecy Fails*, has often been read as demonstrating that, paradoxically, movements are strengthened by the failure of prophecy. The argument draws on the social-psychological theory of *cognitive dissonance*. According to this theory, people find it stressful to hold dissonant cognitions – that is, contradictory beliefs, opinions, attitudes or self-perceptions. Because dissonance is unpleasant, people try to resolve it by changing their cognitions to make them consistent with one another. Festinger used cognitive dissonance theory to explain the behaviour of members of a flying saucer cult. They believed that their leader was in touch with a spiritual being called Sananda, the personification of Jesus Christ. Sananda warned that large areas of the United States would be destroyed on 21 December 1954, but promised that his followers would be rescued by spaceship. The due date arrived, and passed without incident. The crucial point, according to Festinger, is that far from abandoning their beliefs the cult members redoubled their efforts to proselytize at the very moment when their prediction had been disproved. Why did they do so? Because bringing more people into the movement would reduce the dissonance between the leaders' prophecy and the failure of either the cataclysm or the spaceships to appear. If more and more people are persuaded to join, a belief-system becomes psychologically more plausible. Festinger speculates that a similar mechanism may have been at work after Jesus's messiahship ended in crucifixion, the most agonizing and humiliating death the Roman Empire could devise.

There are many reasons to doubt that this interpretation stands up, as Bainbridge (1997: 134–8) has pointed out. The flying saucer cult Festinger and his colleagues studied had a tiny membership. The impact of Festinger's research team on the group's behaviour was probably very great. The researchers appear to have contributed unintentionally to the group's vitality and sense of its own importance. The news media were also pressing for a statement from the cult about the failure of its prophecy. There is no evidence of sustained proselytizing endeavour by cult members. Far from it: after a period of turmoil the movement soon fizzled out. The evidence points the other way to the conventional interpretation. A catastrophically failed prophecy caused the movement to fold after a brief posture of defiance.

Other studies have failed to confirm this thesis of cognitive dissonance theory. The point surely is that a failed prophecy is a serious problem that has to be overcome. Failed prophecies cause people to leave movements, not join them. When prophecy fails, the movement has to devote considerable cultural work to repairing the damage. For this reason, Stark has added the following proposition to his theory of religious growth: 'New religious movements are likely to succeed to the extent that their doctrines are non-empirical' (Stark and Iannaccone 1997: 143). This is a comparative advantage that Mormonism has held over Jehovah's Witnesses. While there have been problems in reconciling the Book of Mormon with historical and archaeological evidence, and in accounting for anachronisms – did native peoples of North America really have weapons made of steel? – at least the LDS church has not issued disconfirmed prophecies about the end of the world.

Nor, on a rational calculation of organizational benefit, is there any need for a religious movement to predict exactly when the world will end. In religious terms a prophecy does not have to entail a prediction. Prophets are not necessarily seers or clairvoyants. The essence of prophecy is that the prophet calls down God's judgement on the world. The prophet's core activity is to forth-tell God's will, not foretell the future. One of the ways in which religious movements cope with failed predictions is to emphasize their prophetic element. So, even though 1975 was not the end, it remains obvious to Jehovah's Witnesses that we are living in the last days. A few minutes watching the news on TV is all it takes to prove this.

The failure of the 1975 prophecy set the movement back (Stark and Iannaccone 1997: 142–4). Some members were demotivated, some defected, the movement's growth rate slowed down, and there was a crisis among the leadership over the failed prophecy (Penton 1985). Only with considerable effort did the movement re-establish its rate of growth. It appears that the society is unlikely to set a new date for Armageddon. The conclusion is the converse of the one conventionally drawn from Festinger's study. It is not that failed prophecies stimulate religious growth, but that strong movements can survive failed prophecies.

To succeed in growing, a religious movement has to retain most of its existing members, successfully socialize their children, and attract a significant flow of new recruits. A crucial consequence of the growth rate of Mormons and Jehovah's Witnesses is that at any given time a high proportion of the members are relatively recent converts. Probably more than 60 per cent of today's Jehovah's Witnesses joined the movement after 1975. The society has less need to explain to them why prophecy failed. In their spiritual autobiography it is pre-history. High rates of growth help movements to live down past problems.

However successful they are in winning recruits, Jehovah's Witnesses and the LDS church are likely to remain *voluntary* religious movements. They are not politically motivated to seize command of the state's instruments of power. Perhaps, then, they will have only a weak impact on the societies in which they operate. They have reached an accommodation with their host societies, even though in the case of Jehovah's Witnesses a high level of latent tension remains. The spectacular growth of these minority movements does not necessarily give us any reason to abandon the secularization thesis, it has been argued. Wilson, Berger and others see epistemologically authoritarian sects as the form of religion best adapted to survival in a secular environment. Sects are protests against modernity, but they lack the capacity or even the will to transform the world. In Wilson's terminology, Jehovah's Witnesses and the LDS church are *revolutionist* movements. They look forward to the end of the present world order, but do so passively. Their rhetoric can be fiery but the reality is law-abiding. These people are not revolutionaries.

For world-transforming potential, perhaps we should turn to the resurgence of so-called fundamentalist movements within the mainstream of great world religions.

Not Revolutionary – not going to do anything to bring down man because they are not interested in man, only God.

6

The Resurgence of Fundamentalism

The nature of fundamentalism

Religious movements labelled 'fundamentalist' are often poorly understood by liberal western commentators. Fundamentalism has become a pejorative term, implying ignorance, bigotry and fanaticism. In France, the term *intégriste* – which has some of the same associations as fundamentalism – is routinely used to characterize assertive forms of Islam. Both these terms originated, however, as *positive* assertions of *Christian* faith. Protestant fundamentalists in the United States claimed the title from a series of pamphlets entitled *The Fundamentals*, which were published between 1910 and 1915. The pamphlets called for a return to what were claimed to be the core doctrines of the Christian faith. As for *intégrisme*, it embodied the aspiration of traditionally minded and politically conservative French people to fuse state and society into an organic union based in the Catholic faith.

It is doubtful whether fundamentalism is a useful term for analysing contemporary movements in Islam and Judaism. Within Christianity it has denoted a claim to orthodoxy. Fundamentalism in the original sense of the term is a formal belief-system predicated on an assertion that the Bible is without error and its truths valid for all eternity. Fundamentalism entails belief in the Virgin Birth, the deity of Jesus Christ, and the biblical miracles including Christ's bodily Resurrection (Barr 1977). These beliefs are used as shibboleths, acid tests to distinguish between true believers and 'nominal' Christians – the 'liberals'. The doctrine of the Virgin Birth is a key instance of how this works. From a rational point of view, the Virgin Birth is hard to accept. It has all the qualities of a myth, a suspicion confirmed by

anthropological evidence of myths of virginal conceptions worldwide
(Leach 1969). If it were not in the Bible, who would believe it? Here, then,
is an ideal test for smoking out the liberals. For Protestant fundamentalists
that is precisely the function of the Virgin Birth (Aldridge 1992). Ironically, Mary has only a minor role in the Virgin Birth. All that matters about
her is that she was submissive to God's will and her hymen was unbroken.
She is not an object of devotion, and plays no part in the spiritual life of
fundamentalist Protestants. The culture of fundamentalism is assertively
masculine, subordinating women and abhorring homosexuals.

Fundamentalism is characteristically Christian in that it formulates lines
of division between the righteous and the unrighteous in terms of what they
believe. Christian history can be written as a series of schisms over correct
belief, and as the triumph of self-proclaimed orthodoxy over heresy. When
we turn to the assertive forms of Judaism and Islam outlined below, they
differ from Christianity in the priority they give to everyday practice. Key
symbols here are what you eat and how you dress. To the faithful and their
opponents these are not the trivial matters they may seem to the rationalist.
They are the basis of identity. The sartorial style of ultra-Orthodox Jewish
men – long black Lithuanian-style coat, black fedora, beard and earlocks –
is liable to inspire admiration or provoke contempt. The same is true of
traditional Islamic dress, particularly for women. The *hijab*, the headscarf
or veil, the *chador*, a long black cloak and veil, and the *burqa*, a voluminous garment which swathes the body, leaving simply a lattice to enable the
woman to see out, are potent symbols of gender and sexuality.

A second problem in applying the term 'fundamentalism' outside a
Christian context is the nature of the Christian Scriptures. To fundamentalists, the Bible was inspired by God and therefore contains no errors. If the
Bible says that Noah took all the animals into the ark two by two, then that
is exactly what he did. This is not a flippant example, since taking these
events literally is essential to fundamentalist belief. Abandon belief in
Noah's ark and the whole edifice of fundamentalism collapses with it: it is
all or nothing. The Bible is read as an exact record of historical events. Of
course it contains other elements such as poetry, prophecy and visions. But
the historical record is the core.

There are many other ways of reading the Bible. Brief passages may be
chosen as food for meditation, as in contemplative religious orders. Some
people read the Bible straight through from beginning to end, others dip
into favourite passages as the mood takes them. Jehovah's Witnesses read
the Bible through the lens of the society's literature; it is a reference work.
Some Christians have used the Bible as an oracle, opening it at random and
reading a passage as a guide to decision-making – a Christian version of the
sortes Virgilianae, the oracles of Virgil, where the educated classes used

the works of the Latin poet to the same end. The churches have their lectionaries – extracts from the Scriptures to be read out in public worship on a regular cycle throughout the year. Although fundamentalists claim to be letting the Bible speak for itself, theirs is simply one system of interpretation alongside others. They chose what to read / quote to suit argument

The contrast with Islam is particularly marked. If one insists on trying to use the term 'fundamentalism' in the Christian sense, then all Islam has to be labelled fundamentalist, despite the wealth of cultural variety within Islam worldwide. The case for saying that Islam is inherently fundamentalist is this. The Qur'an is not simply the Muslims' bible. Muslims believe that the Qur'an is uncreated and coexistent with God. Qur'an means recitation, and the text is the word of God delivered to the Prophet Muhammad by the Angel Gabriel. Strictly, it is untranslatable from Arabic. In Christian terms, the Qur'an functions less as the Bible than as Christ. It is an object of reverence in ways that the Bible usually is not, even to Christian fundamentalists. The Qur'an is not primarily a historical narrative, and it is not arranged in chronological sequence. Disagreements about the seaworthiness of Noah's ark, and reports that it has been discovered in Turkey, have no parallel here. In the case of the Qur'an, it is not possible to distinguish between liberal and conservative interpretations in the Christian sense.

Islam, like Judaism, puts great emphasis on the religious law, much of which lies outside the Qur'an itself. In Islam as in Judaism, the law began as an oral tradition that was later codified and set down in writing. This means that Islam and Judaism are inherently less scripturalist than Protestantism (Sharot 1992: 28–30), so that divisions within them do not turn on the interpretation of the sacred texts. Within Christianity itself, much the same could be said of Catholicism. Even the reactionary Catholic traditionalism of Cardinal Lefebvre was not fundamentalist.

Although 'fundamentalism' is an inappropriate term to describe it, the mid-1970s saw a sea-change within Judaism, Christianity and Islam (Kepel 1994). Certain key events crystallized the realignments that were taking place.

In 1977, the Labour Party failed for the first time in the history of the state of Israel to win enough seats in a general election to be able to form the government. Until that point, the Israeli state had been underpinned by secular socialist values. Power passed to the Likud Party led by Menachem Begin, who depended for support on parties representing Orthodox Judaism. To the Orthodox, Jewishness must not become simply an ethnic identity or an emotional attachment to a set of folkways. Instead, the essence of Judaism is obedience to the Jewish law, strict observance of all the ritual prescriptions and proscriptions, and unblinking acceptance of dogma.

In 1978, Karol Wojtyla was elected Pope and took the name John Paul II.

He reasserted traditional Catholic ethical teaching, particularly on sexual morality, reaffirming the church's opposition to artificial contraception, artificial insemination, abortion, homosexual acts, and new reproductive technologies such as *in vitro* fertilization. His pontificate coincided with the growth of charismatic movements within the Catholic church. Their goal, in Kepel's words (1994: 7), was 'to proclaim the futility of a society dominated by reason alone, show through communal experience the need to rediscover God and so save mankind, and suggest how society can be rebuilt on a foundation of Christian teaching'. This fitted well with the Pope's unflinching opposition to communism, bred through the bleak post-1945 experience of Poland. Liberal-minded Catholics in the west have felt alienated from this resurgence of traditional Catholicism.

Mainstream Protestantism was also profoundly influenced by charismatic renewal. In 1976, the born-again southern Baptist Jimmy Carter was elected President of the United States, and embarked on the moral challenge of cleansing the republic of the sin of Watergate. His successor, Ronald Reagan, also a born-again Christian, had come to power with the support of conservative religious groups who looked to him to re-Christianize secular society. Founded in 1979, the Moral Majority saw itself as rescuing America from the depravity of secular humanism, sexual permissiveness and antinomian licence. The movement embodied a deep challenge to the 'wall of separation' between church and state.

In 1979, following the collapse of the regime led by the Shah of Iran, Ayatollah Khomeini returned in triumph to Tehran and proclaimed the foundation of an Islamic republic. Although iconic, this was not an isolated event. In the former Soviet Union, South-East Asia, the Middle East and the urban centres of western Europe, a radically politicized Islam has asserted itself. It denounces post-colonial regimes for spreading degenerate western values in the name of modernization. The everyday life of ordinary citizens is to be totally refashioned on traditional Islamic lines. Significantly, in Islam as in Judaism and Christianity, this includes a strict gender division of labour and an unapologetic subordination of women to the authority of men.

The revival of conservative faith has occurred against the backdrop of a crisis of modernity which has seen the fall of communism and mounting unease at the problems unleashed by scientific and technological progress. Conservative religion has a double task (Kepel 1994: 191). First, it seeks to explain to its own adherents, in categories drawn from traditional faith, the nature and causes of the crisis in modernity. Second, it plans to change the world, bringing the social order into compliance with the commandments of the Jewish Holy Scriptures, the Bible or the Qur'an. Only thus will truth and justice prevail.

A common ingredient in contemporary conservative religious movements is that they do not reject science and technology as such. This is despite their hostility to the emancipation of reason from faith, and notwithstanding their opposition to some modern inventions, particularly in the field of reproductive technology. The point is that they regard reason as God-given, so that scientific discoveries, rightly directed, can be put at the service of God's people.

While they have much in common, the implications of the rise of conservative religious movements vary according to the religion concerned and the social context in which it operates.

Judaism

In the 1970s a strong current in Jewish culture called for *teshuvah*, a repentant 'return to Judaism' and to observance of the *halakah*, the Jewish law. Assimilation is the enemy. As the chosen people, Jews should insulate themselves against Gentile culture. The means to this end is strict observance of the *mitsvot*, the 613 injunctions listed in the Torah, comprising 248 prescriptions and 365 prohibitions which regulate the whole of life. This is at variance with Reform Judaism, which sees the *halakah* as in need of revision to accommodate contemporary values and lifestyles.

Various socio-cultural changes in the west contributed to the rise of Orthodox forms of Judaism. Until the 1960s Orthodoxy had been eclipsed. In America, the Conservative and Reform branches of Judaism had been in the ascendancy. In Europe, the Shoah (the Holocaust) had obliterated the old centres of Orthodoxy, and also delegitimated the isolationist life of the ghetto or *shtetl* (rural village) as a capitulation to anti-Semitism. 'Never again' was the watchword of the heavily armed Israeli state and its supporters worldwide. But in the aftermath of the 1960s counterculture many disillusioned Jewish ex-hippies sought their identity in religious roots. Some of them found their way into *yeshivot* (Talmudic colleges), often becoming fervent converts to Orthodoxy and keen supporters of Israel's territorial claim to the whole of the biblical Promised Land.

The rise of Black Power in the United States had important consequences for Jewish identity. It broke the alliance between blacks and Jews as opponents of the White Anglo-Saxon Protestant establishment. In its most extreme forms, Black Power was unmistakably anti-Semitic, employing crude derogatory terms and identifying Jews as part of the dominant white society. Here was a further reason for Jews to dissociate themselves from the Gentiles.

In France, the balance of power in the Jewish community shifted away from the Ashkenazi Jews, who had migrated from central and eastern Europe, to Sephardic Jews from Spain, Portugal and Arab countries in the area of the Mediterranean basin. There was a mass migration into France of Jews from Algeria, Tunisia and Morocco. A similar shift was also under way in Israel itself, with migrations from Morocco, the Yemen and Iraq. The Sephardim were in general far less influenced by secular modernism than their Ashkenazi co-religionists.

Israel's victory in the Six Day War of June 1967 was a military triumph achieved by the secular Zionist state. Even so, it was a turning-point in the fortunes of Zionism. Israel's territorial acquisitions meant that it now controlled most of the Bible lands promised to the Jews in a divine covenant valid for all eternity. Here was a powerful symbol to rekindle Orthodoxy. The Arab offensive of 1973, launched on *Yom Kippur*, the Day of Atonement (the most solemn day in the Jewish calendar), was a military and psychological blow to the Israeli state. It undermined the secular progressives and greatly strengthened conservative movements such as Gush Emunim (the Bloc of the Faithful), formed shortly after the Yom Kippur War. It also served as a warrant to conservative groups to found Jewish settlements in the Occupied Territories.

The distinctive feature of revival of Orthodoxy in Judaism, which sets it apart from conservative revivals within Christianity and Islam, is that it is aimed entirely at fellow Jews and has no mission to proselytize outside the Jewish community. Its primary objective is to resist assimilation and combat Enlightenment universalism. A specific object of scorn is the *Haskalah*, the Jewish Enlightenment of the eighteenth century, which aimed to enrich Jewish culture by opening it to secular influences. The ultra-Orthodox groups – the *haredim*, meaning those who 'tremble' at God's word – base their communities around strict observance of the *mitsvot*. The *haredim* are a minority of a minority, representing some 30 per cent of Orthodox Jewry, which itself is only 15 per cent of the 12 million Jews worldwide. *Haredim* see themselves as the true Jews, standing in an unbroken line from Abraham to the present day. Heilman and Friedman (1991) describe them as 'contra-acculturative activists', while Sharot (1992) prefers 'neo-traditionalists'. The essential point is the same: the *haredim* are self-consciously committed to a vision of the past, specifically an idealized image of life in central and eastern Europe before the Holocaust. They actively resist anything which is inimical to the reaffirmation of this tradition. A sharp division exists between their world and the *chukos ha goyim*, the ways of the Gentiles. Interestingly, *haredi* groups are typically dependent on guidance from their *rebbe*, who wields far more power than the rabbis of the rest of the Jewish world, since a *rebbe* acts as an authoritative interpreter of the sacred tradition. Sharot argues that the traditions of the *haredim* are invented traditions, and that the role of the *rebbe* is to reinvent the tradition in the light of contemporary cultural change.

One prominent group of *haredim*, the Lubavitch, have their own demanding system of dietary prohibitions, the *glat-kosher*, which sets them apart from other Jews. They make strenuous efforts to socialize their children into Orthodox belief and practice. In Lubavitch primary schools in France, the only non-religious subjects taught are French and mathematics. As Kepel remarks (1994: 200), 'Cultural interaction with the non-Jewish world is reduced to its most basic terms: you learn to read and add up. Here we see the communal phenomenon at work in its most absolute expression.'

Christianity

The task of banishing secularism from the west is far harder than it is in the Jewish and Muslim worlds. Secularism is a western product, deeply entrenched, and has complex links with Christianity – which itself contains powerful secularizing as well as anti-secularizing forces. Decades of church decline have left millions of people, above all the young, with no anchorage in the Christian faith. They are ignorant not only of Christianity's basic teachings but also of its rituals and symbols, those essential elements which Durkheim called 'the cult of the faith'. It is a situation without parallel in the Jewish and Muslim worlds.

Christian conservatism is dualistic. It recognizes Christ's distinction between things that are Caesar's and those that are God's. There is a valid secular realm as well as a sacred one. Christianity has no equivalent of *halakah* or *shari'a*. Of course there are the Ten Commandments, but they are not intended by Christians to replace the laws and constitutions of secular society.

At the fringes of Christian fundamentalism are groups which espouse violent means to pursue their objectives. This has been seen in the emergence of right-wing fundamentalist militias, and in violent attacks on abortion clinics and the murder of doctors who have worked in them. Despite this, the main conservative Christian movements are committed to the democratic process and forswear political violence. This sets Christian movements apart from some of their Jewish and Muslim counterparts. The Gush Emunim regarded democracy as a system to be exploited in order to bring about a society in which the *halakah* would be enforced by the state. Islamists reject democracy even more emphatically, and seek the imposition of *shari'a* law. Both are monist faiths dedicated to organizing human life in accordance with divine law – the only valid law there is.

Modern representative democracy is a product of Christian culture, even if the relations between them have not lacked conflict. Democracy cannot be rejected as alien, as it is to Islamists and ultra-Orthodox Jews. Thus the New Christian Right in the United States has used the democratic process in pursuit of social change. The fundamental aim is to combat secularism, reinfuse culture with a Christian content, and thus prevent the faith from being pushed into the private sphere of life. Even under communist persecution, as Kepel notes (1994: 198), Christian movements did not turn to violence.

Bruce's (1988) study of the New Christian Right in the United States in the 1970s and 1980s charts the rise and fall of the movement's political fortunes, using a resource mobilization approach as one component of the analysis. He points to the activity of professional right-wing organizers, lobbying by political action committees, use of information technology for direct mailing to solicit funds and mobilize commitment, preaching by television evangelists, and use of congregational networks among Baptist ministers. All of these resources were mobilized in an ultimately unsuccessful attempt to overcome the deep-rooted aversion of fundamentalists to 'politics'.

Bruce argues that explaining how potential supporters are sensitized, politicized and mobilized is only one part of the story. It needs to be complemented by wider considerations, including the question, why was there was a market for the movement in the first place? He accounts for the relatively high proportion of conservative Protestants in the United States compared to other liberal-democratic societies as a product of the sheer size of the North American subcontinent and of its decentralized political system, which allowed the formation of geographically based subcultures such as the 'Bible belt' in the south (Bruce 1988: 25–49). The conservative subculture felt itself threatened by a dominant urban culture which was promoting the 'secular humanist' values of liberalism, cosmopolitanism and sexual permissiveness. The constitutional 'wall of separation' between church and state was increasingly seen by conservatives as a device to impose secular humanism on civil society. At the same time, whereas parts of the industrial north were in decline, the south was enjoying economic prosperity and the greater political influence that came with it. This gave to many conservatives a sense that the time had come to redress the balance against liberalism in favour of the old virtues and values.

In the eyes of many conservative Christians, the political sphere is irredeemably corrupt. Christians must therefore shun political engagement and cultivate their own personal piety, a position epitomized in the stock phrase, 'keeping politics out of religion'. This stands out in Bruce's study as a crucial element in cultural resistance to mobilization. It also explains why supporters of the New Christian Right became rapidly disillusioned with Ronald Reagan's administration. He had campaigned energetically on Moral Majority issues as a born-again Christian, but once he achieved office in 1980 he was perceived to have reneged on his campaign promises because of exactly the same considerations of political expediency which drive all politicians.

Islam

Conservative revival groups in the Muslim world have identified as a principal target what they see as the degenerate regimes installed in power after independence from the colonial powers. In the name of Islam they challenged the political and cultural systems imported from the west by the post-colonial elites in their drive to modernize. Nor had the Soviet model delivered prosperity to the newly independent countries which tried to adopt it. Its legacy was the financial burden of uncompetitive heavy industries.

The outcome of the 1973 Yom Kippur War was a turning-point in the Arab countries as it was in Israel. The myth of Israeli invincibility had been shattered, and the balance of power had tilted toward oil-rich Gulf states, whose economic cartel led by Saudi Arabia had dramatic repercussions in the west. Once viewed as backward, the Saudis came to be seen as prime movers in the resurgence of Islamic culture. Throughout the Muslim world, secular revolutionary Marxist movements were swept aside by a tide of religious fervour.

A key concept for re-Islamization was *jahiliyya*. This refers to the age of pagan ignorance, idolatry and barbarism which prevailed in Arabia before the time of the Prophet. Islamist movements applied this concept not only to the west but also, with telling effect, to existing Islamic societies.

Islamist groups have a monist ideology. The whole of life is to be ordered solely on Islamic principles, since there is no other valid path except submission to Allah. These groups are therefore utterly opposed to democracy. Their condemnation goes beyond criticism of the sham democracies, the military dictatorships and one-party states under which much of the Muslim world has toiled. All democracy, including the western representative kind, is evil. Democracy means the rule of the *demos*, the people or mob. Islam requires the rule of the *umma*, the community of the faithful, through a government whose duty is to implement the *shari'a*, the Islamic law. Political violence has played a significant part in movements seeking to re-Islamize society.

The objective of Islamist movements is not just to defend Muslim identity but to spread Islam throughout the world. Like Christianity but unlike Judaism, Islam is a conversionist faith. Thus the *Jama'at al Tabligh*, the Society for the Propagation of the Faith, was founded in India in 1927 to ensure the survival of Islam in the mainly Hindu subcontinent. Pious Muslims were urged to break with the godlessness around them and to imitate the conduct and spiritual life of the Prophet. The Tabligh has drawn the core of its supporters from the poor and the unemployed. The aim is to construct networks of self-help, forming a self-sufficient Muslim community as a base from which to convert the world.

Islam in the west

The rise of assertive Islamic movements in the west has raised critical questions about the nature of citizenship and social exclusion in multicultural societies. Kepel's comparative study of the USA, the UK and France (Kepel 1997) shows how movements organized around the denial of full citizenship to ethnic minorities have revealed deep fault lines in western society. These movements combine social and political demands with affirmation of an Islamic identity.

USA: the Nation of Islam

The Black Muslims in the United States, members of the Nation of Islam formerly led by Elijah Muhammad and now by Louis Farrakhan, are a dramatic example of a radical Islamic movement.

After the Civil War, 'Jim Crow' legislation legitimized the exclusion of black Americans from full citizenship, segregating the 'races' in public places and unleashing vigilantes and lynch mobs against blacks who claimed their rights as citizens. The black churches became the most powerful vehicles of political aspiration, as witnessed by the prominent role within the civil rights movement of ministers such as Martin Luther King and Jesse Jackson.

The discourse of the Nation of Islam is extreme, branding Christianity and Judaism as 'religions of the gutter', white man's religions that blacks must repudiate. Anti-Semitism has been a prominent feature of the movement, though its spokespeople deny it. Farrakhan is clearly anti-Zionist, having aligned himself with the Palestinians and questioned the legitimacy of the state of Israel. He has gone further than this, however (Kepel 1997: 62–70), denying that Ashkenazi Jews are 'Semitic', and claiming that blacks, not Jews, are the chosen people. Most tellingly of all, the Nation of Islam seeks to reinterpret the Holocaust in order to replace it by the slave trade as the supreme symbol of genocide. It plays down Jews as victims of the Holocaust in order to relocate them as prime movers of slavery, the black Holocaust.

The Nation of Islam calls on black people to cast off the false identity into which they have been brainwashed by evil white society. Islam is their cultural birthright, stolen from them by the whites. The culture of the ghetto is demythologized: it is not the vibrant culture that liberals imagine but a brutalized world of crime, gangs, illiteracy, drugs and prostitution. The official authorities are unable to deal with social problems in the ghettos, so the Nation of Islam has set up vigilante groups to 'clean up' their own neighbourhoods.

The universalistic principles of the civil rights movement are repudiated. What the Nation of Islam offers instead is the vision of a radically other society, a disciplined, self-sufficient social order with strict rules of dress, diet and sexual conduct. This society will have nothing to do with the world of the whites. The vision is the inverse of the American dream of assimilation. It is segregation glorified.

France: the challenge to laïcité

In October 1989, three young Muslims were expelled from a public secondary school at Creil in France for wearing the *hijab*, the traditional headscarf worn by Muslim women. The so-called 'headscarf affair' escalated to become the subject of an intense national debate, with charges of racist discrimination countered by accusations of fundamentalist obscurantism (Kepel 1997: 184–9; Boyle and Sheen 1997: 298–300). Ironically, this took place in the year in which the nation was celebrating the bicentennial of the French Revolution.

A noteworthy feature of the headscarf affair was that it focused on young women. Here as elsewhere – as for example in debates over the ordination of women to the priesthood in the Anglican (Episcopalian) and Roman Catholic churches – women are socially constructed as a problem.

France is a republic which, like the United States, has a constitutionally guaranteed freedom of religion and separation between church and state. *Laïcité* is a key concept which has no exact equivalent in English, though the 'wall of separation' between church and state in the USA is an approximation to it. The school is seen as an 'emancipatory space'. Pupils are required to leave symbols of political, ethnic and religious allegiance on the outside, so that all may benefit equally from the intellectual enlightenment which the French educational system provides.

Although students in French schools are officially forbidden from wearing religious symbols, the ban has been interpreted in different ways. Many Muslim students have worn the *hijab* without facing discipline, just as young Jewish men have worn a skullcap (the *kippa*) and Christians the cross or crucifix on a necklace. At Creil, the head teacher had launched the disciplinary issue to a wider public by announcing his decision to the local press.

The furore that erupted in France was deeply revealing of the dilemmas of church and state in multicultural societies. Islam was portrayed as the oriental Other: irrational, fundamentalist and fanatical, in contrast to western rationality, individualism and civilized tolerance. Wearing the *hijab* was taken to be a defiant act of Muslim fundamentalism, threatening to undermine the long-standing policy of cultural assimilation of ethnic minority groups from France's former colonies (Boyle and Sheen 1997: 296–7). French secular opinion, divided on the question of whether the *hijab* should be permitted or not, was united in defence of the values of the French education system. The leader of the anti-racist pressure group *SOS-Racisme*, Harlem Désir, was quoted as saying: 'Whether they wear a veil or not, these children will best learn how to resist obscurantism in the school of Rousseau, Voltaire and the Enlightenment' (Kepel 1997: 184).

In modern nation states, conflicts over religion are often focused on the education system – unsurprisingly, given the role of schools in the transmission of cultural values. Exclusive Brethren refuse to study computer science. Jehovah's Witnesses reject theories of evolution. Many conservative Christian groups want creation science taught alongside Darwinian evolution as a legitimate scientific alternative. Legislation developed in the west over the course of centuries and designed to deal with the rights of Protestants, Catholics and Jews now faces unenvisaged challenges.

The French republic, in contrast to the United Kingdom, is not prepared to tolerate the formation of separate communities on regional, linguistic, ethnic or religious lines. The French state pursues a policy of assimilation and integration, using the education system as the instrument for transmitting shared cultural values to all citizens of the republic. Unlike Britain, which confers different levels of citizenship depending on national origin, France grants either full citizenship or none at all. Full citizenship does not, however, guarantee social acceptance or equality of opportunity. The rise of a radical Islamist movement, the FIS (Islamic Salvation Front), in France's former colony Algeria, has made available to Muslims living on the French mainland a set of symbols on which they can draw to combat the *laïcité* of the French state. These symbols have a particular appeal to the *beurs* – people born in France of immigrant parents, many of whom have experienced social exclusion from the society whose citizenship they hold.

Britain: blasphemy and the establishment of religion

The affair of *The Satanic Verses*, culminating in the *fatwa* pronounced by Ayatollah Khomeini against its author, Salman Rushdie, has reverberated round the world. It has been a dramatic demonstration of globalization. Islamists have been mobilized in response to the threat that the price of inclusion in a global system dominated by non-Islamic cultures is surrender of the core belief in the immutable sacredness of the Qur'an. Islamists are seeking not to reverse globalization but to shape the global reality (Beyer 1994).

Within this global context, *The Satanic Verses* affair remains distinctively British. Its origins can be traced to British rule in India, and its contemporary unfolding reflects the British approach to 'race', ethnicity and religion. The affair could not have taken the same course in the USA or France.

A complex piece of fictional literature in the postmodern genre known as magical realism, *The Satanic Verses* is a profound comment on racism, migration and identity. It picks up on, but does not endorse, medieval Christian vilification of Muhammad as a mad and promiscuous impostor. No one has ever claimed that the book is easy to read. At the height of the controversy, selected passages, allegedly salacious and insulting to Islam and the Prophet, were translated into Urdu and circulated among Muslims.

The satanic verses themselves refer to an 'underground' tradition that Muhammad, under the influence of Satan, introduced into the Qur'an certain verses which included praise for the three female deities who were part of the polytheistic religion of Mecca at the time of Muhammad's prophecy. The story of the satanic verses is dangerous because it threatens both the integrity of the Qur'an and the character of the Prophet.

In February 1989 the affair reached a crisis when Ayatollah Khomeini pronounced his *fatwa*, a legal ruling that Salman Rushdie was an apostate whose blood should be shed. The timing and nature of the *fatwa* were designed to bolster support for the Ayatollah's regime in Iran and to lay claim to a pre-eminent role in Islam worldwide. Strictly, the *fatwa* could only be considered applicable to those among the Shi'ite community who recognized the Ayatollah's authority. Also strictly, it could not apply outside *dar al-islam*, the Muslim world. The *fatwa* pronounced by the Ayatollah went beyond both these principles, since it was addressed to 'all intrepid Muslims in the world', calling them to act against the author and his accomplices 'wherever they may be' (Kepel 1997: 139–40). It was a personal tragedy for the author, and a focus of deep division in British society.

The majority of Muslims who migrated to Britain came from India, Pakistan, Bangladesh, Uganda and other East African countries. The legacy of the Raj is a significant factor. The British rulers of India, perhaps of necessity, treated Muslims as a separate group and a separate electorate from the Hindu majority, so that Muslim politicians needed to appeal only to Muslim voters. Whether as a planned or unintended consequence, this recognition of two main faith-communities in the Indian subcontinent made the development of pan-Indian nationalism impossible, and paved the way for the partition which established Pakistan as a nation-state in its own right.

In Britain, the stance adopted by progressive white liberals has been to celebrate the multicultural nature of British society. There has not been, as in France, a concerted centralized drive to assimilate ethnic groups into a homogeneous national culture. Instead, communalism has been encouraged in contemporary Britain as it was in the Raj. This can be interpreted from a Marxist perspective as a strategy by the state to achieve two ends: to transfer some of the financial burden of welfare provision from the state to ethnic communities themselves, and to ensure that the working class is divided on ethnic lines. One consequence has been the emergence of rival community organizations and leaders, each tending to claim to speak for the Muslim community as a whole. *The Satanic Verses* affair gave a public platform to a number of these spokespersons, with media attention focusing on the more militant factions. A vicious circle rapidly established itself. Muslims were blamed indiscriminately for the crisis and regularly labelled 'fundamentalist'. The hostility of the wider society acted to reinforce feelings of persecution, thus strengthening the community's resolve to defend its honour – *izzat* – against defamation. In this context it is worth noting that Islam gives no warrant to pacifism and has no equivalent to the Christian concepts of 'turning the other cheek', loving your enemies and submitting voluntarily to humiliation as a transfigured victory. Because of its foundation myth (in the sense of a sacred story, not necessarily a fictitious one), in which crucifixion leads to resurrection, Christianity has a capacity to thrive on persecution – something utterly contrary to the spirit of Islam.

The controversy over *The Satanic Verses* reveals some essential features of church–state relations in Britain. This can be crystallized by considering two interrelated issues: the laws of blasphemy, and the establishment of the Church of England.

Britain's blasphemy law is the legacy of a bygone era. It had fallen into disuse, joining the deposit of laws which are simply inoperative. However, the law on blasphemy was revived in 1976, when Mary Whitehouse, founder of the National Viewers' and Listeners' Association, successfully prosecuted the magazine *Gay News* for publishing a poem depicting a

Roman centurion's homoerotic feelings for the crucified Christ. In his summing-up the judge said: 'Blasphemous libel is committed if there is published any writing concerning God or Christ, the Christian religion, the Bible, or some sacred subject, using words which are scurrilous, abusive or offensive and which tend to vilify the Christian religion (and therefore have a tendency to lead to a breach of the peace)' (quoted by Ruthven 1991: 49).

Only mainstream Christianity is covered by Britain's blasphemy law. The *Gay News* case and the *Satanic Verses* affair have provoked two diametrically opposed calls for reform. On the one hand, it is argued that Britain should abolish the law on blasphemy, since it is a relic of a once-Christian culture and has no relevance to contemporary conditions. The state should be secular and neutral, as in France and the USA. On the other hand, there are calls for the law on blasphemy to be extended to protect all the major faiths. This second solution would raise a familiar problem: where to draw the line between major faiths and the rest?

What evidence there is suggests that the predominant view among Britain's ethnic and religious monopolies is not in favour of the first option, the route of secularity (Modood 1997). The same appears true for disestablishment (Davie 1994: 141–9). Muslims and other communities are not opposed to the established church. They see it as a key player in the common fight against secularity and the secular despisers of all religion. It is a mood well captured by the heir to the throne, who said in a television interview that his role might better be styled not 'Defender of the Faith', as at present, but rather 'Defender of Faith'. So too the Chief Rabbi of the Orthodox Jewish community in Britain argued that disestablishment would make matters worse. It would not introduce neutrality but would remove a powerful symbolic legitimation of faith, thereby increasing the potential for social divisions between faith-communities. Britain is characterized by highly developed Christian ecumenism, both between Christian denominations and with other faiths – probably more so than any other European country, as Modood remarks.

To many commentators, the establishment is not a controversial matter. They argue that neither the established church nor its clergy are unpopular. The Church of England is not a 'state church' as Americans might think, nor is it in French terms *intégriste*. Many people retain a sentimental attachment to the Church of England, manifested particularly at Christmas and in times of trouble. Citizens are entitled to call on the services of the established church for rites of passage, without needing to demonstrate much by way of religious belief or commitment. Support for disestablishment comes from two quarters: from secularists opposed to any fusion of church and state, and from activists within the Church of England who resent the occasional political interference in church affairs and the way in which the church is used by what they see as 'nominal Christians'. These are minority groups with no political muscle.

Against this view, it is possible to argue that the position of the established church is not wholly secure. A feature of the Thatcherite programme from 1979 onwards was an onslaught on what was taken to be a liberal and socialist establishment: nationalized industries, trade unions, universities, state schools and the liberal professions. The Church of England was itself a target, and was caught up in a series of public conflicts with the government, not least over its refusal to mount a patriotic victory celebration after the Falklands/Malvinas war. The established church was seen to align itself with resistance to the Thatcherite project of radical reform through the marketization of social relationships. Arguably, some of the same dynamics continue to operate under the Labour government elected in 1997. The change of government has not interrupted the drive to modernize the United Kingdom. Some have argued that a republican mood is becoming more prevalent, with calls for a bill of rights, freedom of information and a more open, less secretive society on American lines (Hutton 1995). It remains an open question how far the modernization programme will proceed and which social institutions will be its targets. The British monarchy has already taken the message that it must modernize, at least symbolically, or else go under. The same may be true of the Church of England.

Secularization and religious revival

To describe the phenomena discussed above as 'fundamentalism' is inappropriate, pejorative and misleading. There are many differences between them, reflecting the different faiths and societies concerned. There are commonalities even so. We have seen a revival of conservative faith, reasserting a particular tradition even if this means reinventing it in the process – hence the term neo-traditionalist is particularly apt. These are calls to faith, and calls to a return to faith: for black Americans to reclaim their inheritance, Islam; for Jews to turn repentantly back to the Jewish law; for the Christian Moral Majority to reassert the fundamentals of the faith. All of them utterly reject the universalist values espoused by western Enlightenment rationalism. They offer certainty of belief and practice, 'clear-cut answers as to what to do in an era which has abandoned final authorities' (Giddens 1991: 142).

It has been said that none of this affects the secularization thesis in any way. In the case of Judaism, the revivals discussed above are clearly aimed at revitalizing Jewish culture, not at converting the Gentiles. In the case of Christianity, Bruce (1988) has argued that conservative Christianity lacks the ability to transform First World societies. It cannot fully mobilize its core supporters, the evangelical Protestants, whose tendency toward personal piety resists politicization. Nor can it form stable alliances with conservative Jews and Catholics, since more divides than unites them. Its target, secular humanism, is ill defined, but in any case cannot be dislodged. Conservative Christianity's heartland is the private sphere, which is where it must remain in a secular society. As for Islam, any aspiration to convert the world flies against the evidence. The vision of a radical break between *dar al-islam*, the sphere of Islam, and *dar al-harb*, the sphere of war, is belied by the power politics of the Middle East, where Muslim countries have fought one another. Militant Islamic groups in the west are a minority unrepresentative of the wider ethnic communities. Islam will not be able to insulate itself from the fruits of the Enlightenment. The faith will become a voluntary internalized commitment located in the private sphere (Ruthven 1997: 144–6). For Bruce, Islamist revivals are the product of Third World modernization, not First World modernity, and thus are completely irrelevant to the secularization thesis.

This may be so. It is difficult, none the less, to see events in the Middle East and Islamic movements in the west as unimportant for the sociological study of religion. Perhaps one might conclude that there is more to the sociology of religion than the secularization debate, and leave it at that.

7

Sacralization of Modernity: Civil and Political Religion

Ritual and social integration: the legacy of Durkheim

In an influential article analysing the role of political ritual in contemporary societies, Lukes (1975: 291) proposes the following definition of ritual: 'rule-governed activity of a symbolic character which draws the attention of its participants to objects of thought and feeling which they hold to be of special significance'. Three aspects of this definition deserve emphasis. First, it does not couple ritual to organized religion. Second, Lukes's definition carries no implication that ritual is 'irrational' – itself a deeply problematic concept. Finally, it tries to avoid including all human action as ritual. The defining characteristics of ritual action are that it is rule-governed and symbolically charged.

But how to interpret ritual? On the one hand, we cannot simply accept what Leach (1968: 523) calls the 'rationalizations of the devout'. Nor, on the other hand, are we totally free to dismiss actors' accounts as rationalizations. As Lukes puts it (1975: 291), actors' accounts are 'both indispensable and non-definitive'. They clearly cannot be definitive, since different interest groups tend to give conflicting accounts of the 'same' ritual.

Durkheim's theoretical work on ritual has had a deep influence on later studies. For Durkheim, ritual is an essential dimension of religion, since it is only through ritual that we can be brought into contact with the sacred. Ritual also has a cognitive function. The social world is represented to us through the symbols used in ritual action; or, putting the same point more sharply, we understand the social world through symbols. We create, dramatize and reinforce social realities through ritual action. Rituals play a vital part in social integration, literally holding society together. Without them society risks disintegration. Durkheim thought that his own society was in an unhealthy pathological state. One cause, symptom and effect of this, he believed, was the lack of public rituals.

Many sociologists have argued that Durkheim underestimated the vitality of ritual in contemporary societies. Drawing on a rather one-sided interpretation of Durkheim, these writers have analysed a range of rituals in the modern world, such as the coronation of Queen Elizabeth II (Shils and Young 1953), the investiture of the Prince of Wales (Blumler et al. 1971), Memorial Day (W. L. Warner 1959, 1962), the mourning for President Kennedy (Verba 1965), and the ceremony surrounding the inauguration of a new President of the United States (Bellah 1967).

What these studies have in common is an emphasis on the role played by ritual in expressing and reinforcing consensus on ultimate values, a consensus which the writers take to be essential to social integration. Thus for Shils and Young the coronation of Queen Elizabeth II in 1953 was 'a great act of national communion' through which ordinary citizens were able to experience contact with the monarchy as the repository of the sacred values of British society. This is a clear restatement of Durkheim's theory that religion is 'society worshipping itself'. The grief and mourning which followed the assassination of President Kennedy is similarly treated by Verba as a set of rituals which rededicated the American people to allegiance to their political community. Blumler et al. saw in the investiture of Charles Windsor as Prince of Wales a ceremony through which fundamental values of family solidarity and national pride were symbolically enacted and reaffirmed. Similarly, Warner's famous studies of 'Yankee City' interpreted Memorial Day as a modern cult of the dead, specifically those who fell in the Civil War – a cult which unifies people into a sacred community, the nation.

The most influential of all these studies is Bellah's. He uses the inauguration of a new President as a vehicle for analysing what he calls 'civil religion' – a religious dimension which, once again, puts citizens in touch with the sacred. Bellah's work is examined more fully below.

Lukes points to a number of problems with these neo-Durkheimian theories of ritual. Four closely related issues are particularly important.

First, the neo-Durkheimian approach overstates the role played by value consensus in holding societies together. It plays down coercion, political manipulation and pragmatic compliance.

Second, the writers select for analysis those rituals where the argument for value consensus is at its most plausible. But surely there are rituals which express and reinforce social divisions? What of such rituals as Orange parades and Republican funerals in Northern Ireland; neo-Nazi marches displaying the symbols of the Nazi era; burning the American flag in anti-Vietnam war protests, or the burning by Muslims of Salman Rushdie's *The Satanic Verses*? These rituals reinforce social solidarity among the subcultures which support and participate in them, but they are deeply divisive at the level of the nation state.

Third, analyses assume that official interpretations are the same as popular ones. So, for example, Shils and Young's comments on the British monarchy reflect uncritically the perspectives of the royal family's public relations entourage. A people devoted to the Crown and the symbols surrounding it is a key element in a vision of Britain which is useful for marketing. The archaism of the symbols is part of the message: it goes with thatched cottages, unarmed police on bicycles and London fog swirling round 221b Baker Street.

Fourth, the neo-Durkheimian approach to ritual underplays the exercise of power. It is not just that it gives undue attention to rituals associated with institutions which have lost most of their direct political power, such as the British constitutional monarchy. More fundamentally, it ignores the use to which rituals are put, including the deliberate creation and dissemination of rituals for political purposes. To treat rituals as beyond time is to accede to their own mythology.

The issues raised in the critique of neo-Durkheimian writings on ritual are examined in the case studies which follow. Particular attention is given to ritualized expressions of social conflict, and to ritual as a mode of exercising power.

In God We Trust: civil religion in the United States

Bellah's seminal article on civil religion in America drew explicitly on Durkheim's theories of religion and ritual. The term 'civil religion' was taken from Rousseau's classic text of political philosophy, *The Social Contract*, first published in 1762. Rousseau argues that the social integration of any healthy society depends on a set of basic religious dogmas. These are: belief in God, belief in a life after death, and the conviction that virtue will be rewarded and vice punished. The good society also commits itself to the practice of religious tolerance.

Bellah adapts Rousseau's concept of civil religion and applies it to the contemporary United States. He argues that civil religion is a pervasive religious dimension of American political life existing independently of the churches. All American citizens are expected to take part in civil religion. Atheism is not a popular option. Paradoxically, this does not violate the right to freedom of religious worship and assembly guaranteed by the First Amendment to the Constitution: 'Congress shall make no law respecting an establishment of religion, or prohibiting the free exercise thereof; or abridging the freedom of speech, or of the press; or the right of the people peaceably to assemble, and to petition the Government for a redress of grievances.' American citizens enjoy religious liberty in their private devotion and in their voluntary activity. Civil religion applies to the public sphere, manifesting itself in calendrical festivals such as Thanksgiving and the Fourth of July, in rituals such as reciting the Pledge of Allegiance, and in ceremonies such as Presidential inaugurations. Freedom of religion does not lead to social disintegration, thanks to the socially integrative role played by civil religion. Civil religion provides a unifying set of symbols which integrate a geographically, ethnically and religiously diverse society.

In Durkheimian fashion, Bellah argues that American civil religion is made manifest in the great rituals of public life. He takes Presidential inaugural addresses as a case study. For example, the address to the nation by President Kennedy after his inauguration in 1961 referred to God three times. Importantly, although Kennedy was a Catholic he made no allusion to Catholic symbolism: no Our Lady, no mass, no prayers for the dead. Civil religion embraces Protestants as well as Catholics as part of its integrative function. The constitutional separation of church and state means that civil religion cannot be a vehicle for religious divisions but must transcend them.

American civil religion goes further, embracing not just Christianity but also Judaism. Hence the God that is invoked is the God of the Hebrew Scriptures that make up the Christian Old Testament. Presidential inaugurals do not normally include specifically Christian references. If they do, as in President Reagan's first inaugural in 1981, an equivalent Jewish reference must also be supplied. Thus Reagan referred to 'Arlington National Cemetery, with its row upon row of simple white markers with crosses and Stars of David, adding up to only a tiny fraction of the price that has been paid for our freedom'.

Presidential inaugural addresses draw on and play into the complex set of symbols that make up American civil religion. The symbols include sacred texts such as the Declaration of Independence and the Gettysburg Address; sacred heroes such as Washington, Jefferson and Lincoln; sacred places, such as the Lincoln Memorial; and sacred historical events, such as the War of Independence and the Civil War.

American civil religion accords a unique role to the United States. The American nation has a special historic mission to liberate the whole of humanity from bondage – a belief which Britain held of itself in its imperial heyday, but which is now confined to extremist right-wing groups in the UK (Lane 1981: 258–9). America is the new Zion, God's chosen people. Washington was a Moses leading the people out of captivity into the promised land. Lincoln is a Christ-like figure, sacrificed for us all. Like Israel, America plays a crucial role in God's redemptive plan for the human race. This theme was particularly prominent in Ronald Reagan's 1981 inaugural, at the height of the 'Cold War' against what Reagan called the 'evil empire' of the USSR. Asserting that Americans enjoy more liberty than any other people, Reagan said: 'We are a nation that has a government – not the other way around. And this makes us special among the nations of the Earth.' The quasi-biblical nature of this last phrase was of course entirely fitting as an expression of civil religion.

It might be thought that civil religion is simply a mechanism for providing the state with religious legitimation. Bellah argues, however, that it is also a cultural resource on which citizens can draw to call down God's judgement on the nation. There is, then, a *priestly* role for civil religion in celebrating national achievements, and a *prophetic* role in calling the nation to account for breaking its covenant with the Almighty (McGuire 1992: 180–1). At the height of the anti-Vietnam war protests, Bellah sharply criticized the way in which the military dictatorship in South Vietnam became sacralized in civil religious discourse as 'the free people of South Vietnam and their government'. Senator William Fulbright, in Bellah's view, was a prophet calling the nation to judgement. So too were Martin Luther King and other civil rights activists, who drew on American civil religion to point up the contrast between the nation's self-image and its actual achievement.

American civil religion transcends the state and secular institutions. In so far as it legitimizes them, it does so only conditionally. If we apply the Durkheimian formula that religion is society worshipping itself, the American case shows, according to Bellah, that the object of worship is not necessarily the society as it exists, but may be 'a higher reality which upholds the standards that the republic attempts to embody' (Bellah 1990: 418). The prophetic role may take precedence over the priestly. In a deregulated religious economy, civil religion is a resource available to prophets. While this can find its supreme expression in great crusades such as the campaign for civil rights, it can also result in witch-hunts against ordinary citizens for 'un-American activities', as in the McCarthyite era of the 1950s, or even against the powerful, as in the claim that President Clinton's covert sexual affairs amounted to 'high crimes and misdemeanours' requiring his impeachment.

Happy and Glorious: the British monarchy

For Shils and Young, as already mentioned, the coronation of Queen Elizabeth II in 1953 was 'a great act of national communion'. Through this ritual

British people entered into communion with one another and with the monarchy as a 'vessel' of sacred values.

With hindsight, the immediate post-war period was a golden age for the British monarchy. The controversies of earlier ages had been erased from collective memory while the problems to come were scarcely envisaged by anybody (Cannadine 1983).

The 1939–45 war had given added intensity to civil religion. This was experienced as a 'total war' in which all citizens could play a part in the war effort. The royal family emerged from the war with its popular prestige greatly enhanced. King George VI had remained in London throughout 'the blitz', and from this was forged the symbolic link between the royal family and the working-class communities of the East End of London.

With the fall of many of the royal houses of Europe, the House of Windsor survived as the only example of a constitutional monarchy enjoying both popular support and the full paraphernalia of monarchical symbolism. The anachronism of the symbols – the royal carriages, the Queen riding side-saddle, the horse guards – was an essential part of the monarchy's sacred aura. As Britain's standing as a world superpower ebbed away, this unique monarchy stood as a symbol of national prestige offsetting economic and political decline.

The rapid spread of television after the war meant that state pageants became national events that could be witnessed as they happened rather than belatedly, as with the newsreels. Television, as Cannadine remarks, was the medium without which it would not have been possible for the coronation to be a nationwide communion.

The royal family had recognized the power of the mass media from an early stage. The monarch's Christmas broadcast to the nation began in 1932, and immediately became as 'traditional' as turkey and Christmas pudding. Television coverage of ceremonies such as the coronation emphasized the colourful pageantry of these occasions and the unrivalled consummate skill with which the British brought them off. Until the 1980s, the national press exercised extensive self-censorship in its coverage of the royal family, suppressing or at least greatly understating potentially discreditable information, such as Edward VIII's sympathetic view of the National Socialist regime in Germany.

Shils and Young's treatment of the monarchy as a repository of sacred values is curiously static. History is effectively suppressed, since traditions are treated as if they were beyond time. No effort is made to analyse the invention and stage management of tradition. As Cannadine points out, Shils and Young ignored the fact that historically the monarchy experienced periods when it was deeply unpopular. Its fortunes were revived by the rise of the British Empire in the nineteenth century, symbolized most potently in the title Empress of India, bestowed on Queen Victoria in 1877.

Similarly, looking forward, the monarchy has been the subject of mounting controversy from the 1980s onward. Many of the anachronistic symbols have turned sour: the royal family's involvement in socially exclusive sports such as polo and controversial field sports such as grouse shooting and fox hunting; the symbolism of a profligate extended family migrating between the royal residences at Balmoral, Sandringham, Windsor and Buckingham Palace; and, perhaps above all, the exposés of sexual infidelity. The House of Windsor had used the mass media to disseminate a carefully nurtured idealized image of a close-knit loving family. These same media shattered the illusion.

The death of Diana, Princess of Wales in August 1997 unleashed a torrent of public grief in a society whose citizens are famed for their emotional reserve. Although the coverage perhaps exaggerated the breadth and depth of the mourning, it cannot simply be dismissed as something conjured up by the media. The American commentator Neil Acherson wrote that 'The spontaneous appearance of great crowds on the street is always important in any country, and especially in a society as controlled as Britain' (*Independent on Sunday*, 7 September 1997). An element in the public mood was righteous indignation directed against the royal family's use (or neglect) of symbols: the fact that Diana had been deprived of the title HRH (Her Royal Highness) after her reluctant divorce from Prince Charles; the silence of the Queen, and her tardiness in returning from Balmoral to London; the bare flagpole outside Buckingham Palace (technically showing that the monarch was not in residence), when people unaware of arcane royal protocol expected to see a flag flying at half-mast as a mark of respect. In the funeral which followed, the royal family was displaced from centre-stage, and their advisers found themselves not deferred to over the planning of the mourning. The British monarchy is now seeking advice on how to modernize its image, and is engaged in a gradual process of judiciously publicized reform, including the introduction of greater informality in ritual events.

Symbolic division in society: the case of Canada

Canada is an interesting case of a modern democratic society which has no overarching civil religion expressing social, cultural and political unity. In Kim's (1993) analysis, the absence of a pan-Canadian civil religion is attributed to regionalism and biculturalism.

Taking Canadian regionalism first, Kim sees it as a product of three sets of factors. Geographically, Canada is a vast country with a sparse population concentrated in cities hundreds and even thousands of miles apart. Historically, Canada's regions were settled by different migrant ethnic groups at different times in the nation's history. Politically, extensive powers have been devolved to the provinces from the relatively weak federal government in Ottawa.

Canada is a bicultural society. The crucial divide is between Anglo- and French Canada, two non-native founding cultures which continue to struggle for supremacy. Biculturalism is multidimensional, manifesting itself in language, schooling, religion, cuisine and the media. The 'third force' of Canadians from ethnic backgrounds other than these two has not successfully organized as a significant challenge to the two dominant cultures.

Symbolism inherited from Britain, including the link to the British monarchy, reminds French Canadians of their colonial defeat by the British. Despite the fact of a national flag depicting the maple leaf, at public ceremonies in Quebec it is common to see only the Quebec flag flying. More remarkably still, the national anthem, *O Canada*, only achieved official status in 1980.

The Canadian landscape plays a prominent part in the nation's self-image. The beaver and the maple leaf are evocative, as is the imagery of a ruggedly beautiful northern country. However, Kim argues, these images and symbols have not been fully sacralized. They have remained closely tied to the natural realm, and have not achieved a transcendent significance. They do not point beyond themselves to abstract qualities that define national history, character and identity. The Canadian beaver is not invested with the deep symbolic meaning of the American bald eagle, the Russian bear or the British bulldog.

According to Kim (1993: 269), Canadian national identity contains some powerfully negative elements, including 'defeat, division, the difficult ecological challenge, and an uneventful or uninteresting history'. The heroic strand that is so prominent in the civil religions of the USA and former imperialist countries such as the UK is absent from Canadian culture.

Symbols of nationhood in Canada are divisive and deeply contested. Not only is there a lack of shared sacred symbols of national identity, there is also disagreement on how to characterize the essence of Canada as a nation state. Is it one Canada? Is it a dual culture? Is it a cultural mosaic? Fundamentally, Kim argues, the absence of pan-Canadian civil religion intensifies the threat of Quebec separatism and signals a failure of nation-building.

Symbolic division in society: the case of Northern Ireland

'The Northern Ireland conflict is a religious conflict' (Bruce 1986: 249). Explanations that try to reduce the conflict in Northern Ireland to something other than religion – for example to class conflict, in Marxist fashion – are unconvincing.

This does not mean that the conflict is purely religious, since religion as a social phenomenon is never 'pure'. In Northern Ireland, the religious divide coincides with and reinforces social divisions based on education, occupation, neighbourhood, social clubs, sport, newspapers and political parties (McGuire 1992: 197). These divisions are actively maintained. On the one hand, the Catholic church hierarchy supports the continuation of separate schooling for Catholic children, to insulate them from Protestant as well as from secular culture. On the other hand, the Protestant majority has discriminated against Catholics in housing, employment and the police service. Discrimination has been reinforced by political gerrymandering to weaken the democratic impact of the Catholic vote. The Protestant working class struggles to maintain its dominant position in skilled manual occupations. In 1974, a hardline Unionist organization, the Ulster Workers' Council, used intimidation by loyalist paramilitaries to cause what was referred to as a 'strike' by Protestant workers against the British government's attempt to give more political power to Catholics. This brought the province to a virtual standstill and killed off the new power-sharing Northern Ireland Executive.

The conflict between Catholics and Protestants is not primarily over doctrine or theology. Most people are not and do not want to be theologians. The conflict is not between theologians or church leaders, who have little power to control it. Rather, it is a conflict of civil religions (McGuire 1992: 205–9).

Catholic civil religion in Northern Ireland – or, in its own terms, the North of Ireland – is Irish, republican and nationalist. It opposes British colonialism, and celebrates the heroes and martyrs, and the sacred myths and symbols, of Irish rebellion against British rule. It is not anti-Protestant, however.

Protestant civil religion, by contrast, is explicitly anti-Catholic. This is particularly marked in the Free Presbyterian Church led by the Reverend Dr Ian Paisley (Bruce 1986). In Paisleyite ideology, Roman Catholicism is not merely in error but deeply evil. The Roman Catholic Church is not and never will be Christian. It is the continuation of Babylon and a perversion of the gospel. The papacy is the Antichrist.

Free Presbyterians share with Jehovah's Witnesses and other fundamentalist Protestant groups the belief that the Roman Catholic Church is described in the Bible, most graphically in chapter 17 of the Book of Revelation. It is worth quoting from this at some length, as Bruce does, as a reminder of anti-Catholic sentiments which mainstream Protestants elsewhere have long abandoned and almost forgotten.

> And there came one of the seven angels which had the seven vials, and talked with me, saying unto me, Come hither; I will show unto thee the judgement of the great whore that sitteth upon many waters: With whom the kings of the earth have committed fornication, and the inhabitants of the earth have been made drunk with the wine of her fornication. So he carried me away in the spirit into the wilderness: and I saw a woman sit upon a scarlet coloured beast, full of names of blasphemy, having seven heads and ten horns. And the woman was arrayed in purple and scarlet colour, and decked with gold and precious stones and pearls, having a golden cup in her hand full of abominations and filthiness of her fornication: And upon her forehead was a name written, MYSTERY, BABYLON THE GREAT, THE MOTHER OF HARLOTS AND ABOMINATIONS OF THE EARTH. And I saw the woman drunken with the blood of the saints, and with the blood of the martyrs of Jesus; and when I saw her, I wondered with great admiration.

The text goes on to decode some of the symbolism of this passage. Among other things, it explains that the seven heads 'are seven mountains, on which the woman sitteth'. Rome is a city set on seven hills. The chapter ends: 'And the woman which thou sawest is that great city, which reigneth over the kings of the earth.' Within the logic of fundamentalist Protestantism, it is impossible to deny that this abomination is the Roman Catholic Church.

Free Presbyterianism embraces a conspiracy theory in which the Roman Catholic Church is both devious and highly effective. Rome has worked consistently to persecute true Christians and to subvert democratic institutions which owe their existence to the Protestant faith. For example, the Vatican promotes the ecumenical movement as a means of sapping the vitality of Protestantism. The same is true of European union. The Pope has voiced his longing for a united Europe. The 'Schuman plan' which established the European Coal and Steel Community in 1951 was drafted by Konrad Adenauer, Jean Monnet and Robert Schuman – all Catholics. The founding charter of European union was the 1957 Treaty of Rome – where else? The UK's membership of this crypto-catholic organization is one among many threats to the democratic rights of the Protestant people of Northern Ireland.

Northern Ireland is the stage for a conflict of civil religions. Crucially, this conflict is asymmetrical. In Bruce's words (1986: 258), 'The conflict in

Northern Ireland involves a nation on the one hand and an ethnic group on the other.' Irish republicanism is nationalist. Most Catholics in the North see themselves as part of the Irish nation. Committed Ulster Protestants, in contrast, are not straightforwardly British. Though 'loyalist', their loyalty is strictly conditional on the British government's delivering them what they want. Their loyalty is to the sacred symbols of the Crown, not to the secular politics of the government in Westminster. The Britain revered by loyalists is an idealized nation which disappeared in the nineteenth century, if indeed it ever existed. The contemporary British mainland is offensively liberal, permissive and irreligious. Most Ulster Protestants would prefer provincial self-determination within Britain to complete integration with the British mainland (Bruce 1986: 251–3).

Ulster Protestants, in Bruce's analysis, are members of an ethnic group. They possess a distinctive culture with a shared history, traditions, values, beliefs, lifestyles and symbols. It is characteristic of ethnic groups that they foster what Weber called 'ethnic honour', including an abiding sense of the superiority of their culture and the inferiority of alien cultures. Ulster Protestantism constitutes itself by a set of virtues recognizably embodying the Weberian Protestant ethic: 'respectability, uprightness, honesty, order, respect for authority, work ethic, cleanliness and tidiness, modesty and informality in social relations, social and political conformity' (Ruane and Todd 1996: 182). These virtuous traits contrast with the vices attributed to Catholics, such as fecklessness, dishonesty, subservience and disloyalty. Furthermore, the Protestant virtues can be presented to employers as valid grounds for preferring Protestant to Catholic workers, and to the security forces as an entitlement to be treated with respect as a good citizen.

Their Protestant faith is the one secure basis of their cultural identity as an ethnic group. Evangelical Protestantism is 'the only identity that can make sense of their history and that justifies their separation from the South' (Bruce 1986: 262). They increasingly feel embattled. They suspect that the British government sees Northern Ireland, politically and economically, as a liability rather than an asset. Demography is also a concern. The 1991 census shows Catholics at 43 per cent of the population, a significant increase over the decade since the previous census. This is accounted for by the higher birth rate among Catholics and by higher rates of emigration among Protestants (Davie 1994: 99).

A key characteristic of public ritual in Northern Ireland are the loyalist and republican parades. Jarman (1997) provides a richly detailed analysis of these. Each year there are approximately 3,500 parades, most of them passing without violence. Parading was once widespread in Europe and North America, but gradually died out as these societies became industrialized and urbanized. In maintaining a vigorous tradition of parading, Northern Ireland is self-consciously anachronistic.

Loyalist and republican parades differ both quantitatively and qualitatively. Each year there are over 2,500 loyalist parades, compared to a little over 300 republican ones; the remaining parades are not linked to either cause. There are revealing differences between them. Loyalist parades draw heavily on militaristic symbolism. Spectators are strictly segregated from participants: a parade marches past its spectators. Participants are male. They are divided into independent quasi-regimental units. The parades are a triumphalist assertion of loyalist culture, of the civil rights of the loyalist community including the right to 'walk', and of Protestant military defeat of Catholics. The intense emotion invested in and generated by loyalist parades reflects the Protestant community's sense of being under siege.

Republican parades, in contrast, are less formal, less structured, and open to anyone to take part, including women. They are far less militaristic. Unlike loyalist parades, they may include American-style marching bands. They also draw on the tradition of funeral processions – a tradition which, as Jarman points out (1997: 153–5), feeds into IRA funerals. In 1981, an estimated 100,000 people lined the route of the funeral procession of Bobby Sands, who led the Hunger Strikers in the H Blocks of Belfast's Maze Prison and was the first to die. The emphasis is on honouring fallen heroes.

This theme of martyrdom is powerfully expressed in the republican Easter parades (Jarman 1997: 153–5). In Easter 1916, a group of nationalists and republicans took control of key buildings in Dublin and proclaimed the formation of an Independent Irish Republic. After heavy bombardment by the British army the rebels were forced to surrender. Fourteen of their leaders were executed. These events are celebrated by republicans as the Rising: a clear symbolic echo of Christ's Resurrection. The parallel is further reinforced by their relocation in the calendar. The 1916 Rising took place on 24 April, which was Easter Monday. However, the events are commemorated on Easter Sunday, the day of the Resurrection.

To Protestant loyalists, the Easter Rising of 1916 was a treacherous stab in the back to Britain at a crucial moment in the First World War. Protestants respond by commemorating the battle of the Somme, which took place in July 1916 and in which the Ulster Division suffered terrible casualties. Commemorating the Somme stands in symbolic opposition to the Rising as a powerful statement of loyalty and sacrifice to the Crown.

Parades do not merely reflect community identity, they re-enact and recreate it. In Northern Ireland, these rituals are 'a cultural medium for constructing the collective Other' (Jarman 1997: 261). They reinforce the sense of difference between the communities, obliterating the memory and recognition of things they have in common.

Creating new symbols: the French revolutionary calendar

Twentieth-century revolutionaries drew some of their inspiration from the French Revolution of 1789 and the events which followed. The French Revolution included an attempt to create a ritual system and a set of symbols appropriate to the new world order.

Time itself was to be reordered. A special commission led by Fabre d'Eglantine devised a new calendar for the republic. It was introduced in October 1793, during the Terror, and remained in official use until 1806. Its use was briefly revived in Paris in 1871 by the Paris Commune. It was, in Schama's words (1989: 771), a bold attempt 'to reconstruct time through a republican cosmology'.

A key objective was to replace the superstitious symbolism of the familiar Gregorian calendar with a rationally planned nomenclature celebrating the agricultural year. The revolutionary year began in September, marking the foundation of the French Republic on 22 September 1792. Henceforth the years would be dated from 1792 and not from the birth of Christ. The new months were named as follows:

vendémiaire, month of the wine vintage
brumaire, month of mist
frimaire, the cold month
nivôse, month of snow
pluviôse, month of rain
ventôse, month of wind
germinal, month of germination
floréal, month of blossom
prairial, month of meadows
messidor, month of harvest
thermidor, month of hot weather
fructidor, month of fruiting

In keeping with the rational spirit of egalitarianism, the republican months were equally divided into thirty days. They were arranged into three ten-day weeks, each ending with a rest day. Owing to the arithmetically unhelpful period of the earth's orbit, there were of course five or six days left over. These would be devoted to festivals in honour of such virtues as talent, industry, heroism and ideas. One planned outcome of this calendrical restructuring was to make it difficult for the faithful to observe the Christian Sunday, since it coincided very rarely with the official rest day – only five times a year, in fact.

Not just the months, but each day of the year was given a new name, once again on a rationally planned system that celebrated rural life. The days of the week were given the names of crops, vegetables, fruit and flowers, except that every fifth day was named after an animal and every tenth day after an agricultural implement.

As Schama points out (1989: 774), although the revolutionary calendar might appear innocuous, it was an integral part of the aggressive pro- gramme of anti-clericalism, iconoclasm and 'dechristianization' unleashed by the Jacobin Terror.

Political religion: the Soviet Union

An elaborate system of public ritual flourished in the former Soviet Union from its foundation in 1917 to its collapse in 1991 (Lane 1981; Binns 1979, 1980). The Soviet state invested heavily in its ritual system as a conscious political policy. Here was a situation full of ironies. Soviet political ideology emphasized rationality, materialism, atheism, and the triumph of science over religion. In the Russian context, this meant specifically attacking the Orthodox Church, which the Soviet regime saw as doctrinaire, obscurantist and backward-looking. The Orthodox Church was seen to have collaborated all too willingly with the reactionary policies of the autocratic Tsarist regime.

Relations between Russian intellectuals and the Orthodox Church were deeply antagonistic throughout the nineteenth century (McLellan 1987: 90–2). This fed into Lenin's writings, which were contemptuous of reli- gion. Religion and the clerics who profited from it were to be the target of revolutionary political action. Lenin equated religion with superstition and ignorance. Religion is 'spiritual booze' – a cheap intoxicant cynically doled out to the masses by the clerical lackeys of the ruling class. In a significant coarsening of Marx's famous epigram, Lenin called religion an opium not *of* but *for* the people.

The Soviet ritual system was partly designed in order to provide substi- tutes for religious rituals. The system had a number of dimensions:

Calendrical festivals

The Soviet calendar was an important feature of life in the USSR. Al- though the calendrical reforms were far more modest than those introduced by the Jacobins after the French Revolution, they were none the less significant. The structure of days, weeks and months remained un-altered, but the Soviet authorities adopted the Gregorian calendar, which had been promulgated by Pope Gregory XIII in 1582 and which was gradually adopted throughout the west, despite Protestant qualms about its Catholic provenance (for example, it was not accepted in England until 1752). The highly traditional Orthodox Church retained the Julian calen-dar, as devised by Julius Caesar in an earlier effort at rationalization. This meant that church rituals were often out of step with secular ones. The pre-revolutionary use of the Julian calendar explains why the Orthodox celebrate Christmas in January, and also why the anniversary of the Octo-ber revolution falls in November.

Some Soviet rituals were in direct competition with Christian equiva-lents. For example, from the 1960s onwards there were new Soviet holi-days contending with Easter and Whitsun. However, direct competition on the same day ran a high risk that people would opt for the religious celebra-tion in preference to its Soviet rival. What the regime therefore tried to do was to strip out all the popular folk elements from religious rituals and transfer them to the Soviet equivalents. A good example of this (Lane 1981: 137–9) was the celebration of the Soviet New Year. This involved the lighting of a 'Christmas' tree, gift-giving to children, exchange of greetings cards, alcohol-assisted revelling, and the revival of traditional festive fig-ures such as Grandfather Frost and the Snow Maiden.

Built into the Soviet calendar were days celebrating the work of key groups, such as border guards, which had an ideologically central role in building and safeguarding the Soviet way of life.

Rites of passage

The various initiation ceremonies sponsored by the Soviet regime had a mixed reception (Lane 1981: 243–8). Some were relatively late introduc-tions – for example, initiation into the working class, into the peasantry and into the armed forces – and so had little time to establish themselves. As for the family-oriented rites of passage, the wedding rite appeared to be the most popular. The rite of Solemn Registration of the New-Born Child gained some acceptance, but the funeral rite was far more problematic. This may be evidence of the regime's problems in providing answers to the ultimate questions of meaning in human life.

Mass parades

In the revolutionary euphoria which followed the October revolution, grassroots community gatherings were often spontaneous expressions of popular enthusiasm (Binns 1979). People had a good time. However, in the politically troubled years after Lenin's death, with the gradual ascendancy of Stalin, mass events lost their freshness and spontaneity and came under the control of the state apparatus. Permanent raised tribunes were built in every city, so that political leaders could harangue the masses and review parades of Soviet organizations, troops and military equipment. The most famous of these was the May Day parade in Moscow, a reminder to the world of Soviet military capability.

A leadership cult

In his own lifetime, Lenin was concerned about the personality cult which was already beginning to develop around him. After his death in 1924 a number of crucial decisions were taken which reinforced this cult (Binns 1979). St Petersburg had already become Petrograd during the First World War; it was renamed Leningrad. The date of Lenin's death, January 21, became a day of national mourning. Monuments to Lenin were erected in all the major cities of the Soviet Union. His body was embalmed, and placed in a mausoleum constructed under the Kremlin wall among the graves of the fallen warriors of the October revolution. His collected works were published – a New Testament to match the Old Testament scriptures of Marx and Engels, which together formed the sacred canon of Marxism-Leninism.

Places of pilgrimage

The principal site of pilgrimage in the Soviet Union was Lenin's mausoleum. It was open to the public and entry was free. A quasi-religious devotional atmosphere was preserved in this sacred place. Visitors were required to move in respectful silence around the corpse. Reverence was enforced by the security guards, who prevented all talking – even rational expositions of Lenin's scientific socialism were forbidden. This place of pilgrimage has been so successful that when the Vietnamese leader Ho Chi Minh died his body was also embalmed, with the aid of Soviet experts, and displayed in a similar mausoleum in Hanoi.

Studying Soviet ritual is a means to strip aside political ideology in order to uncover the social reality which the ideology in part conceals. In contrast to the revolutionary rhetoric of the Soviet regime, what Soviet rituals displayed was a profoundly conservative symbol system. Soviet ritual sacralized the Soviet world – the supposedly good society in operation, or 'actually existing socialism' as it was known officially. The ritual system did not cultivate Marx's vision that the state would 'wither away' once communism was fully achieved. Rituals idealized labour productivity, not the liberation of workers from the dull compulsion of alienated labour. The cult of the leader, seen not only in the central cult of Lenin and the subsequent cult of Stalin, but also in minor cults of successive leaders such as Khrushchev and Brezhnev, was a conservative force that deviated from the progressive rationalistic ideology of Marxism-Leninism.

A final key feature of Soviet ritual was that it was literally that: *Soviet* ritual, not for export to other countries, not even to the former communist societies of eastern and central Europe. Communism's internationalist rhetoric contrasted with Soviet ritual, which was profoundly nationalistic, patriotic and militaristic. Thus Soviet ritual was deployed to legitimize the Stalinist policy of 'Socialism in One Country'. Significantly, the capital had been moved east from St Petersburg, the country's most cosmopolitan city, to Moscow, architecturally and culturally a more distinctively Russian city. According to Binns (1979), Lenin's mummified body became a further symbol of the nationalization of Marxism. A popular belief in the Orthodox tradition is that the body of a saint will not putrefy. By scientifically embalming Lenin, the Soviet authorities had made a symbolic gesture against this popular superstition, while paradoxically elevating Lenin to saintly status.

This was not the only irony in the Soviet ritual system. The 1960s saw a flourishing of new rituals, particularly ones designed to channel family life and leisure pursuits in politically desired directions. This appears to have been a conscious effort by the state to shore up a political religion in decline. By the 1960s, the October revolution was a distant memory, and even the heroic defence of the motherland in what Russians call 'The Great Patriotic War' against Hitler's invasion in 1941 had lost its immediacy as a symbolic resource for the regime. Young people were beginning to look more knowledgeably to the west for images of the good society. They saw the attractions of consumerism. The new Soviet rituals of the 1960s were probably counter-productive. Despite the political objectives of the regime, the rituals tended to reinforce individualism and consumerism. Filtering out the official propaganda, as Soviet citizens could skilfully do, people took advantage of unofficial aspects of the rituals such as meeting friends and joining in the festivities (Binns 1980). These gratifications contrasted with and underlined the greyness of everyday life in the USSR.

Lane (1981) argues that the ritual system of the former Soviet Union should be seen not as civil religion but as political religion. Civil religion represents transcendent categorical truths on which people and interest groups can draw not only to support existing political institutions but also to protest against them, evoking religious legitimation for their protest. In western liberal-democratic societies, civil religion is also constrained by norms of tolerance: the civil rights and liberties of people of all faiths are to be respected.

This was not the case in the USSR. Political religion was consciously planned and rationally administered by the regime as a system of symbols and rituals sacralizing Soviet society and the Soviet state. It fused political ideology and religion into an indissoluble entity – hence the term political religion. The Soviet state held a monopoly on sacred values: dissidents were tantamount to heretics, and crimes against the state were sacrilege. The ritual system was a vehicle of top-down 'cultural management'. In Geertz's terms (1968: 7), rituals were 'models for' rather than 'models of' social relationships: they did not arise organically out of social relationships, but were ideologically driven models of what those relationships should be, and therefore designed to mould society in the desired direction.

The collapse of the communist regime in 1991 led to a rapid abandonment of most of the symbols of the Soviet era. Even the cult of Lenin was profoundly affected. Many of the statues of Lenin were dismantled, discreditable facts about his life were publicly aired, and Leningrad reverted to its former Tsarist name St Petersburg. Interestingly, though, Lenin's corpse still rests in its mausoleum. President Yeltsin has indicated that he would like to see Lenin buried literally as well as figuratively. However, there is quite widespread political and popular opposition to this ultimate act of anti-Soviet sacrilege.

Political religion: Nazi Germany

There are many parallels between political religion in the former Soviet Union and Nazi Germany (Lane 1981: 273–9). Although Hitler's thousand-year Third Reich only lasted from 1933 to 1945, it produced an abundance of sacred symbols and rituals including rites of passage, calendrical festivals and mass rallies. Both regimes celebrated the following: the seasons, infusing popular holidays with pagan associations; familial life-cycle rites; the incorporation of young people into social and political organizations such as the Komsomol and the Hitler Youth; labour, and the individual's contribution to the economy; the anniversary of the foundation of the new political order; a sacred history of fallen heroes; and a cult of the leader.

Despite these common features in the ritual systems there were also marked dissimilarities, reflecting profound ideological differences between the two regimes. Whereas the Soviet Union was committed to rational (though inefficient) planning, Nazi Germany was profoundly irrational (though bureaucratic).

The irrationality of Nazism manifested itself in many ways. One of the most striking was the cult of the Führer, which far from being antithetical to the regime was of its very essence. Unquestioning obedience to the visionary charismatic commands of the Führer was powerfully symbolized in the Hitler Salute. Although, ironically, neither Hitler himself nor many of his associates resembled the physical ideal of the 'Aryan' male, the cult of the leader emphasized his physical appearance and prowess – linking to the key Nazi symbols of blood and 'race'. All manner of mystical powers were attributed to Hitler. For example, it was popularly believed (Gruberger 1991: 121) that if a house was destroyed in an Allied bombing raid one wall would remain standing: the wall bearing Hitler's portrait.

Another crucial difference between the two regimes was in the treatment of organized religion. In the Soviet case, repression and persecution alternated with periods during which the state simply waited for religion to wither away of its own accord. Nazi Germany, on the other hand, had a deeply ambivalent relationship with Christianity and the Christian churches. For some members of the Catholic hierarchy in the occupied countries, anti-Semitism and hostility to communism united to dispose them to collaborate with the National Socialist programme. Some German Protestants, the Deutsche Christen (German Christians), co-operated in fusing Nazi and Christian symbols into a new religious system. To Nazi ideologists, Christianity was a religion for slaves, emphasizing meekness, humility and care for the weak. These were not National Socialist virtues. Similarly, Christ as a crucified saviour, a suffering servant, and moreover a Jewish man, was not a suitable symbol for Aryan heroes.

In the Soviet case, there were very few rituals surrounding the Communist Party itself. Since party members were ideologically mature they were thought not to need rituals. Rituals were devised and administered by the party for the masses – ironically, a Marxist-Leninist opium for the people. It was quite otherwise in Nazi Germany, where the party itself was saturated with symbolism and surrounded with ritual. Lane's analysis suggests, then, that whereas the Soviet regime found ritual *politically useful*, in the case of National Socialism it was *culturally essential*.

Character and society

Much of the analysis of civil religion has located itself in the Durkheimian approach to ritual and symbolism. Yet Bellah's own work draws its inspiration not only from Durkheim but also from the tradition stemming from de Tocqueville. As discussed in chapter 5, de Tocqueville saw religion as essential to any republic of free citizens. Bellah (1990: 415) echoes this, arguing that a despotism will have despotic customs and a republic republican customs – ones which are conducive to public-spiritedness and commitment to the public good.

De Tocqueville's influence is explicit in the widely read study *Habits of the Heart*, which Bellah co-authored with Madsen, Sullivan, Swidler and Tipton (1996). Their aim is to explore the relationship between character and society, the private and the public sphere. Does the private sphere prepare people for participation as citizens in public life? And does public life meet people's private aspirations? Answers to these questions are seen as crucial to gauging the health of the republic. De Tocqueville said that the 'tyranny of the majority', an oppressive egalitarianism, was the greatest threat to the American social order. For Bellah and his colleagues, this is no longer the case. Instead, rampant individualism is now the gravest danger, carrying with it the prospect of social disintegration. The integrity of the social order depends upon the continued vitality of the republican and biblical traditions, both of which are key components of a civil religion which transcends individualism in the name of the public good. Thus in Bellah's perspective civil religion is much more than a 'lowest common denominator', as Bruce (1986: 233) has it. The role of civil religion is to forge a connection between character and society.

8

Brainwashing, Consumer Protection and the State

Brainwashing – old and new

Minority religious movements, particularly those of the world-rejecting type, have faced persecution throughout their history. Many movements – including Mennonites, Shakers, Hutterites and Doukhobors – fled Europe to escape persecution and pogroms, seeking asylum in a New World which held out the promise of religious tolerance backed by a constitutional guarantee of freedom of worship and assembly. The New World itself gave rise to a rich diversity of home-grown movements which have had an impact internationally, including Christian Science, Seventh-day Adventism, Jehovah's Witnesses and the Church of Jesus Christ of Latter-day Saints.

Even in the United States, there is a long though largely forgotten history of persecution of minority religions (Bromley and Shupe 1981: 6–20). Faiths which have achieved respectability were once vilified similarly to the Moonies of today. Persecution of religious minorities is usually legitimized by what sociologists have called 'atrocity stories'. Just as warring nations accuse one another of crimes against humanity – rape, torture and massacre of innocent civilians – so too religious minorities are the target of atrocity stories, both true and false. The bloody history of confrontations between Mormons and the wider society is one of the most dramatic cases.

Less graphic but no less telling is the case of Roman Catholicism. Bromley and Shupe (1981: 11–15) identify five themes in anti-Catholic polemics in the history of the United States.

Deception and coercion   Roman Catholics were thought to be indoctrinated by priests, nuns, Jesuits and other agents of papal authority, who used confession as a means of extracting guilty secrets to use as blackmail against the hapless victim.

The illegitimacy of Catholic beliefs In the ultra-Protestant version of history, the Protestant Reformation of the sixteenth century restored the true Christian faith which had been betrayed by heretical Catholic beliefs and practices. Backed solely by the illegitimate doctrine of papal infallibility, these beliefs and practices had no foundation in the Bible. A prime example is the cult of the Virgin Mary, seen by ultra-Protestants as pure paganism.

Sexual perversion The celibacy of priests and members of religious orders was portrayed as repressing natural sexual drives which would inevitably find an outlet elsewhere: using the services of prostitutes, homosexual acts, seducing young people, sexually abusing children. Convents, abbeys, monasteries, priests' houses, seminaries – all were allegedly hotbeds of perversion.

Political subversion Catholicism was seen as a conspiracy bent on undermining democratic institutions and freedoms, replacing them with the unfettered autocratic power of the Vatican. Successive waves of migration from Catholic Europe to the New World were part of a papal design to seize power in the United States. This theme of political subversion lives on, as we have seen, among fervent Protestant loyalists in Northern Ireland.

Financial exploitation The Catholic church was portrayed as extracting large donations from its members, duping them into believing that this would relieve their sufferings in this world and the next. An extreme example was the practice which grew up in the late Middle Ages of selling indulgences. At considerable cost, people could buy indulgences from professional 'pardoners'. Purchasing an indulgence would reduce the time the sinner would have to spend in purgatory before entering heaven. The money raised was often devoted to construction projects: most notably, it contributed to the cost of building St Peter's in Rome. Eventually banned by Pope Pius V in 1567, the highly commercial activities of the pardoners, who were in effect selling salvation as a commodity, were held up by the Protestant reformers as a powerful symbol of Catholic corruption.

The five themes identified by Bromley and Shupe recur in atrocity stories told about contemporary religious movements. In that sense, there is nothing new in the accusations made against Moonies and others. However, these atrocity stories are given a specifically modern inflection. Moonies are accused of thought reform, mind control and brainwashing.

The term 'brainwashing' was originally used to describe the experiences of US military personnel who were taken prisoner and indoctrinated by the Chinese communists during the 1950–3 Korean war. This indoctrination, it was argued, built on and intensified techniques of persuasion which the communists had already successfully used on their own people. American prisoners of war were subjected to a variety of techniques: inadequate and unbalanced diets; sleep deprivation and disruption; ideological indoctrination; psychotropic drugs; repeated interrogation; beatings and torture; and threats of beatings, torture and execution. This brutality was aimed at reducing prisoners to a state of physiological dysfunctioning, and psychological disorientation and suggestibility, which would leave them susceptible to deep-seated attitude change. The American public was shocked to see films of prisoners of war making zealously pro-communist statements and denouncing western capitalism and American imperialism. How had these dramatic ideological conversions come about? The answer: mind control through coercive and powerful techniques of brainwashing. In a body of academic literature (Sargant 1957; Lifton 1961) published during the era of the Cold War, techniques of brainwashing were analysed as mechanisms of social control characteristic of totalitarian societies.

When the activities of world-rejecting religious movements came under scrutiny in the west from the late 1960s onwards, a parallel was drawn between their socialization practices and the techniques of persuasion used by the Chinese communists on prisoners of war. Brainwashing in religious movements has been said to involve the following:

- use of deception to conceal the movement's identity and true purpose
- sleep deprivation brought about through long, exhausting and irregular work schedules
- an unbalanced diet, particularly one excessively high in sugar, which produces a state of euphoria known as 'sugar buzzing'
- disruption of sexual activity
- denial of privacy
- repetitive chanting of mantras and ideological slogans
- participation in childish team games
- disruption of contact with the outside world
- intense displays of love, admiration and concern (love bombing)

Assuming that these techniques have indeed been used by minority religious movements, how effective are they? Sociological studies give a clear answer: they are remarkably ineffective and short-lived. A well-known demonstration of this is Barker's study of the Moonies (Barker 1984a: 145–8). In a survey of over a thousand people who attended a two-day workshop in the London area in 1979, she found that only one in ten actually joined the movement for more than a week. From the perspective of the Unification Church this is a poor rate of take-up, especially since the people who attended the initial workshop were not a random cross-section of society but a highly self-selected sample of seekers – good prospects, in other words. People drop out of the movement at regular intervals. After one year, only 7 per cent of the people who had joined were still members; after two years the figure had fallen to 5 per cent, and by the end of four years it had fallen still further to 3.5 per cent at most. This drastic rate of attrition shows that the Moonies' techniques of persuasion are extremely ineffective, and hardly warrant the grandiose title of brainwashing. The rapid turnover of members reflects the movement's recruitment strategy, and its targeting of relatively unattached young people who can enjoy the luxury of a brief interlude of 'time out' before re-entering the mainstream of society. However, as Barker points out, both the Moonies and their opponents have a vested interest in exaggerating Moonie successes.

Returning to the Chinese communists and their prisoners of war, even here the achievements of the brainwashers were less than was once thought. Scheflin and Opton's book *The Mind Manipulators* (cited in Bromley and Shupe 1981: 99–100) showed that of the over 3,500 Americans taken prisoner during the Korean war only about fifty made pro-communist statements and only twenty-five refused repatriation to the USA when the war ended. Obviously, many of the pro-communist statements were motivated by self-preservation rather than ideological conversion.

The power of the brainwashing metaphor

When the accusation of brainwashing is applied to religious movements it evokes deep-seated fears and anxieties. Thus the debate about brainwashing sheds light not only on minority religions but also on the wider society. A number of closely related fears can be identified.

Fears of psychological manipulation

The debate about brainwashing taps into broader fears about the capacity of new technologies to manipulate people's thoughts, emotions and desires. This has been a common theme in science fiction and in dystopian novels generally. The panic about subliminal advertising is an illustration of this fear. Vance Packard's popular classic, *The Hidden Persuaders* (1957), gave a chilling account of the way in which the advertising industry drew

on depth psychology in order to deploy powerful and sophisticated techniques of non-rational persuasion of which consumers were unaware. At
stake are the autonomy and integrity of the individual. Packard's book
ended with a warning (1957: 226): 'the most serious offence many of the
depth manipulators commit, it seems to me, is that they try to invade the
privacy of our minds.'

Fears of charismatic leadership

Jim Jones of the People's Temple, David Koresh of the Branch Davidians
at Waco, Marshall Applewhite ('Do') of Heaven's Gate, Luc Jouret of the
Ordre du Temple Solaire, Shoko Asahara of Aum Shinrikyo: all of these led
their followers to disaster. The shock of the mass suicide of the People's
Temple at Jonestown in 1978 transformed public sentiment in the west.
Minority religions were all subject to the suspicion that they would follow
the apocalyptic example of the People's Temple and induce their members
to commit suicide. In each of the cases cited above, a deranged charismatic
leader was seen as possessing extraordinary mental powers, en-abling him
to take control of the mind and the will of his followers.

Fears of collectivism

It is no coincidence that allegations of brainwashing have their roots in the
Cold War. The threat posed by the apocalyptic ideology of communism,
backed by the Soviet Union's formidable nuclear arsenal, and the longer-
term menace of communist China, indirectly coloured thinking about the
'new' religions of the late 1960s and the 1970s. Critiques of new religious
movements often show what Robbins (1988: 73) calls an 'atomistic bias',
since they assume that authentic religious experience must necessarily be
deeply personal and individual. Movements in which the religious community provides a powerful mediation and reinforcement of spirituality
risk being seen as manipulative and inauthentic. Individual autonomy is
threatened just as much by religious collectivism as by atheistic communism.

One illustration of anti-collectivism is the hostility displayed towards
mass wedding ceremonies performed by the Unification Church. The first
such ceremony in the west was a small-scale affair by later standards:
thirteen couples were blessed in Washington, DC, in 1969. In the 1970s
and 1980s, intense publicity surrounded these ceremonies. In 1982, 2,075
couples were blessed by the Reverend Moon in a mass ceremony in Madi-

son Square Garden, New York, a figure that was more than doubled in Seoul later the same year, when 5,800 couples were blessed (Barker 1984a: 65). These large-scale collective wedding ceremonies, involving arranged marriages in which the partners are ostensibly selected by Moon himself, strike a symbolic blow at western individualism and its faith in romantic love. They are an expression of the Unification Church's affirmation of community service and duty rather than individual self-realization.

Ironically, the Unification Church is fiercely anti-communist. In the early stages of his career Moon had been imprisoned and ill-treated by the communist authorities in North Korea. Part of the Moonie message to the west is that the United States has been the leader of the free world in a deadly struggle with godless communism.

Fears of the alien 'other'

The explosion of new religious movements and a new religious conscious-ness in the west from the late 1960s onwards gave rise to a wide-ranging debate in sociology and in the media about the social significance of these apparently new phenomena. The term 'cult' became widely used to charac-terize the new religions and the personal relationships operative within them. While 'cult' may have been understood neutrally by sociologists, it was certainly used negatively by journalists and other commentators. Part of what it connoted was an alien intrusion into 'our' culture. At least the sects were home-grown! For all the problems they are thought to present, Jehovah's Witnesses take their place on the far wing of extreme conser-vative Protestantism, just as the Mormons, despite all the doubts about the authenticity of the Book of Mormon and the justification for polygamy, are a recognizably American movement rooted in American history and suf-fused with conventional American values – clean living, the nuclear family, the success ethic. But Hare Krishna? The Divine Light Mission? The Moonies? What were *our* young people doing joining *them*?

What new religious movements offer their recruits

One feature of the accusation of brainwashing, as has often been pointed out, is that it takes attention away from the content of religious beliefs and practices, and refocuses on the processes through which believers are brought to a state of passive dependence on the movement. In doing so, it carries the implication that these movements have nothing of value to offer their members. From a sociological view, however, we cannot simply dismiss out of hand the benefits which members claim to experience. Following Barker (1995: 25–31), six main types of benefit may be distinguished; as one would expect, movements usually offer more than one of these. These factors are not unique to minority religions, though many who join say that they did not find them in mainstream religion.

Success in careers It is mainly the world-affirming religious movements which provide techniques of self-improvement promoting the achievement of worldly career goals. These movements offer their services to individuals and also to business corporations interested in improving the motivation and commitment of their personnel.

Improved health and longevity Again, this claim is common among world-affirming movements. Health is typically viewed holistically as embracing mental, spiritual and physical well-being. Cartesian dualism, with its strict division between mind and body, is rejected.

Community Some movements, especially the world-rejecting type, provide communal living for their devotees. Even where this is not the case, members develop affective ties of friendship and loyalty. Family imagery is very common, with fellow worshippers being called brothers and sisters and the leaders mother and father (as in the Unification Church, where Moon and his wife are referred to as 'True Parents').

Kingdom-building World-rejecting movements often attract idealistic young people with the promise that they will be building a better world, even the kingdom of God on earth. Fired by religiously inspired altruism, members may engage enthusiastically as unpaid volunteers in labour-intensive community projects, recruitment drives and fund-raising activities. However, disillusionment can set in if the member comes to feel that recruitment and fund-raising are the dominant goals, leaving the social action programmes and charitable work as little more than a public relations exercise.

Self-development This theme is particularly strong among world-affirming movements. The distinction between secular self-advancement and spiritual development is often unclear. Some people start out with straightforwardly this-worldly success goals, but then discover as they progress in the movement that the spiritual dimension gradually takes priority. Equally, self-development is not incompatible with altruism. For example, Transcendental Meditation teaches that if a critical mass of people engage in TM it will have positive benefits for the whole of their society. It is on this basis that the Natural Law Party, the political wing of TM, has fielded candidates in general elections in the UK.

Religious experiences   New religious movements cultivate a variety of religious experiences, and, crucially, offer a forum in which religious experience is validated. This can be attractive to people who feel that mainstream religion is spiritually barren, or that the wider culture is hostile to spirituality (Hay 1987). Barker found that over three-quarters of the Moonies she interviewed claimed to have had religious experiences before they joined the Unification Church (Barker 1984a: 218). The majority had never told anyone about these experiences, for fear of being ridiculed or branded as a fanatic. New religious movements offer, then, an outlet for repressed spirituality.

Disengaging from new religious movements

Members of new religious movements typically cite the benefits discussed above. In evaluating their accounts, we need to recognize that they are just that – accounts, which seek to make sense of social phenomena and social processes (Beckford 1978). Like any account, they are not simply spontaneously generated: they are called forth in certain contexts, retold to certain audiences, and they are also learned. Becoming a member of a religious movement is a complex process in which the prospective convert is socialized into appropriate motivation, behaviour and discourse. For these reasons, any conversion account is in part scripted, which does not imply that it is insincere or untrue.

Precisely the same considerations apply to accounts of deconversion given by people who have left a religious movement. In the sociological literature these people are often called apostates – an unfortunate term, since in religious discourse it can carry implications of defection and heresy. Apostasy in that framework is the religious equivalent of military desertion, a serious disciplinary offence. In the early Christian church, apostasy, murder and fornication were the three sins considered unpardonable if committed by a baptized Christian. Later in western Christianity, the term was applied more specifically to the unpermitted renunciation by monks and nuns of their lifelong vows. In Islam, apostasy is a grievous sin, potentially punishable by death in some Islamic cultures. Significantly, the freedom to change one's religion is not recognized as a human right by any Islamic state (Boyle and Sheen 1997: 8–9).

Although sociologists are supposedly using the term neutrally, much of the sociological literature, as Beckford (1985: 146) points out, tends to be dismissive of apostates' accounts of their experiences. To avoid the pejorative associations, the term ex-members is preferred here.

Ex-members are prominent among those who tell atrocity stories about new religious movements. Their testimony gains credibility from being firsthand. They claim to be in a position to reveal the sordid truths which outsiders, including sociologists, have failed to uncover. Some ex-members have been active in anti-cult movements, while others simply recount their experiences to family and friends. A theme running through some of these stories is that the ex-member was brainwashed. Not all accounts, however, conform to the brainwashing paradigm. Beckford's work on the Moonies (1985: 149–217), based on interviews with ex-members and their families, provides telling insights into the appeal and also the drawbacks of the rhetoric of brainwashing.

The crucial point in Beckford's analysis is that when a committed member leaves the Moonies she or he is likely to find it a harrowing experience. First, the Unification Church does not make it easy. From the church's perspective there is no valid reason for leaving. Seekership is not legitimate: ex-members cannot say that their spiritual quest is leading them elsewhere. There is no legitimate mode of exit; hence, the church makes no provision for the spiritual welfare of those it sees as apostates. People who leave the church therefore do so suddenly and unexpectedly. Even if they had been harbouring misgivings for a long time, they would have found it risky to share them with fellow Moonies for fear of rejection or betrayal. Defectors are stigmatized, and their example is held up to members as evidence of the power of Satan to seduce the faithful. The Unification Church tries to prevent ex-members from communicating with their former friends in the movement – the mirror image of its efforts to disrupt communications from members to their family and friends.

Second, family and friends unwittingly place additional strains on the ex-member. As Beckford points out, most ex-Moonies are likely to return to the parental home. It is a situation fraught with embarrassment, confusion and mutual suspicion on both sides. The period during which the ex-Moonie was active in the movement is likely to have caused worry and anguish to the parents, doubly so if they were themselves facing a mid-life crisis in relationships or career. Involvement in new religious movements is also widely regarded in western culture as foolish and immature – scarcely an enhancement of anyone's curriculum vitae. While welcoming their children back, parents typically seek an account not only of why they joined the movement but also of why they left it. In rendering an account, the ex-Moonie is not merely telling a story but restoring a balance, making reparations for a breach in the social order. The account is expected to paint a harsh picture of life in the Unification Church. Brainwashing and mind control fulfil this role, enabling blame to be attributed entirely to the church. Ex-Moonies are required to renounce their Moonie past, obliterating it from their c.v. as a condition of their relaunch into the mainstream of social life.

The rhetoric of brainwashing can offer a way forward to ex-Moonies, enabling them to discount their Moonie past as the product of brainwashing, and to re-enter social life virtually at the point where they left it. More than that, some ex-Moonies have made a career in the anti-cult movement, offering themselves as experts on brainwashing.

Beckford's evidence shows, nevertheless, that many ex-Moonies have problems with embracing the brainwashing rhetoric wholeheartedly. Ex-members often feel guilty about leaving the church, fearing that they have let down their Moonie companions. They also typically experience a sense of failure, since they were unequal to the challenge of living the Moonie life. Despite their doubts, they may not have abandoned all hope that Moon is the promised Messiah. They may well have pleasant memories of the good times: the spiritual support, the kingdom-building, the companionship of a close-knit community. These experiences, after all, were what the movement offered them in the first place, meeting needs which they had been unable to satisfy before they joined. Now, it seems, they are required to deny that there was anything good at all about being a Moonie. They are under pressure to make a full confession in order to be absolved, clearing the path for a fresh start. If, however, they believe that the Unification Church has betrayed the trust they showed by being spiritually 'open' when they were members, they are likely to be wary of repeating that mistake. They may also feel they are being treated as incompetent – back to childhood with a vengeance.

Disengagement from new religious movements is often a solo performance, and in that sense a taxing virtuoso act. Movements like the Unification Church provide no support, while the contribution of family and friends, however well intentioned, is frequently counter-productive. Ex-members may lack a 'cultural script' for disengagement, unless they adopt the brainwashing account scripted by deprogrammers and the anti-cult movement.

Since Beckford's study, a significant development in the UK has been the establishment in 1988 of INFORM, the Information Network Focus on Religious Movements (Barker 1995: 141–4). INFORM is a registered charity that has received funding from the Home Office and mainstream churches. It defines as its primary aim 'to help the public by providing information about new religious movements that is objective, balanced and up-to-date'. To guard its independence it will not accept any funding from new religious movements themselves, nor will it employ members of those movements. Non-political and non-sectarian, it does not engage in theological debate about the truth or falsity of religious belief. It seeks to judge each case on its merits, forswearing sweeping generalizations hostile to 'cults' as a blanket term of abuse.

INFORM seeks a middle way. As well as disseminating impartial information, it promotes direct contact with new religious movements on the grounds that this often allows a constructive dialogue between parents and children which can help in resolving difficulties. INFORM's middle way explicitly rejects two extremes. On the one hand, it is opposed to the use of forcible deprogramming involving physical restraint. There are two reasons for this: forcible deprogramming is an illegal violation of individual liberty and, in so far as it has any effect at all, on balance it does far more harm than good. On the other hand, INFORM also rejects the non-interventionist policy of complete laissez-faire. Laissez-faire is too risky, since some situations are potentially threatening to the well-being and even the lives of members of new religious movements. Barker (1995: 137) lists six warning signs:

- a movement isolating itself off from the wider society geographically or socially
- dependence on the movement for one's definition and sense of reality
- a movement drawing a sharp, non-negotiable divide between 'us' and 'them'
- important decisions being taken for members by the leadership
- charismatic leaders claiming divine authority
- leaders and movements determinedly pursuing a single goal

The characteristics of destructive religious movements will be examined later in this chapter.

Consumer protection and the regulation of abuses

Robbins (1988: 164–8) has argued that, at least in the United States, controversy about new religious movements is fuelled by their status as *privileged enclaves*. Although the state is gradually extending its regulatory control into all areas of social life, transforming private troubles into public concerns, religion and religious movements enjoy legal privileges which insulate them from state interference in their affairs. This is one reason why so many social movements have been determined to claim a religious identity. What Robbins calls a 'regulatory gap' is opening up between tightly regulated secular organizations and their privileged religious counterparts.

As long as religious movements are content with a privatized role, cultivating members' inner spirituality (as in world-accommodating movements), their privileges are unlikely to cause controversy. The regulatory gap only becomes an issue when religious movements broaden their scope to include more and more areas of social life. Scientology and the Unification Church have been at the cutting edge of church–state tension precisely because they are highly diversified organizations with a myriad of activities. They are not unlike multinational corporations. Activities listed by Robbins (1988: 166) include commercial and financial stakes in publishing, education, child care, residential establishments, nursing homes, political lobbying, healing and psychotherapy. When the state's regulatory grip is relaxed, their status as religion is seen to give them an unfair competitive advantage over their secular rivals.

Consider two examples of intervention by the state to regulate abuse. First, the Moonies (Barker 1995: 214–16). The Unification Church owns a wide range of commercial operations. It has machine tool and ginseng businesses, a large fishing fleet, and owns the *Washington Times*. It trades under a number of names which conceal its identity. These entrepreneurial activities have attracted the attention of the authorities. Moon himself has been imprisoned in the USA on several occasions, most notably on an entirely secular charge of tax evasion.

Second, the Rajneeshees (Barker 1995: 201–5; Bruce 1996: 178–9). In 1974, Bhagwan Shree Rajneesh founded a community at Poona in India. Thousands of pilgrims from the west travelled to the ashram in order to enter the guru's presence and receive enlightenment. From the very outset the movement was both fashionable and controversial, mainly because its techniques of meditation routinely resulted in group sex. A folk myth has become widespread that the title 'Bhagwan' means 'Master of the Vagina'. In fact, it means 'the High God'. It is indeed offensive – but as a blasphemy, not an obscenity as the secular western imagination supposes.

In 1981, Rajneesh abruptly left Poona and moved to the United States, where he purchased a 64,000-acre ranch in Oregon, building a community called Rajneeshpuram, which incorporated an elaborate nuclear bunker. Despite the movement's celebration of love and peace, Rajneeshpuram was run on totalitarian lines. Relations with the local community degenerated into violence and intimidation. Rajneesh's secretary, Ma Anand Sheela, was imprisoned for a variety of criminal offences. Rajneesh himself was caught trying to leave the USA, imprisoned, and then deported for violation of US immigration laws. Refused entry by a number of countries as an undesirable alien, Rajneesh returned to Poona, where he died in 1990.

Evading taxes and violating immigration laws are quintessentially secular offences carried out for financial gain. In acting against them, the state is not identifying heresy but regulating abuses. Brainwashing falls into the same category as tax evasion and illegal immigration, except that it is harder to prove. It is constituted as an infringement of the liberty of the autonomous individual, and an abuse which the state is required to eliminate. It is not the state but the world-rejecting religious movement which has transgressed against the separation of church and state.

The modern liberal-democratic state has extended its regulatory grip to include, in Beckford's words (1985: 284), 'virtually all aspects of commerce, manufacturing, hygiene, and safety in places of work, health hazards in therapeutic practice, and the use of land and buildings'. Beckford argues that new religious movements have not been singled out for special attention because they are religions; it is simply that any movement, secular or religious, which aims to cater comprehensively for its members, revitalizing the host society in the process, is bound to come into conflict with the modern state.

State surveillance of new religious movements in western societies is 'indirect, piecemeal, administrative, *ad hoc*, and liberal' (Beckford 1985: 288). It is not driven by a coherent underlying social policy, nor do the various state agencies act in concert to achieve clearly identified goals (except perhaps in Germany, where after the Nazi era the need to protect the state against any threat from totalitarianism was made a constitutional imperative).

All social systems, according to Habermas (1973), have a need for mechanisms which give them legitimacy in the sense of respect and active commitment that go beyond mere compliance. Contemporary capitalism requires extensive state intervention to regulate economic and social life. The state gains a high degree of legitimacy through its role in consumer protection. Although state intervention in a liberal-democratic society can give rise to what Habermas identifies as a 'legitimation crisis', in that the state increasingly interferes in its citizens' private lives, this intervention is rendered legitimate by the claim that its rationale is to defend the autonomous individual against abuse.

Returning to the example discussed above of state action against the Moonies and the Rajneeshees, a crucial point is that these interventions were popular with the general public. Also significant was the open humiliation of the movement's charismatic leader. If there is a legitimation crisis in the contemporary state, acting against world-rejecting minority religions and their leaders can be a cost-effective way of gaining popular support.

Cult scares and the anti-cult movement

Much of the sociological work on new religious movements has sought to defend them against critical onslaught and the legislative curbs proposed by anti-cult groups. A classic example of such a defence is Bromley and Shupe's 1981 publication, *Strange Gods*. Significantly subtitled *The Great American Cult Scare*, this book was written in the aftermath of the tragedy of the People's Temple at Jonestown in 1978. It concludes (1981: 203–20) with a 'hard look' at the cult controversy.

Bromley and Shupe argue that new religious movements are the subject of crude stereotyping and unsubstantiated myths propagated by anti-cultists in an attempt to arouse public indignation. The agenda of debate has been dominated by an anti-cult crusade which is in many ways more dangerous, and more threatening to civil liberties, than the movements it attacks. To redress the balance, Bromley and Shupe are deliberately more critical of anti-cultists than of the new religions themselves.

Anti-cultists exaggerate the numerical significance and social impact of new religious movements, implausibly claiming that virtually anyone is at risk of falling victim to their techniques of brainwashing – whereas in fact very few people join. According to Bromley and Shupe, the abuses perpetrated by new religions are not the lurid scandals of popular imagination but relatively minor offences – for example, street soliciting for funds while concealing the movement's true identity. Leaders of the movements are neither more nor less sincere than the leaders of mainstream churches, Bromley and Shupe assert. It is incorrectly assumed that they wield absolute power, whereas they have to deal continually with doubt, dissent and the threat of factionalism.

For anti-cultists, new religious movements have no positive features. Bromley and Shupe argue, in contrast, that new religions embody fresh sources of meaning reflecting emergent needs and aspirations among significant sections of society. They are part of a normal cycle, in which an era of stability is followed by a period of revitalization. Instead of breaking up families, new religious movements more commonly help to resolve family and inter-generational conflicts. In the late 1960s and the 1970s, they played an important part in weaning young people from the drug counterculture. Movements such as the International Society for Krishna Consciousness provided a bridge back into the social mainstream, reaching out where mainstream Christianity so often failed to do so. In reinvigorating society, they also challenge the mainstream churches to reassess their own evangelical and pastoral policies.

The anti-cult movement fails to see new religions in historical perspective. The danger they represent is exaggerated now as it was in the past. New religions are invariably seen as subversive – as Christianity was in the Roman Empire, and as the Protestant Reformation was to the Roman Catholic Church.

In our own times, the persecution of new religious movements is justified by unfounded allegations of brainwashing which legitimate forcible deprogramming. This cure is ineffective, illegitimate and far worse than the problem. Anti-cultists and deprogrammers constitute a greater threat to civil liberties and democratic pluralism than the new religions do. Ironically, persecution of new religious movements tends to reinforce their cohesion and sense of solidarity. Instead of trying to legislate morality it would be better to leave new religions alone, so that those movements which did endure would gradually accommodate to the mainstream and evolve into an approximation of the denominational form.

The example of the People's Temple at Jonestown is treated as a unique tragedy that cannot be generalized to other movements. Bromley and Shupe's conclusion is that the controversy surrounding new religious movements in the USA is a 'scare' and even a 'hoax', in that it is an unnecessary panic generated primarily by anti-cultists. 'In the final analysis', they say, 'the campaign against the new religions is better understood as the product of the anticultists' interests rather than as a civic crusade to save the rest of us from a dark, evil conspiracy' (1981: 213).

Doomsday cults: five case studies

Since Jonestown, there has been a series of highly publicized disasters in which members of new religious movements have taken their own lives, or died by the hands of their co-religionists, or perished in the aftermath of intervention by the authorities. Concern has grown about the threat posed by these destructive and violent 'doomsday cults'. What are the characteristics of these movements? And do they confirm that writers like Bromley and Shupe were too sanguine, whereas the anti-cultists were right all along?

The People's Temple at Jonestown

In November 1978, US Representative Leo Ryan led a delegation to the agricultural community known as Jonestown, which had been established four years earlier in virgin territory in the socialist republic of Guyana. Jonestown was a project of the People's Temple, whose leader was the Reverend Jim Jones.

Congressman Ryan's purpose in visiting Jonestown was to investigate the truth of stories circulating in the United States that members of the People's Temple were being kept in Jonestown against their will. A small number of people agreed to return with him to the US. However, when they arrived at the airstrip for their flight home, Ryan and four other members of his party were shot dead by People's Temple security guards. After the news of this was broadcast in Jonestown itself, over 900 people, 30 per cent of them children, either participated voluntarily in a mass suicide, drinking Kool-aid laced with cyanide, or were shot dead or killed by lethal injection. Their bodies were found scattered in little huddles on the ground. They had often practised the ritual of 'revolutionary suicide' before, but this time the poison was real.

Jim Jones had a long history as a preacher and religious leader. In 1953, he established an inter-racial congregation in Indiana. By 1964, his church was affiliated to the Disciples of Christ. In 1966, Jones and some of his followers moved to California, where they built up congregations in San Francisco and Los Angeles. They also became active on the fringe of Democratic Party politics. On the one hand, their cultivation of Democrat politicians and their engagement in inter-racial community programmes earned them respectability. On the other hand, Jones faced allegations of financial misconduct, sexual impropriety and faking miraculous cures for life-threatening illnesses such as cancer.

The apocalyptic theme was established early in Jones's career as a key element in his theology. The initial move from Indiana to California was justified by the belief that Redwood Valley would survive the impending nuclear holocaust. In California, Jones became increasingly preoccupied with what he saw as the CIA's plan of genocide of black people. Relocation to socialist Guyana was a bid to escape the clutches of American capitalism. In the last days at Jonestown, Jones contemplated a further move to Cuba or the USSR.

The Branch Davidians at Waco

In 1993, US government agents of the Bureau of Alcohol, Tobacco and Firearms (ATF) launched an armed attack with helicopter support on the Branch Davidians' Mount Carmel settlement at Waco, Texas. Their objective was to arrest David Koresh for firearms violations. An exchange of gunfire resulted in the death of four ATF agents and six Branch Davidians. The FBI took over from the AFT; there followed protracted negotiations with the Branch Davidians over the course of a siege lasting fifty-one days. At the end of this period, the FBI advanced on the settlement in armed vehicles equipped with battering rams. They penetrated the walls of the compound and launched CS gas. Fires erupted, possibly set off by the Branch Davidians themselves. The separate sources of fire combined into a huge conflagration which engulfed the compound. Most of the members of the settlement perished, including Koresh.

The Branch Davidians are an extreme offshoot of the Davidian Seventh-day Adventists, who had separated themselves from the Seventh-day Adventist mainstream in 1935 (Anthony and Robbins 1997). When the Waco crisis broke, the Seventh-day Adventist Church made strenuous efforts to disown the Branch Davidians (Lawson 1997).

It was in 1981 that Vernon Howell joined the Branch Davidians. In 1987, he and his followers took control of the movement. In 1990, Vernon Howell changed his name to David Koresh: David after King David of Israel, Koresh the Hebrew name for the Persian King Cyrus, who defeated Babylon (Bainbridge 1997: 113). He identified himself as 'the Lamb' who would open the seven seals, after which Christ would return to earth and the war of Armageddon would be unleashed, a war in which the Branch Davidians would play a key part.

The Branch Davidians had accumulated an arsenal of weapons at Waco, ostensibly for self-defence against the forces of 'Babylon'. Under Koresh, the Mount Carmel settlement at Waco was prophetically renamed 'Ranch Apocalypse', reflecting his belief that the compound would be the site at which the war of Armageddon would begin. The two attacks on the compound confirmed Koresh's prophecy that the cosmic struggle between good and evil would lead the Babylonians to mount an onslaught on the Lamb and his elect.

L'Ordre du Temple Solaire

In October 1994 the emergency services were called to a fire at a farmhouse in Cheiry, Switzerland (Hall and Schuyler 1997). A total of twenty-three people were found dead. They proved to be members of the Order of the Solar Temple, a movement founded in 1977 by Luc Jouret. Twenty-one of them had been shot, and the remaining two had died of asphyxiation. Ten of the twenty-three had plastic bags over their head. In some cases there was evidence that a struggle had taken place. Following an investigation the authorities concluded that three of the members had been murdered as a reprisal for allegedly betraying the movement.

At the same time, some sixty kilometres away in a complex of villas at Granges-sur-Salvan, a further twenty-five bodies were found, many of them burned beyond recognition. They included two of the movement's leaders, Joseph DiMambro and Luc Jouret himself. These incidents were found to be connected with the earlier mysterious death in Morin Heights near Montreal of five people, including a three-month-old infant who had had a wooden stake impaled in his heart.

The Order of the Solar Temple was a secret society, one in a long line of esoteric movements which fancifully trace their descent to the Rosicrucians, an occult brotherhood supposedly founded in the fifteenth century, and the medieval Knights Templar, who originally guarded the routes for Christian pilgrims to Jerusalem. The Order's members were affluent, middle class, francophone and lapsed Catholic. The movement's belief-system mixed together environmentalism, homoeopathy, numerology, astrology, Christian symbols and reincarnation.

Fire was a central symbol in their belief-system. They believed that the world would be consumed by fire, and that in order to move on to another world they themselves would need to die by fire. Documents recovered from the farmhouse at Cheiry referred to 'the Transit'. Death is an illusion: those who 'died' thought they were moving to a higher plane of existence located on a planet orbiting Sirius, the Dog Star.

Aum Shinrikyo

In 1995, the lethal nerve gas sarin was released on the Tokyo underground (Mullins 1997). Twelve people died and more than 5,000 were injured. This appears to have been the work of Aum Shinrikyo, a little-known new religious movement founded in the 1980s by Chizuo Matsumoto, who later adopted the 'holy name' of Shoko Asahara. The title Aum Shinrikyo is a hybrid of Japanese and Sanskrit roots, whose meaning is that the movement teaches the Supreme Truth about the creative and destructive power in the universe. In 1989, Aum Shinrikyo was registered in Japan as a religious organization.

Initially, Aum Shinrikyo presented itself as an eclectic Buddhist movement, offering its members liberation from illness and suffering, and ultimately enlightenment. The movement's vision was to transform Japan into a utopia. As the movement developed, however, an apocalyptic strand grew more and more prominent, drawing on the prophecies of the sixteenth-century monk Nostradamus and the Book of Revelation. The vision of the utopian transformation of Japan was replaced by the need for Aum to prepare to survive an inevitable nuclear war. Asahara travelled forward in time to interview survivors of World War Three. As part of the movement's new imperative, Aum was reorganized into divisions mimicking the departments of the Japanese government, with Asahara as Supreme Leader. Here was a government ready to take power after the apocalypse.

Two days after the atrocity in Tokyo, the police raided twenty-five Aum centres across Japan. Aum claimed that it was being persecuted as a religious minority, and that it was the victim rather than the perpetrator of gas attacks. Asahara, who had been in hiding, was arrested two months later.

He is currently under trial.

Reflecting on these events, Mullins refers to Ellul's emphasis on 'the democratization of evil' in contemporary societies. Weapons of mass destruction are, potentially, more widely available than in any previous civilization. Access to instruments of random indiscriminate slaughter has in that sense become democratic.

Heaven's Gate

The movement was founded in the 1970s by Marshall Applewhite and Bonnie Nettles, who gave themselves a series of fanciful names beginning with Bo and Peep, before finally settling on Do and Ti, musical notes in the tonic sol-fa system. After its initial phase of development as a UFO cult – they waited in the Colorado desert for a spaceship which failed to arrive – the movement went underground, travelling around to different locations in the USA until eventually settling in a large rented property, which they called their monastery, near San Diego. Members were cut off from contact with friends and family, many of whom became deeply worried about their welfare and the increasingly volatile and apparently deranged behaviour of Applewhite himself.

In common with many other Ufologists, the movement held that UFOs are interstellar spaceships crewed by extra-terrestrial beings whose motive in visiting Earth is to bring humanity to a higher plane of existence. It is a familiar notion, one frequently explored in science fiction. Heaven's Gate combined this belief with prophecies they derived from the Book of Revelation concerning two witnesses who were killed, but subsequently revived and taken up into the heavens. This prophecy concerning 'the Two' was interpreted as referring to Ti and Do.

The movement held to a dualistic philosophy according to which the human body is a temporary and debased container of the human spirit. The spirit could be detached from its physical vessel by a carefully timed act of suicide, through which members would attain the Kingdom Level of existence, transcending the limitations of mundane human existence.

Sexuality was a key theme in the movement: the Kingdom Level would be free from gender identity and sexual activity. Sexual relations between members were forbidden, and a number of men in the movement, at Do's prompting and following his example, agreed to be castrated. There is evidence that Applewhite, who was gay, was profoundly troubled about his own sexual orientation and had unsuccessfully sought therapy to change it.

The appearance of comet Hale-Bopp in 1997 was interpreted as a sign from Ti, who had died of cancer in 1985, that the time had at last come to evacuate planet Earth and join the extra-terrestrials aboard a spaceship concealed on the far side of the comet. Thirty-nine members of the movement, including Applewhite, committed suicide. A videotape they left behind shows they did so voluntarily, in excited expectation of their future life.

Apocalypse, charismatic leadership and self-destruction

In a famous article, Bromley and Shupe (1980) warned of the threat posed by the Tnevnoc Cult. This movement preyed on impressionable young women. New recruits were stripped of their individual identity and their material possessions. They were given a new exotic name, and were required to shave their head and wear a drab uniform. They were isolated from family and friends in an encapsulated community. Their lives were closely regulated, involving an ascetic discipline of self-denial and repetitive prayer. They were also required to undergo a ritual marriage with the cult's charismatic founder, who had been resurrected from the dead.

Tnevnoc is, perhaps somewhat obviously, convent spelled backwards. Although a spoof, Bromley and Shupe's article was deeply serious. The socialization practices which take place in Christian religious orders clearly qualify as brainwashing in anti-cult terms, yet few people in the west regard them as life-threatening or would wish to see them outlawed.

It seems unlikely that sociology will ever develop a formula or algorithm that will enable us to predict which religious movements will end in self-destruction or violent confrontation with the wider society. Certainly the anti-cult movement failed to do so. What it did instead was to launch an indiscriminate broadside attack on a multitude of religious movements including many which were long established and whose members were upstanding citizens. Far from predicting such disasters as Jonestown or Waco, the anti-cult movement prevented a clear understanding of them and in some cases may even have made matters worse.

Despite these caveats, there are some critically important factors which can be discerned in the case studies of destructive cults outlined above.

Catastrophic millenarianism

A millenarian religious movement is one which expects that the present world will come to an end in the immediate future, to be replaced by a new world order.

There are many versions of millenarianism. In the Christian tradition, the millennium refers to a thousand years of blessedness. Some conservative Christian movements believe that the world was created 6,000 years ago; 4004 BC was one widely canvassed date, as originally calculated from biblical data in the seventeenth century by James Ussher, Archbishop of Armagh. To God, who created the world in six days and rested on the seventh, one day is as a thousand years. The millennium, therefore, will commence at the end of the period of six thousand years since the creation.

Although mainstream Christian churches look for the second coming of Christ, in most cases this is not a belief which actively influences the lives of rank-and-file members as a lively expectation that the world is about to come to an end literally at any moment. It does however play that role for Jehovah's Witnesses, Christadelphians and Seventh-day Adventists. These movements are fired by a sense of urgency: we are all living at the end of time, in the last days. Their perspective on history is drastically compressed: nothing significant happened between New Testament times and their own foundation. Although they see themselves as the bearers of eternal truth they are not oriented to tradition; their focus is, rather, on the present and the immediate future (Wilson 1981).

In conventional theological treatments, Christian millenarian movements are divided into two basic types. The post-millennialists believe that the millennium is a period during which righteousness will spread progressively throughout the world, preparing the way for Christ's second coming at the end of the millennium. The pre-millennialists believe that the second coming of Christ will be a time of the Great Tribulation, often involving a battle (the War of Armageddon) between the forces of good and evil. Only after the final defeat of evil will the millennium commence. Among pre-millennialist groups there is disagreement about what will happen to righteous people during the tribulation: will they be rescued, or will they have to endure it?

The theological distinction between pre- and post-millennialism, tied as it is to specifically Christian thought and practice, is not well suited to sociological analysis of religious movements more generally. For sociologists, Wessinger (1997) has argued, a more productive distinction is between progressive millenarianism and catastrophic millenarianism. The progressive millenarians believe, optimistically, that collective salvation on earth will be achieved by humans working in accordance with the divine or transcendent plan. For example, some groups believe in a peaceful transition from the troubled Age of Pisces to the Age of Aquarius, a period of harmony and understanding. The catastrophic millenarians believe, pessimistically, that evil is so deeply entrenched in the present world order that only an impending catastrophe can destroy it.

The propensity for violent destructive acts is at its greatest among catastrophic millenarian movements.

The religious movement as agent of the apocalypse

Jehovah's Witnesses, Christadelphians and Seventh-day Adventists are all catastrophic millenarian movements. The second advent of Christ is a dominant article of faith which shapes members' lives. For example, it is because these are 'the last days' before the War of Armageddon that Jehovah's Witnesses are motivated to go out on their door-to-door ministry, offering people a chance to come into the truth before it is too late. Hundreds of thousands of ordinary Jehovah's Witnesses do this every week, despite the predictably contemptuous insults they incur.

This does not mean, though, that Witnesses, Christadelphians and Seventh-day Adventists are likely to engage in acts of violence against themselves or others. These are movements which, having survived for over a century, have become rationalized and routinized, adopting longer-term strategies for self-perpetuation including the socialization of their own children. In Wilson's (1970, 1975) terminology they are not revolutionaries but *revolutionists*. It is not they but God who will act to bring an end to the evil world order. Until God chooses to do so, the task of the faithful is to obey his commandments, be law-abiding (render unto Caesar the things that are Caesar's), bring up their children in righteousness, and spread the good news to those in the world who will listen to it. Although they play a crucial role in God's plan, the success of the plan does not depend on them.

The situation is radically different when a movement comes to see itself as an agent of the apocalypse, actively bringing it about for themselves or others.

Exemplary dualism

Anthony and Robbins (1997) argue that destructive religious movements are characterized by exemplary dualism. By this they mean that the movement divides the world and the people and organizations in it into two mutually exclusive and warring entities, good versus evil, Christ versus Antichrist, the Israelites versus Babylon. There are no shades of grey and no compromises. The religious movement and its leaders are idealized, while conversely its alleged enemies are demonized. Exemplary dualism is not a philosophical abstraction but a principle actively shaping members' lives and the policies and actions of the movement toward the wider society.

The charismatic leader

Movements with an exemplary dualist orientation are potentially volatile – even more so when they have a charismatic leader who sees himself as a saviour or messiah (for, although women have played leadership roles in many movements, the leaders of destructive movements have invariably been men) (Anthony and Robbins 1997: 276). Charismatic leadership is inherently less stable than systems of authority based either on tradition or on legal-rationality. Charismatic leadership is legitimized by the extraordinary qualities either claimed by the leader or attributed by the followers to him or her. This can be a licence for antinomianism (exemption from external moral restraint – literally anything goes), allowing the charismatic leader to indulge in sexual, financial or violent excess.

Despite this apparent freedom the charismatic leader lacks institutional support: if the followers lose faith the leader's authority simply evaporates. The possibility of defection and betrayal is therefore inherent in charismatically led movements. Paradoxically, a charismatic leader can come to feel trapped by his or her own followers, who may demand miracles or worldly success which the leader simply cannot deliver or regards as irrelevant to the mission. When Muhammad was asked for miracles to prove that he was the Prophet, he reportedly referred to the Qur'an as miracle enough.

As Weber said, a charismatically led movement will survive only if its members fare well. At Jonestown, the pioneering agricultural project ran into a number of difficulties and was clearly struggling. The stresses on the leader will be compounded if he or she is in declining physical or mental health (Robbins and Palmer 1997: 21). This appears to have been the case with Shoko Asahara, Jim Jones, Marshall Applewhite, Joseph DiMambro (whose cancer Luc Jouret was unable to cure) and David Koresh (who was painfully shot during the first gun battle at Waco).

The small encapsulated community

The destructive movements under consideration here involved an encapsulated community of believers who had cut themselves off from contact with friends and family. Core members had become highly dependent on the movement not just for sustenance but for their very sense of reality. They were also members of a small, face-to-face community, a *Gemeinschaft*, in which the charismatic leader was able to exercise close personal control over his disciples.

An external threat

The expectation of persecution is a time-honoured mechanism for reinforcing social cohesion in religious movements. That fact of persecution is regularly held up to members as a sign that they have the truth. It fits well with exemplary dualist views of the world.

The threat may not be real, but it is enough that it is perceived. Luc Jouret was threatened with an inquiry into firearms offences, as was David Koresh. Aum Shinrikyo, which is accused of perpetrating the Tokyo sarin gas atrocity, counter-attacked by accusing the state of using nerve gas against the movement. Jim Jones was under growing pressure from allegations of a wide range of scandalous and illegal activities; the visit from Congressman Ryan, with its invitation to defect, was the final catalyst for the community to implode.

Given the critical role played by external intervention in a group's activities, there is always a danger that the authorities will unwittingly play their part in an apocalyptic doomsday script. Since Jonestown, the most vivid illustration of this has been at Waco. The initial assault on the Mount Carmel community met unexpected armed resistance leading to injuries and deaths on both sides. During the ensuing siege, there were lengthy negotiations between the authorities and the Branch Davidians. To the authorities, Koresh was a charlatan and a fanatic, a trader in illegal firearms and probably a sexual abuser of children. Koresh meanwhile was grappling with the theological exegesis of the Book of Revelation. It is worth noting that although the movement became widely known as the Branch Davidians the members normally called themselves Students of the Seven Seals. This did not refer, as some among the FBI were reputed to have thought, to aquatic mammals. It was a reference to Revelation, chapter 5:

> And I saw in the right hand of him that sat on the throne a book written within and on the backside sealed with seven seals. And I saw a strong angel proclaiming with a loud voice, Who is worthy to open the book, and to loose the seals thereof? And no man in heaven, nor in earth, neither under the earth, was able to open the book, neither to look thereon. And I wept much, because no man was found worthy to open and to read the book, neither to look thereon. And one of the elders saith unto me, Weep not: behold, the Lion of the tribe of Judah, the Root of David, hath prevailed to open the book, and to loose the seven seals thereof.

A few days before the siege ended in the catastrophic fire, Koresh received a revelation from God that he should write a description of the seven seals and then surrender with his followers to the FBI. Koresh's unfinished text was carried out of the compound on floppy disc by one of the few survivors. To the authorities, Koresh had been simply engaging in a delaying tactic. And from the standpoint of New Testament scholarship, Koresh's exegesis is worthless. It was none the less serious to him. Wrestling with the mystery of the seven seals was not a crude bargaining chip, but what his movement was all about.

9

Religious Identity and Meaning in the Modern World

One truth about the modern world is, as Beckford (1989: 169) remarks, deceptively simple: 'we no longer live in industrial societies of the kind depicted by the founding generation of Western sociologists.' Recognition of this undeniable fact has given rise to a ferment of theoretical reassessment and reorientation within sociology. Major new themes have emerged as sites of sociological interest: detraditionalization, globalization, risk society, postmodernity. This ferment has begun to make itself felt within the field of sociology of religion (Heelas 1998; Hoover and Lundby 1997; Flanagan and Jupp 1996). Whether or not we call the new situation 'postmodern', there are good grounds for reassessing the place of religion in the world.

The contemporary world is often portrayed as an unsettling place. It gives rise to what Giddens (1991: 181–208) calls 'tribulations of the self', existential dilemmas which confront us all. One of these is the choice between authority and uncertainty. In a detraditionalized culture there are no final authorities. Radical doubt is always with us, insinuating itself into every corner of the life-world. Fundamentalism, so called, is a possible haven, though a precarious one. Pursuing a theme developed by Berger, Giddens argues that reflexivity affects even fundamentalism: it is hard to escape the uneasy acknowledgement that fundamentalism is itself a cultural choice from a range of options. Fundamentalism's strident denunciation of its opponents is a sign of its weakness. For Giddens, as for Berger, dogmatic authoritarianism is a pathological mutation of faith.

The opposite pole to fundamentalism is radical doubt. The danger here is that doubt can collapse into paranoia and a complete paralysis of the will. The healthy individual has the task of navigating between dogmatic authoritarianism and *accidie*. Underlying all the tribulations of the self is the threat of meaninglessness produced by 'a technically competent but morally arid social environment' (Giddens 1991: 201) – an obvious echo of Weber. Death, as Berger insisted, is the ultimate test of meaning (Mellor and Shilling 1993). Death is sequestered: hidden from view in hospitals and hospices, an individual event with an individual cause, and reduced to a technical concern of the medical profession. If contemporary life is a project of the self, it is a project that is never completed, because death brings it to a definitive close. Since salvation cannot be achieved through aerobics or a Mediterranean diet, there may be scope for religion in Giddens's high modernity.

In this chapter, the condition of contemporary religion is examined by focusing on four issues: consumerism, challenges to religious authority, sex and gender, and New Age religion. Each of these can be interpreted as corrosive of religion; conversely, they can be seen as challenges which will lead to religious renewal and the re-sacralization of society.

Religion and the consumer

In contemporary societies, as Davie remarks (1994: 39–41), the relationship between consumerism and religion is profoundly ambivalent. On the one hand, consumerism and religion are often held to be incompatible. Bocock, for example (1993: 50), defines consumerism as 'the active ideology that the meaning of life is to be found in buying things and prepackaged experiences'. Consumerism is an ideology which locates meaning not in things held sacred but in the profane pursuit of self-gratification. It is calculative, self-seeking and materialistic – the polar opposite of religion, which is moral, altruistic and spiritual. The consumer and the Almighty cannot both be sovereign. As Heelas (1994: 102) succinctly puts it, 'Religion would appear to be the very last thing that can be consumed.'

Bocock concludes his book with an attack on unbridled consumerism, which he sees as threatening ecological catastrophe. Both consumption-oriented capitalism and the military-industrial complexes of the former communist societies have exploited the natural world unsustainably. Lust for economic growth is now gripping the Third World. Even so, the world's great religions remain capable of expressing the values and spiritual life of common humanity – something which intellectuals' atheistic positivism has failed to do. Bocock therefore calls upon atheists and agnostics to abandon their futile preoccupation with critiques of religion. Instead, they are urged to join religiously inspired conservationists in a rainbow alliance to defend the planet against despoliation by consumerism, 'the main ideology of the future' (Bocock 1993: 119).

Critiques of consumerism and consumer values have been recurrent in European commentaries on religion in the United States. A powerful expression can be found in Wilson's *Religion in Secular Society* (1966). Wilson considers the case of the United States, which appears to be a counter-example to secularization, in that religious institutions are flourishing, the vast majority of citizens confess a belief in God, and national culture is characterized by an overtly Judaeo-Christian civil religion. Even so, Wilson argues, American religiosity is 'secularized from within'.

As evidence of consumerism Wilson cites a statement supposedly made by President Eisenhower, that everyone should have a faith but it did not matter which. Wilson also refers to the case of President Lyndon Johnson, a Disciple, and Lady Bird Johnson, an Episcopalian, who were not troubled by their daughter's conversion to Catholicism since they regarded religion as a private matter. This, says Wilson (1966: 117), is an American value, not a Christian one; it has 'no respectability of pedigree in Christianity'. Americans are offered 'the religion of your choice' – a choice, that is, merely between different brands of a virtually identical and rather bland commodity. As for new religious movements, Wilson's judgement is that they exemplify 'the highly privatized preference that reduces religion to the significance of pushpin, poetry, or popcorn' (Wilson 1976: 96).

In contrast to these critiques, consumerism can be presented as a support to the sacred realm. What excuse do religious movements have for not marketing their services efficiently? Why should they not identify and respond to the demands of their clients? Effective evangelism surely requires them to do so? Voluntary associations – the sects, denominations and cults of an earlier generation of sociological theorizing – have always had to promote themselves. The vigour of religion in America testifies to the market mechanism as guarantor of consumer satisfaction. Perhaps it is time for the indolent state-subsidized churches of Europe to compete in the spiritual market-place? For example, as Bruce (1996: 132) points out, a Church of England vicar in the nineteenth century had little financial incentive to recruit a congregation. His income was dependent not on his flock but on the rental value of church land acquired over the centuries. He and they were literally living off the past. His career prospects were determined not by his popularity with his congregation but by the patronage of social superiors who had church appointments in their gift. Preferment, not popularity, was the key to career advancement. It was not a situation designed to spur him to be customer-oriented.

These diametrically opposed views are typical of debates about consumerism. Slater (1997: 13) refers to consumerism's 'double face'. On the one hand it may be culturally disruptive, unleashing insatiable appetites while sanctioning social permissiveness – as in Durkheim's vision of anomic disorder. Conversely, it may produce private contentment and thus contribute positively to social integration – as in neo-liberal celebrations of the triumph of the market system over the command economies of so-called actually existing socialism.

Consumers, too, have a double identity in contemporary social thought. Negatively, the consumer is a cultural dupe or dope: taken in by the tricks of the advertising industry, a victim of every passing fashion, a shallow status-seeker. In religion, the consumer as dupe is represented by the brainwashed zombies of anti-cult theory, and the stereotypically credulous clients of irrational New Age beliefs and practices. Positively, the consumer is a hero: a rational and autonomous individual on whose self-defined needs the legitimacy of social institutions is built (Slater 1997: 33) – as in theories of 'the new voluntarism'. Ethnographic work on shopping has shown that far from being self-indulgent it is a labour of love. It is women's work directed at the welfare of other members of the household (Miller 1998). The very fact that it is socially constructed as women's work is a reason why it is persistently misunderstood and devalued. Despite the mythology, shopping is not selfish but altruistic. It is not the epitome of hedonistic ungodliness, but a devotional ritual serving the cult of domesticity.

Slater (1997: 24–32) identifies seven key themes in sociological theorizing about consumer culture. Each theme has a negative and a positive polarity.

A culture of consumption   The implication is that consumption determines the core values of society. Consumer culture may be characterized negatively as hedonism and narcissism (the culture of the masses) or positively as choice and autonomy (the culture of empowered citizens).

The culture of market societies   The market is the mechanism for supplying consumers with goods and services in the form of commodities produced specifically for exchange in the market. In Marxist terms this is the capitalist culture of the cash nexus, alienated labour and commodity fetishism. Religion functions in the capitalist system as an opiate to deaden the pain of the masses. For Adam Smith, in contrast, the ascendancy of the market swept away political and religious regulation of consumption. It brought an end to medieval Europe's sumptuary laws: codified prescriptions and proscriptions on consumption – of food, drink, clothing, gambling, hunting – according to the individual's status in a divinely ordained hierarchy stretching from the monarch down to servants and common labourers.

A universal and impersonal culture   Consumer culture implies mass production and mass consumption, in which goods and services are produced for national and now increasingly global markets. The consumer is not a known client but an anonymous impersonal object, the target of advertising and marketing campaigns. Negatively, this is dehumanizing, reducing humans to objects; positively, it is liberation from oppressive social control.

Freedom as private choice   The consumer is free to make choices without being accountable to the authorities for how his or her money is spent. Positively, the private sphere is an arena of freedom from interference, a realm of the 'sovereign consumer' whose demands are an engine of the economy and the foundation of the legitimacy of the political order. Negatively, the private sphere is both constricted and stripped of public significance. Citizens have shrunk to the diminished status of mere consumers, whose trivial and manipulated tastes in consumption are their sole exercise of an illusory liberty.

Consumer needs as unlimited and insatiable   Commodity production depends upon the continual stimulation of consumer demand. Positively, this can represent the good society: comfortable, affluent, leisured. However, as Slater points out, in most cultures and in all the great religions the possibility of insatiable desires has been seen as socially and morally pathological. This finds its reflection in sociological thought. Thus, for Durkheim, the breakdown of normative constraints on individual desire is a social pathology unleashed in transitional periods of rapid social change. For Marx, the system is unsustainable – as predicted in his theory of the falling rate of profit.

Identity and status in post-traditional society   According to theories of post-traditional society, it is increasingly for each individual to construct her or his own social identity. People no longer have an immutable position in a fixed status order. Not only is social mobility a reality, but the status order itself is fluid and constantly changing. Our patterns of consumption are not constrained by sumptuary laws – relics of feudalism which were swept away by the rise of commercialism and market exchange. Social class, the bedrock of identity in industrial society, has diminishing significance for an individual's lifestyle and sense of identity. The decline of heavy industry has brought with it the disappearance of tight-knit occupational communities. The purchase and display of consumer goods play an ever more important role in the social construction and negotiation of identity. Again, there are varying interpretations. On the one hand, some commentators lament the decline of community entailed by detraditionalization, and diagnose a growing rootlessness of contemporary culture. In this perspective, secularization equates to a multiple loss of meaning: loss of historical continuity, of a sense of place and of community. Conversely, detraditionalization can be interpreted as a gain in democratic freedoms for the mass of ordinary citizens.

Culture and the exercise of power   On the one hand, as outlined above, consumption is the supreme site of individual liberty and autonomy. It is also an aesthetic realm, in which people artistically create their own style of life, fashioning their identity according to their own taste rather than the dictates of others. As consumers we are relatively free from social constraint. Against this, consumers are the targets of powerful multinational corporations shaping consumer demand and largely unaccountable to the elected governments of nation states. A few trivial aesthetic choices, made from a range predetermined by these corporations, hardly constitutes the Enlightenment ideal of freedom.

The seven themes which Slater distinguishes are closely related to one another. Underlying them is a dialectic between freedom and constraint, and at the theoretical level between free will and determinism, agency and structure. Given this, it is unsurprising that many of the contemporary debates about religion are also debates about consumer culture.

Consumerism repudiated: the Prayer Book Society

In 1980, the Church of England published the first edition of the Alternative Service Book (ASB). The ASB, as its title implied, was put forward as an alternative in modern English to the traditional services of the 1662 Book of Common Prayer, which until then had been the sole official service book of the Church of England. The Book of Common Prayer had been first published in 1549. It was conceived by Thomas Cranmer, Archbishop of Canterbury, as a convenient, comprehensive and authoritative compendium of services in English. Cranmer later became a Protestant martyr, burned at the stake for heresy in 1556 during the reign of Mary Tudor.

The launch of the ASB provoked a wide-ranging controversy (Aldridge 1986). In anticipation of the trouble to come, the Prayer Book Society had been founded in 1975 with the aim of upholding 'the worship and doctrine of the Church of England as enshrined in the Book of Common Prayer', ensuring that it remained 'a major element in the worshipping life of the Church of England'. The Prayer Book Society developed into a well-organized and effective pressure group. From the outset, however, it was trying to hold together two incompatible strands in its campaign for the defence of the Book of Common Prayer.

One strand was consumerist. The argument was that the ASB was supposed to be just that: an alternative, not a substitute for Cranmer's original. In this spirit, the Prayer Book Society supported a Bill in Parliament which would have enabled churchgoers in any Anglican parish to ensure that the Book of Common Prayer would be used at least once a month for the main Sunday service. The proposal put before Parliament was justified as guaranteeing that churchgoers would have the Prayer Book available to them – an argument from fair competition and consumer choice. The Prayer Book Society claimed therefore to be acting as the legitimate mouthpiece of the consumer. Church leaders, including the Archbishops of Canterbury and York, were quite happy to support this aspect of the campaign.

The second – and dominant – strand was anti-consumerist. The introduction of the ASB was held to be entirely unnecessary. Cranmer's original text was, contrary to its detractors, easy to understand, and the few problems its majestic English presented were an occasion for theological reflection and debate, not bewildered incomprehension. The ASB was ridiculed for its clumsy, unevocative, prosaic English. Not just the language but the theology it conveyed was a feeble watered-down version of Cranmer's robust original. The ASB was what economists call an 'inferior good': nobody would buy it unless forced to do so through lack of a viable alter-native. Clergy and the church's bureaucracy were the only enthusiasts for the ASB, which they were forcing on an unwilling public.

In its dominant anti-consumerist mode the Prayer Book Society's campaign had several interlinked features worthy of sociological attention.

Defence of legitimate taste   As well as the 1662 Book of Common Prayer, the Prayer Book Society's campaign also included a defence of the Authorized Version (the King James Bible) and the musical settings traditionally used in Anglican services. New translations of the Bible and modern church music were criticized on aesthetic grounds. Here, then, was a campaign in support of high culture or, in Bourdieu's terms, 'legitimate taste' (Bourdieu 1984).

Intellectuals speaking for the people   The Prayer Book Society's campaign was an alliance of intellectuals claiming to speak for the people of England. This alliance included people who were not Anglicans, churchgoers, or even professed Christians. Scholars, politicians, actors, novelists, poets, high court judges, composers, musicians: this elite stratum was invited to sign petitions to parliament and to the church. Far from being a weakness, the constituency's breadth was presented as testifying to the depth of feeling in the nation about the issues at stake in liturgical reform. A cultural elite professed to be speaking for the silent majority.

Appeal to organic community According to the Prayer Book Society, one of Cranmer's great achievements was to produce a book of *common* prayer. The Alternative Service Book, with its extensive menu of options, was by contrast an agent of cultural fragmentation. Each local congregation was free to choose its own pattern of worship customized to its own taste. The result, so the critics alleged, was an inward-turned pseudo-community of like-minded individuals engaged in shallow, clerically orchestrated conviviality (Martin and Mullen 1981: 12). A national church with a parish system rooted in genuine organic communities was at risk. The church was being subverted by sectarianism.

The Prayer Book Society's campaign was far more than a domestic quarrel about liturgical details. It was a public defence of high culture, legitimate taste and organic community. Hence the bitterness of the debate. Liturgical change provoked a similar reaction to other cultural innovations such as proposals for spelling reform, revision of the school curriculum and restructuring of public service broadcasting. A characteristic feature of these debates is the impassioned accusation that people who should be upholding high cultural standards are betraying them – a *trahison des clercs*. The Church of England was reminded of its special responsibility as the established church to defend national identity by ensuring that national culture is passed on to succeeding generations as their inalienable birthright. In this sense, the church was called upon to act as an English counterpart to the Académie Française, and the religious equivalent of the Royal Shakespeare Company, the Council for the Protection of Rural England and the Campaign for Real Ale. The Prayer Book Society's mission was not to uphold consumerism – consumers can display vulgar tastes – but to defend England's cultural patrimony.

Consumerism embraced: Soka Gakkai International

Soka Gakkai – Value Creation Society – is a lay religious movement within Nichiren Buddhism, a branch of Mahayana Buddhism derived from the teachings of the thirteenth-century Japanese monk, Nichiren Daishonin. Mahayana (the 'greater vehicle') is the branch of Buddhism which spread from India to China, Japan, Korea, Nepal and Tibet. Mahayana compared itself favourably to what it called Hinayana – the 'lesser vehicle', represented in the modern world by Theravada Buddhism ('the doctrine of the elders'), which prevails in Sri Lanka and South-East Asia. From the perspective of the Mahayana tradition, Hinayana involved a rigorous set of ascetic disciplines that could be practised only by living as a Buddhist monk, a life suited exclusively to religious virtuosi. Mahayana offers a more inclusive and immediate prospect of salvation to everybody. It was Mahayana which influenced the counterculture of the 1960s. A key role in Mahayana thought and spirituality is played by the *Bodhisattvas*: saintly figures who, though on the brink of enlightenment, deliberately postpone their own attainment of nirvana in order to help other people to salvation. Bodhisattvas are revered in popular devotion as exemplars of compassion. They stand as a symbol to humans of the principle of altruism: people who are more spiritually advanced should assist others who are less so.

Nichiren taught that the essence of Buddhism is captured in the *Lotus Sutra*, held to be the last discourse of Shakyamuni (Gautama Buddha). The Lotus Sutra teaches that enlightenment can be attained by anyone, regardless of their social standing – whether based on caste, class, 'race', education or gender. In Nichiren Buddhism, salvation requires devotees to chant the pregnant mantra *Nam-myoho-renge-kyo*, an adoration of the Lotus Sutra which Barker (1995: 193) unpacks as: 'I devote myself to the inexpressibly profound and wonderful truth – the law of life – expounded in the Lotus Sutra, which embodies the loftiest teachings of Buddhism.' Devotions involve chanting the mantra twice a day in front of the *Gohonzon*, a sacred scroll inscribed with Chinese and Sanskrit characters, the names of the Buddhas and a summary of the law of enlightenment. As with the sacraments in some Christian traditions, chanting is held to have objective effects even if the individual is ignorant of the meaning of the mantra. In revolutionizing the individual's inner spiritual life, these dev-otions are held to lead on to a growing concern with the well-being of other people.

Soka Gakkai has enjoyed rapid growth since its foundation in Japan in the 1930s, and now claims to have over twenty million adherents (Barker 1995: 193). It has attracted favourable publicity through its sponsorship of education and the arts, its ecological concerns and its commitment to world peace. Daisaku Ikeda, who founded Soka Gakkai International (SGI) in 1975, was awarded the United Nations peace medal in 1983. The movement has nevertheless attracted controversy (Wilson and Dobbelaere 1994: 10–12; Barker 1995: 194–5), particularly in the United States and in Japan itself. Soka Gakkai's proselytizing can be very vigorous. In Japan, it has involved an uncompromising approach to conversion known as *shakubuku* – 'break and subdue' – designed, as prescribed by Nichiren himself, to combat and delegitimize all other traditions of Buddhism. Soka Gakkai's critics focus on what they see as its intolerance, and on its overt engagement in Japanese politics.

In Wilson and Dobbelaere's analysis, Soka Gakkai has succeeded, on their evidence from the UK, in expressing the values and lifestyles of contemporary consumerism. Consumer culture reflects a consumer economy: 'The development of *laissez-faire* economics inevitably brought in its wake a *laissez-faire* morality' (1994: 218). This morality is antithetical to asceticism. In place of the character virtues of the Protestant ethic, consumerism celebrates 'hedonism, self-indulgence, and the unending pursuit of pleasure' (1994: 219).

Soka Gakkai's system of beliefs and practices is congruent with the hedonistic ethos of consumerism. It does not impose on its adherents an exacting set of disciplines and commandments. The standards of personal conduct demanded by the Protestant ethic are displaced by a political morality emphasizing world peace, the environment, the plight of refugees, and educational and cultural programmes. Virtue gives way to values. Soka Gakkai endorses individual choice and responsibility, and personal happiness and self-fulfilment, combining these with a range of politicized causes which appeal to the idealism of young people in particular.

Soka Gakkai presents itself as thoroughly compatible with a scientific outlook – more so, indeed, than Christianity ever could be. Science operates less with personal agency than with the impersonal functioning of systems governed by mathematical and statistical principles. An anthropomorphic 'God of the Gaps', called upon only when scientific explanation fails, has diminishing credibility, as do nature-defying miracles performed (or faked) by charismatic leaders. The gradual decline of belief in a personal deity has been matched by an increasing acceptability of belief in an impersonal life force or spirit.

The affinity between science and consumerism is many-sided. Consumerism depends not only on the technological development of consumer goods, but also on scientific management of production and social scientific principles of marketing. Consumers, as Giddens (1991) has argued, are obliged to place their trust not so much in individuals as in abstract expert systems. The licence granted to the professional guardians of expert systems depends not on their location in a traditional hierarchy of status – as with the clergy before the Industrial Revolution – but on expertise grounded in abstract theoretical knowledge. Consumer organizations espouse the values of the Enlightenment, undertaking on behalf of consumers comparative scientific analysis of goods and services and statistically controlled surveys of customer satisfaction (Aldridge 1994).

Whereas the anti-consumerist campaign to defend the Book of Common Prayer appealed to aesthetic criteria, consumer-friendly movements such as Soka Gakkai stress their compatibility with science. An affinity with the scientific world-view is one key facet of Soka Gakkai's congruence with contemporary consumerism. Add to this its successful mobilization of resources for proselytizing, and its rapid growth is unsurprising. It has succeeded in presenting an ancient faith in a modern mode. In Wilson and Dobbelaere's conclusion (1994: 231): 'Well may dedicated members affirm that SGI is a faith whose time has come – a time to chant.'

Authority and individualism: the Roman Catholic Church

One feature of churches is their remarkable internal diversity. This can be both a strength and a weakness. It enables them to embrace a wide range of different orientations to faith and practice, so that people can find a outlet for their various dispositions and talents. Conversely, it raises problems of internal cohesion. No church displays these tensions more sharply than the Roman Catholic.

Hornsby-Smith's studies of Roman Catholicism in England document a profound change since the Second Vatican Council, which sat from 1962 to 1965. Until around that time, Catholicism had constructed itself as a distinctive subculture with a defensive outlook, fearful of incorporation into the wider culture. 'Fortress Rome' was a common way of characterizing this subculture. Roman Catholics in England were socialized to see themselves as set apart from other people by their distinctive beliefs and practices – a view of the world depicted in the novels of Graham Greene and Evelyn Waugh.

This Catholic subculture was marked by deference to authority. It was not nationalistic but ultramontane, looking 'beyond the mountains' to Rome. At the apex of the church hierarchy stood the Roman curia and the Holy Father himself, whose formal pronouncements on matters of faith and morals had been declared infallible by the First Vatican Council of 1869–70. Although not infallible themselves, priests wielded considerable authority over the laity and generally expected to be obeyed. Democratic participation was not on their agenda.

Theological and doctrinal consistency had been secured during the papacy of Leo XIII at the end of the nineteenth century. He encouraged the revival of Thomism, the theology of St Thomas Aquinas, the 'Angelic Doctor' of the thirteenth century. Aquinas's teachings were certainly not irrationalist, since he held that faith is not contrary to reason. He taught, however, that reason is subordinate to faith, and philosophy to theology. This has a political implication: civil authority is subject to the church (McSweeney 1980: 67–74). Although human reason – the province of natural theology – enables us to arrive at fundamental truths about the world such as the existence of God, we can attain the fullness of the faith only through divine revelation, of which the church and its priesthood are the authoritative interpreters. In wake of Leo XIII's reforms, theologians who departed from Thomist orthodoxy were purged from Catholic seminaries and universities.

Aspects of the everyday lives of the Catholic faithful reinforced the maintenance of a defensive subculture. A clear illustration of this is provided by attitudes to 'mixed marriages' (Hornsby-Smith 1987: 98–108). Roman Catholics were discouraged from marrying outside the faith, and this included Protestants. To do so was likely to provoke social disapproval and even ostracism by relatives. The non-Roman Catholic partner was usually required to state in writing that their children would be baptized as Catholics and brought up in the Catholic faith. The Catholic partner was expected to strive to convert the other. If the couple opted to have the marriage service in a Catholic church, they would typically be offered a basic, stripped-down version of the ritual – without music or flowers, for example. Since the Second Vatican Council, these restrictions have been gradually relaxed in practice as well as in theory.

Another key symbol of Catholic identity was the Tridentine mass, named after the Council of Trent (1545–63) which consolidated the Counter-Reformation against Protestantism. The Tridentine mass was a miracle performed by the priest for the people. The priest faced away from the congregation towards the high altar, and murmured the canon of the mass (the prayer of consecration) in so hushed a tone that people often could not hear what was being said. The language they could not hear was Latin. Throughout four centuries, this was the style of worship of the Catholic church worldwide. To its Protestant and rationalist detractors it represented the quintessence of obscurantist mumbo-jumbo – for what else could inaudible mutterings in a dead language possibly be? The answer, from its advocates, was that it conveyed a sense of mystery, of the numinous, of the presence of God and the sanctity of the universal church.

The Second Vatican Council (Vatican II) swept all this away. The mass is now performed in the vernacular. The altar is brought closer to the congregation, the priest faces them and speaks up so that they can all hear. This is no longer a miracle performed for a public of passive spectators; it is a collective act of worship in which all the 'people of God' participate.

These liturgical reforms unleashed controversy, as in the Church of England. The two cases were very different, however. The Church of England retained the Book of Common Prayer as an option, whereas the Roman Catholic Church in effect abandoned the Latin mass. In Anglicanism, a cross-section of the cultured elite rallied to the defence of a nation's patrimony. In the Catholic case, traditionalism was cast as obdurate resistance to change, a benighted refusal of *aggiornamento*. The starkest expression of this was in France, where supporters of Monseigneur Marcel Lefebvre declared their rejection of the spirit and content of Vatican II. In France, ultra-traditional Catholicism is linked to neo-fascist groups whose anti-Semitism has expanded to include hostility to France's Muslim population. In other countries, traditionalism does not carry quite the same ideological freight, even though it does involve an authoritarian opposition to individualism and permissiveness. Traditionalists despair of the abandonment of a deposit of faith and practice which, so they had been taught, was universal and invariant. In this perspective, the Second Vatican Council has changed the unchangeable.

Catholic teaching on abortion and birth control was one area left largely untouched by the reforms of Vatican II. In 1968, to the dismay of the modernizers, Pope Paul VI issued the encyclical on human life, *Humanae Vitae*. Abortion and all forms of artificial birth control were condemned, a position uncompromisingly reaffirmed under the pontificate of John Paul II.

On Hornsby-Smith's evidence, fewer and fewer Catholics in England feel compelled to observe the disciplines of the 'rhythm method' of birth control. Perhaps this shows the truth of Iannaccone's observations on contemporary Catholicism. He speculated that in the United States – and the point could surely be generalized to western Europe at least – the Catholic church has landed itself in the worst of all worlds. It has abandoned that which should have been retained (for example, the Latin mass), while retaining that which should have been abandoned (the ban on contraception and abortion, and the rule of priestly celibacy). It has adopted the fatal combination of general laxity and misplaced strictness.

Hornsby-Smith's research shows that, in England, a relatively unified Catholic subculture has dissolved. Catholics now draw distinctions between different elements of the faith. They continue to hold the basic creedal beliefs, while being less committed to matters of faith which are not in the creeds. The priesthood is still respected, but not as a body of men who can command unquestioning obedience to an unchanging faith. The fear of hellfire and damnation has declined. Catholic laypeople claim the right to follow their own conscience on questions of personal morality. They feel less bound by the church's disciplinary rules on attendance at mass, frequency of confession and intermarriage. A church which was once 'strongly rule-bound and guilt-ridden' (Hornsby-Smith 1992: 131) is no longer so. Official Catholicism has evolved into what he calls 'customary Catholicism': beliefs and practices which, while derived from the church's teaching, are filtered through personal interpretations that have ceased to be under clerical control. Individualism and consumerism are inescapable elements in customary Catholicism.

Alongside *Humanae Vitae*'s pronouncements on reproductive technology and sexual morality, the other major symbol of Catholic resistance to modernity is its refusal to allow women to be priests. Issues of sex and gender have become key boundary-defining issues for Catholic subculture as it seeks to differentiate itself from the wider culture. In the past, other issues served the same function. The *Syllabus of Errors* promulgated by Pope Pius IX in 1864 was preoccupied with church–state relations, and the need to subordinate the latter to the former. By the beginning of the twentieth century, the attention of the Catholic hierarchy had switched to an attack on 'liberalism'. This involved repudiating relativistic 'higher biblical criticism' and, most importantly, the theory of evolution of the species. These issues have lost most of their salience for the Catholic church today, but sex and gender persist as critical symbols of Catholic culture.

Chaves (1997) argues that in the United States there are two belief-systems which legitimize resistance to women priests. One is Protestant fundamentalism, the other Catholic sacramentalism. What they have in common, for all their differences, is the claim to a transcendental point of reference, valid for all times and places, which cannot be subject to secular influence. In the one case, this is an inerrant Bible, in the other, the sacraments. Only a transcendental appeal to an unchanging source of authority can justify the exclusion of women – and even this is under challenge. A few intellectuals, fearing that the Roman Catholic Church will go the way of the Anglican communion and open the priesthood to women, are beginning to look to the Orthodox churches as the only reliable bulwark against the modern world.

Religion, sex and gender

A feature of religions, obvious yet insufficiently studied, is their central concern with sex and gender. Among the classical sociologists only Max Weber (1965: 236–42) was fully alert to the significance of the erotic. He argued that hostility toward sexuality is an essential feature of religion. It is not confined to Christianity, but present in all the great religions of the world. This is because sexuality is the strongest irrational force in human life. Religions are bound to seek to control it. In particular, they aim to tie sexual expression to reproduction. Non-procreative sexual acts are strongly discouraged in Roman Catholicism, and regarded by most Muslims and conservatively minded Jews as forbidden. Hence the abhorrence of homosexuality found in most religions, the Roman Catholic opposition to artificial methods of birth control and the Hebrew Scriptures' curse on the sin of Onan – which was in fact *coitus interruptus*, not masturbation as commonly thought.

Religious control of sexuality takes many forms, ranging from ascetic renunciation, as in vows of celibacy made by religious virtuosi, through strictly confining sexuality to reproduction in the monogamous marriage, to the apparently unbridled but actually carefully controlled and ritualized sexual expression found among the Rajneeshees.

Women's sexuality is typically presented as a threat to men. As McGuire (1992: 115) puts it, in creation myths 'women's presumed characteristics of sexual allure, curiosity, gullibility, and insatiable desires are often blamed for both the problems of humankind and for women's inferior role'. So in the Jewish and Christian traditions it is Eve's seductive influence which leads Adam to disobey God's command not to eat the apple from the tree of knowledge. Evil temptresses are counterbalanced by women of supreme virtue, such the Virgin Mary. Arguably, the former should not and the latter cannot be imitated as role-models.

Gender-blind religion? Quakers, Unitarians and Baha'is

Very few religions or religious movements would even profess to treat women and men equally. Fewer still would aspire to the reversal of traditional gender roles accomplished by the Brahma Kumaris (Barker 1995: 168–70) – Kumari means unmarried woman. Their founder was the wealthy diamond merchant Dada Lekh Raj, known to his followers as Brahma Baba. After a series of revelations, he set up a Managing Committee of eight young women in 1937 and handed over all his assets to a trust administered by them. Most of the positions of authority within the movement are held by women.

Exceptional cases for whom a claim of gender equality might appear plausible are the Religious Society of Friends (Quakers), the Unitarians (and the Universalists, with whom they have in effect merged) and the Baha'is. Other possible cases might be Christian Science, the Salvation Army and some spiritualist movements.

Quakers and Unitarians have a good deal in common, including their commitment to equality of men and women (Punshon 1984; Chryssides 1998). In Wilson's terms they are *reformist* movements. They encourage people to act out their faith through participating with others in movements for social reform such as the Campaign for Nuclear Disarmament, Amnesty International and environmental campaigns. Most members count themselves pacifists. Quakers and Unitarians are opposed to creeds and dogma, leaving it to the conscience and reason of individuals to find their own path to the truth. Science and education are allies in this quest. Neither movement believes in sacraments, and miracles are viewed sceptically. Rites of passage are de-sacralized and tailored to the needs of the individual. They do not have a priesthood or academic theologians, though Unitarians have a trained ministry. Although they have no formal rituals, Unitarian services are usually well planned by the ministers, while Quaker worship, for all its informality, is governed by a set of unspoken norms regulating what is acceptable as Quakerly conduct. They are not actively conversionist movements, preferring instead to make themselves and their publications available to anyone who enquires. They are constituted democratically, giving considerable freedom to individual congregations but combining this with a bureaucratic structure at national and international levels, thereby retaining organizational coherence. The concept of membership is attenuated, so that it is unremarkable for Quakers and Unitarians to take part in services and activities organized by other denominations provided they are liberal and tolerant. Although rooted in Christianity, they are uncomfortable with assertions that any one faith possesses a monopoly of the truth.

Women have played leading roles in the history of the Society of Friends and the Unitarian Church, and this is important to the movements' self-image. Perhaps the most celebrated Quaker of all was the great nineteenth-century campaigner for penal reform, Elizabeth Fry. And arguably the greatest of all feminist tracts is *Vindication of the Rights of Women*, published in 1792 by Mary Wollstonecraft, a Unitarian. Quakers and Unitarians were prominent supporters of the women's suffragist movement. Unitarians began ordaining women to the ministry before the end of the nineteenth century; at the close of the twentieth, women make up approximately half the Unitarian ministers in the USA and one-third in the UK (Chryssides 1998: 112). Quakers, who have no professional ministry, are committed to equality of opportunity within the society.

The implication of all this is that both these religious movements have been pledged to the same objectives as the 'first wave' feminists of the suffragist movement. Suffragists campaigned not just for votes for women, but for full citizenship, equality before the law and equal opportunities in public life. What is less clear, however, is how well attuned either the Religious Society of Friends or the Unitarian Church could be to the demands of 'second wave' feminists, the so-called Women's Liberation Movement, which launched a broadside attack on patriarchy as institutionalized gender inequality endemic to culture and social structure (Whelehan 1995). Contemporary trends in feminism, centred around the politics of lifestyle and the deliberate transgression of conventional cultural boundaries, are likewise problematic for movements which have not shed their Puritan origins. Issues of lesbian and gay rights remain deeply divisive, as they are in mainstream churches torn between Christian love, liberal tolerance and moral condemnation. Yet Quakers and Unitarians are not bound by dogma. It is therefore an open question how far they can accommodate to contemporary cultural change.

The Baha'i faith, which arose in an Islamic context, shows some similarities to these two Christian movements. Baha'is advocate equality of women and men. They embrace science and education. They lack a professional priesthood and formal rituals. They are pacifists. Like Muslims, they are averse to other-worldly asceticism, and specifically forbid the monastic life. They give responsibility to local congregations within a worldwide administrative framework. They are opposed to racism, prejudice and superstition, and claim to be undogmatic.

Despite their progressive credentials it is even less clear than in the case of Quakers and Unitarians that Baha'is can respond to all the challenges brought by feminism. Although the Baha'i faith presents itself as non-doctrinaire it is shaped by divine revelation and divinely inspired authoritative scriptures. It has an authoritarian vein which makes western liberal members deeply uneasy (MacEoin 1997). It is, at root, a conversionist faith, one which engages in rationally planned missionary programmes in pursuit of its vision of a universalist religion uniting all humanity. It does not tolerate plural membership and does not take part in rainbow alliances with campaigning pressure groups. Its scriptures prescribe monogamous heterosexual marriage and oppose divorce. It also takes a conservative stance on abortion and euthanasia. Crucially, it has little warrant to amend these principles. As society changes, the Baha'is risk being left behind in a posture which will seem less and less progressive. In this respect it is probably not gender roles but sexuality which poses the sharper challenge to Baha'i culture.

Gender roles and the symbolic subordination of women

It is not difficult to trawl through the sacred scriptures, rituals and traditional practices of the world's great religions in order to produce abundant evidence of women's subordination to men. Controversy has focused on a number of symbolic cases: the exclusion of women from the priesthood in Catholic and Orthodox Christianity, and the opening of the priesthood to women in the Anglican communion; the veiling of women in some Islamic cultures; the strict gender division of ritual labour in Orthodox and Conservative Judaism; the strong preference for sons over daughters in Hinduism, the financially punitive dowry system which underpins it, the practice of *sati* (self-immolation by a virtuous Hindu widow on her husband's funeral pyre) and the crime of wife-burning in domestic 'accidents' arranged by men intent on marrying again to acquire another dowry.

Conflicts over these practices are marked by a dialectic between the three

Weberian principles of legitimate domination: charismatic, traditional and legal-rational authority. In religious disputes, legal-rational arguments are rarely sufficient by themselves because they are essentially secular. Hence the parties to any given dispute will try to harness charismatic and traditional authority in support of their position.

Consider the debate within the Church of England over the ordination of women to the priesthood (Aldridge 1992). The exclusion of women from priesthood prevented the church from drawing on a pool of talented women who, in secular terms, could obviously do the job at least as well as and often better than men. As the number of men coming forward with a vocation to priesthood declined, the church faced a manpower crisis which had an obvious solution – a situation now facing the Catholic church. However, as a sacred institution the church needed to legitimize any change in non-secular terms. Hence the theological cast to the debate. Opponents of the ordination of women included among their arguments the following. Jesus chose men to be his twelve apostles, and this is a sign that priesthood is open only to men. St Paul taught that women should remain silent in church, and that wives are subordinate to the authority of their husband. In sacramental functions the priest is an icon of Christ, and so has to be male since Jesus in his human aspect was a man. The western Catholic and eastern Orthodox churches have excluded women from the priesthood following the sacred ordinance of God; the Church of England, as one minor branch of Christianity, has no warrant to act unilaterally on a fundamental principle of doctrine and practice.

These propositions were countered by arguments which sought to contextualize the historic exclusion of women from the priesthood. It was pointed out that mainstream Christianity incorporates a doctrine of progressive revelation. The church's traditional practices are not fixed for all time but dynamic: the holy spirit acts in the world to bring the church to a realization of the fullness of faith. Abolition of slavery is an obvious precedent. The ministry of Jesus and the teachings of Paul have to be interpreted in their cultural context, and are not to be taken as signs valid for all eternity. Jesus did not carry his ministry to the Gentiles, even making the disturbing remark that this would be casting pearls before swine. The Christian church clearly cannot be bound by this. So too the symbolism of gender has changed, as has our scientific understanding of sexuality and reproduction. We know, as scholars in the Middle Ages did not, that in reproduction the woman is more than merely a passive breeding-ground for the man's 'seed'. As for Catholicism and Orthodoxy, perhaps Anglicanism's *raison d'être* is to give them a lead?

This debate between what might be called *traditionalists* and *modernizers* has many parallels in faiths other than Christianity. In each of these the core issue is the same. Traditionalists define culture as something separate from religion or faith. The faith as they present it is divinely ordained, unalterable and not to be contaminated by culture, which is a human creation. So Christian advocates of ordination of women to the priesthood, and Muslim opponents of the veiling of women, are accused of 'feminism' – a secular contagion. Modernizers, on the other hand, insist on the interpenetration of religion and culture: there is no such thing as a culture-free religion. In all the major religions of the world, practices vary enormously from one country and historical period to another. Modernizers argue that much of what passes as tradition is in fact recently invented. They also point out that traditionalists are highly selective in their account of the tradition, insisting on some points while overlooking others. For example, slavery and concubinage are permitted under Islamic *shari'a* law but have virtually disappeared in Muslim societies and certainly do not serve as a shibboleth of Islamic life in the way that the veiling of women has come to do (Ruthven 1997: 93–4). Modernizers within Islam often emphasize that some traditional practices, such as genital mutilation of young girls performed in some Muslim communities, have no justification in the Qur'an.

Given that for modernizers there is no such thing as culture-free religion, it follows that they hold the spirit of the law to be more important than its letter. In the case of Islam a good deal of attention has focused on the legal rights and disadvantages of women. In the Qur'an women are legally inferior to men. A woman's testimony in some court proceedings carries half the weight of a man's. Under Qur'anic laws of inheritance women receive half as much as their brothers. A man may marry up to four wives provided he can support them and treat them equally. He may marry a Christian, a Jew or a slave, whereas a Muslim woman cannot have more than one husband and he must be a Muslim. A man may beat his wife if all other methods of discipline have failed, but she must never strike him. Divorce is discouraged, but is far easier for a man to initiate.

Traditionalists argue that the Qur'an, and also the sayings and conduct of Muhammad himself, were more protective of women and gave them far greater legal rights than they had previously under the *jahilyya*, the pre-Islamic age of ignorance, or in other cultures of the period. They sometimes add that Christians should examine their own practice more critically. Against this, modernizers argue that the fact that the Qur'an and the Prophet were caring towards women shows that the same underlying principle should be applied in the changed conditions of the modern world. Their problem is to justify altering the letter of an unalterable law.

Reclaiming the symbols of subordination

In *Alone of All Her Sex*, a historical and cross-cultural survey of the cult of the Virgin Mary from a feminist perspective, Marina Warner (1978) argues that the cult is pathological. It holds up to women a manifestly unattainable ideal, a Virgin Mother who, unlike the rest of humanity, was immaculately conceived – that is, conceived without the taint of original sin. Following the teaching of St Augustine, the medieval church held that original sin was transmitted through the sex act, which inescapably involves sexual desire. Although it is no longer tied to this particular interpretation of original sin, Catholic thinking remains preoccupied with the conditions of conception. This is reflected not only in its prohibition of artificial contraception but also in its official hostility to *in vitro* fertilization, an 'unnatural' technique which necessarily requires masturbation.

According to Warner, the impact of the Mary cult is to induce in women a hopeless yearning and an ineradicable sense of inferiority to men. The myth reinforces itself, creating the very desires, fears and anxieties it purports to assuage. Brought up as a Catholic herself, Warner testifies that for years after she had abandoned her faith she had to fight against 'that old love's enduring power to move me' (M. Warner 1978: xxi).

While emphasizing the impact of the cult of the Virgin Mary on the psyche of the devout, Warner offers a sociological rather than psychological analysis of it. She has little time for Freudian interpretations, dismissing them as crudely reductionist, but she devotes some space to Jungian analyses. To Jungians, the Virgin is not pathological but a healthy expression of an archetype. An archetype involves a tendency for certain qualities and attributes to cluster together in the individual and collective unconscious. The Virgin expresses the mother archetype. Other examples of this archetype are the Hindu goddess Kali, the Greek goddess Demeter, the wicked witch and the stepmother. The mother archetype is composed of positive and negative attributes. Positively, the mother connotes femininity, magical power, caring, wisdom, helpfulness, fertility and sympathy. Negatively, the mother connotes secretiveness, darkness, seduction and devouring.

Warner argues that a Jungian approach to the cult of the Virgin Mary colludes with the objectives of the church's hierarchy. The Vatican, says Warner, proclaims that the concept of the Virgin Mother of God always existed, and Jungians proclaim that all men need a symbolic Virgin Mother. Perhaps the most striking illustration of the Jungian approach is Jung's own view of the Assumption. In 1950, the Pope proclaimed as an official doctrine of the Catholic Church what many Catholics had believed for centuries: that after her earthly life the Blessed Virgin Mary was assumed body and soul into heavenly glory. To Jung this was a momentous development. People had a deep psychological longing that Mary, as intercessor and mediator, should take her place as Queen of Heaven alongside God the Father, the Son and the Holy Spirit. The Trinity came to fulfilment as a Quaternity, as God in four persons – a wildly unorthodox view theologically, but one which for Jung expressed a profound psychological truth. If we take into account popular beliefs as well as official teachings about the Virgin, it is remarkable how many parallels there are between her sacred story and that of Jesus. Jesus's Virgin Birth is paralleled by Mary's Immaculate Conception; Jesus was Son of God, Mary has the title Mother of God; Jesus's Ascension is matched by Mary's Assumption; there is a tradition that Mary's tomb was empty, and early apocryphal texts attested that she too rose on the third day; the cult of Mary as Jesus's mother has its counterpart in the cult of Mary's mother, St Anne, which has been popular in Brittany; the Stations of the Cross are paralleled by the Rosary, and the Man of Sorrows has a *Mater Dolorosa*.

The collusion that Warner detects between Jungians and the Vatican goes deeper than Jung's idiosyncratic endorsement of popular elements of Mariology. Warner's fundamental point is that the cult of the Virgin collapses history into myth, nature into culture. A cult that has been shaped by the interests of the church's hierarchy is turned into something supposedly natural and eternal. Following Roland Barthes's (1972) theory of mythology, Warner argues that this is the basic transmutation wrought by ideology. In becoming natural, the cult of the Virgin is stripped of the interests which shaped and changed it over time. Through the operation of mythology, nothing seems more natural than 'this icon of feminine perfection, built on the equivalence between goodness, motherhood, purity, gentleness, and submission' (M. Warner 1978: 335).

Warner believes that the cult of Mary is a spent force incompatible with contemporary conditions. It will cease to be an active myth and become instead a sentimental legend like Robin Hood – an outcome which she clearly welcomes. Other feminists, such as Rosemary Radford Ruether (1979), have been concerned to 'reclaim' the historical Mary from the church hierarchy. Ruether agrees with Warner that the dominant view of Mary, within Protestantism as well as Catholicism, sees her as the passive recipient of the grace of a male God and his earthly representatives, the clergy. However, Ruether and other Christian feminists believe it possible to assert a different Mary, emphasizing her courage, her struggles and her radical credentials – her song of praise, the Magnificat, speaks of God's elevation of the poor and humbling of the mighty. The aim is to reclaim the woman Mary as a sister, freeing her from centuries of oppressive Mariology, much as in the nineteenth century there was a theological quest

for the historical Jesus, the real man concealed under the weight of theologically sophisticated Christology. Here is another parallel between the
careers of Jesus and his mother.

This same dilemma – to reject a symbol as oppressive, or to reclaim it –
presents itself to women in many faiths. The Mormon concept of a Mother
in Heaven is one example (Heeren et al. 1984). The LDS church interprets
it in a conservative way to legitimize patriarchy. The Mother in Heaven is
an idealized symbol of womanhood and motherhood, and she is subordinate to the Father. Mormon feminists have sought to use the concept to
boost women's self-respect, to vindicate the rights of Mormon women, and
to open up a space within Mormonism for feminist theology.

The veiling of women (*hijab*) in Islamic cultures has been interpreted as
a powerful symbol of patriarchy. To many westerners it is an icon of the
Otherness of Islam, as the *affaire des foulards* in France, the headscarf
affair discussed in chapter 6, makes very clear. At the time of writing, the
Taliban forces in Afghanistan are rigorously enforcing the most stringent
dress codes on women as one component of their policy to exclude women
from public life and encapsulate them in the domestic sphere.

Traditional Muslim dress, as so often with tradition, is a modern invention. It is legitimized as the dress worn by the Prophet's wives to conceal
their hair, their body and most of their face. The implication is that wom-
en's bodies are a strong temptation to men and thus potentially disruptive to
the social order. As Ruthven says (1997: 112–13), *hijab* has become a
shibboleth, a symbol through which a Muslim woman displays her religious and political allegiance. Its supporters say it is liberating, since it
frees the woman from the voyeuristic gaze of male *flâneurs*. Western feminists, in contrast, see the veil as an inherently oppressive symbol which
nullifies the individual and renders women invisible.

To speak of 'the veil' is in fact a gross oversimplification, as Watson
(1994) points out. There is a continuum of veiling from state-regulated
voluminous garments, through colourful peasant attire to fashionable de-
signer scarves worn by affluent women. Underlying each of these is the
symbolic aim not only of preserving the woman's modesty, but of maintaining the cosmologically significant boundary between the sexes.

Religion and New Age spirituality

New Age is a catch-all term for a rich variety of cultural phenomena.
Bainbridge (1997: 390) describes it as 'a cultural fog bank' surrounding
conventional religion. It is resistant to formal definition and formal organization. It can be seen as an amorphous 'cultic milieu' (Campbell

1972). In the terms discussed in chapter 3, New Age groups would be classified as cults, since they are deviant rather than respectable, and see themselves as pluralistically rather than uniquely legitimate. Some revel in their deviance, though it may be more symbolic than material. Luhrmann (1989: 340) points out that, despite the elements of the macabre and the morbid, witchcraft paradoxically provides an extremely safe environment in which its largely middle-class practitioners can indulge their fantasies. As for their sense of legitimacy, New Age groups are strikingly pluralistic. There is no problem in participating in a variety of groups and practices to suit the individual's needs. People who do this are seekers – a self-definition appropriate to the New Age. The concept of 'membership' simply does not apply: that is an authoritarian notion which New Agers attribute to organized religion.

It is mistaken to approach the New Age as if it were an internally consistent set of beliefs. Most belief-systems are less coherent than we like to imagine, as Luhrmann argues (1989: 307–23). In any case, her English witches were not totally absorbed by questions of belief, and rarely discussed them. The core of their involvement was magical practice. The sort of thing they argued about was not the theology of the Horned One but the interpretation of particular cards in the Tarot pack.

New Age groups constitute themselves as either audience cults or client cults, rather than as fully fledged cult movements (Stark and Bainbridge 1985: 26–9). Neither audience nor client cults make exacting demands on the people associated with them. *Audience cults* have only a minimal level of organization, and lack an authority structure through which commands could be issued. In any case, they have nobody to command: they do not have members but an audience of consumers. Audience cults spread their message mainly through the mass media. The New Age is heavily reliant on magazines and books, supplemented by audio cassettes and compact discs, and a loosely structured lecture circuit. *Client cults* are based on relationships between practitioners and their clients. Here too the level of formal organization is limited. Clients are individuals, not a community. In the past, as Stark and Bainbridge remark, client cults offered miraculous cures, clairvoyance and contact with departed spirits. In the New Age, the emphasis switches towards holistic therapy and healing.

The degree of engagement in the New Age obviously varies between people. Heelas (1996: 117–19) distinguishes three levels of commitment. The most deeply committed are those he calls *fully engaged*, people who have given over their lives to the spiritual quest. Some of them have abandoned conventional lifestyles in favour of the counterculture. They are often practitioners providing services to clients, or organizers of New Age events. A lesser degree of commitment is found among the *serious part-*

timers. Their New Age spirituality is compartmentalized as a part of their life, albeit a serious part. It does not prevent them from living conventional lives and pursuing conventional careers. The lowest level of commitment is found among the *casual part-timers*. These are the consumers. They are interested in exotic and esoteric things, but are wary of getting deeply involved. The New Age is fun, 'time out' from the stresses of humdrum living. Other aspects of their lives are typically more important than the New Age. Now, although statistical data are impossible to obtain, it seems clear from Heelas's extensive research that the fully engaged are a small minority. The New Age is largely peopled by serious and casual part-timers. It is this last group, and the consumerist values it embodies, which threatens the New Age from within. For Heelas, the authority of the consumer is incompatible with the authority of the transcendent. Religion cannot be consumed; if it is, it is no longer religion.

In many ways the New Age is not new at all. Similar elements flourished in the Victorian and Edwardian eras, when spiritualism and the occult were fashionable, and when there was a 'turn to the east' for spiritual enlightenment. An example is the Theosophical Society, founded in 1875 in New York by Madame Helena Petrovna Blavatsky and Colonel Henry S. Olcott (Wilson 1970: 157–9). Theosophy was an eclectic system of occult philosophy drawing particularly on Hinduism and Buddhism. It was energetically promoted in the twentieth century by Annie Besant, who identified a young Indian man, Krishnamurti, as messiah – a status he later disowned. Theosophy was a major influence on Anthroposophy, an esoteric system of beliefs and practices based on quasi-scientific principles adumbrated by Rudolf Steiner, now known above all for its philosophy of education.

The New Age claims a lineage stretching back well beyond Christianity to paganism, and drawing on the wisdom of ancient civilizations and native peoples untouched by Christian influence. This self-image is rarely endorsed by independent scholarship. Thus Luhrmann says, rather bluntly, that modern witchcraft was created in the 1940s by a civil servant, Gerald Gardner, who derived his vision from Margaret Murray's book, *Witchcult in Western Europe* (Luhrmann 1989: 42–4). According to Murray, witchcraft was an organized pre-Christian fertility cult, falsely branded as devil-worship by the medieval church. Witchcraft was a popular practice driven underground by persecution.

In the view of most scholars, Murray's account has no historical basis. The women who were burned as witches in the Middle Ages were not only innocent of the satanic abominations which the fantasies of the demonologists attributed to them, they were also guiltless of involvement in any magic, however harmless (Thomas 1971; Macfarlane 1970). Such scholarly scepticism cuts no ice with many New Agers, who are convinced they belong to a secret tradition hidden from official history. Others accept the scholarly version but, in postmodern spirit, could not care less. If this is an invented tradition, so what?

The New Age may be too elusive to define, but a number of salient themes within it can be identified. Superficially, these would appear to show that New Age thought is out of step with the ethos of western rationality.

Rejection of scientific methodology   Scientific investigation is predicated on hypothesis-formation, observation, experimentation, measurement, prediction, replication. Its spirit, if not always its practice, is detached, clinical and objective. Science proceeds by conjecture and refutation. Whole branches of knowledge are discarded as worthless, a fate which has befallen alchemy, astrology and phrenology. In contrast, New Age spirituality emphasizes subjectivity. Personal testimony that a technique or therapy works is definitive. If science cannot back it up, so much the worse for science, whose limitations are thereby exposed (Bruce 1996: 196–229; 1995: 103–23).

Questioning of professional expertise   Science is only one embodiment of abstract expert systems. The New Age calls into question all forms of professional expertise. Professionals are seen as having closed minds. They are wedded to western rationality and blind to the wisdom of ancient traditions. Worse still, they disempower their clients.

Rejection of organized religion   The term 'religion' sits uneasily with New Age thinking and practice. Organized religion as conventionally understood in the Judaeo-Christian tradition is rejected as authoritarian and spiritually arid. Luhrmann's study of witches in England (1989) found that what attracted them was the emotional and imaginative intensity of witchcraft. They could enjoy the solemnity of religion without its authority structures.

Perennialism   New Age thought appeals to ancient wisdom: paganism, witchcraft, the knowledge and spirituality of native peoples. According to Bruce (1995: 107) this is legitimization by tradition. The older the tradition the better. Legitimization by tradition is the converse of the scientific method, which perpetually destroys old knowledge in favour of the new. However, Bruce's interpretation is misleading, in that New Agers are averse to traditions, which bring with them authoritative creeds and moralities. In that sense New Agers are detraditionalizers. What they do is plunder the world's traditions for the hidden core, the ancient wisdom, the arcane and esoteric secrets. Distinctions between traditions are obliterated. Truth is perennial, surviving persecution and the clash of rival dogmata (Heelas 1996: 27–8). Perennialism is a radically different conception of history from the linear view of the Judaeo-Christian tradition and its secular counterpart, a belief in progress.

Holistic rejection of Cartesian dualism   The New Age embraces holistic philosophies which see the human being as an entity which cannot be separated into material and spiritual components. It utterly rejects the dualism of Cartesian philosophy. To Descartes, the mind and the body are separate, and it is the mind which is of the essence of humanity – as revealed in his great deduction, 'I think, therefore I am'. According to Descartes non-human animals do not think, but are simply mechanical automata.

Commitment to ecology   Whatever else they are, as Bruce (1996: 210–11; 1995: 108–9) remarks, New Agers are 'green'. Their commitment to ecology has two features which distinguish it from more conventional environmentalism. First, environmental problems are seen as bound up with personal problems. A fundamental transformation of personal values and human relationships is the key to living in harmony with the environment. Second, the earth is revered as Gaia, an animate organism which, like the elements within it, has rights.

Affirmation of feminine imagery   Among the reasons why New Agers are often lukewarm about organized religions is their treatment of women. In terms of symbolism, as numerous feminist commentators have observed, Christianity has tended to offer a choice between woman as saint and woman as whore, the humility of an inimitable Virgin Mother or the power of an evil seductress. In terms of career, Christian churches have offered women subordinate support roles, excluding them from professional ministry as the Catholic and Orthodox churches resolutely continue to do. The Anglican communion is gradually admitting women into the ministry, but they face constant reminders that their presence is causing a good deal of trouble and even threatening schism within the body of Christ. Many of the most successful new religious movements, such as Jehovah's Witnesses and the Mormons, are organized on firmly patriarchal lines with an all-male leadership. The New Age has rekindled interest in the Goddess principle, placing it in a feminist context. Women are also prominent among the fully engaged participants in the New Age. Within Christianity itself, it is significant that women have had leadership roles in gnostic movements offering a new esoteric interpretation of Christianity. In these, revelations have often been delivered to a woman: for example, Mother Ann Lee, founder of the Shakers; Ellen White, prophet of Seventh-day Adventism; and Mary Baker Eddy, founder of Christian Science.

Despite the apparent conflict between New Age thinking and western rationality, it can be argued that the continuity between the two is at least as significant as the divergence. This is shown in the growth of interest in alternative therapies and complementary medicine. Orthodox medical practitioners and their professional associations are losing the capacity to stigmatize as unscientific 'quackery' alternative therapies which attract ever larger numbers of clients, many of them from the professional classes. Levels of reported satisfaction with alternative therapies are typically high. Consumer organizations increasingly treat them seriously. Some forms of alternative practice are deeply rooted in and legitimized by minority ethnic communities – for example, Ayurvedic medicine, which serves the Asian community, and traditional Chinese medicine. In these cases it is not possible to separate out the 'religious' element in the therapy, even if religion is defined narrowly – which is difficult to do when dealing with Hinduism and Tao. Faith healing is an important element in alternative practice; integral to Pentecostalism, it has become more respectable in the Christian mainstream as a result of charismatic renewal. The growth of alternative medicine and its relocation in the cultural mainstream call into question narrow definitions of religion and science and sharp distinctions between them (Saks 1998).

As Heelas shows, few of the people associated with the New Age are fully engaged in it. The serious part-timers compartmentalize it as one part of their lives, while the casual part-timers treat it as little more than a set of experiences to be sampled or discarded at will. Since the New Age has no means of shaking off its free riders, it is likely to be undermined by them. Hence the medium-term future of the New Age may be absorption into the cultural mainstream as one attenuated and commodified stylistic option alongside all the others. The New Age can be commercialized, as the popularity of aromatherapy and the success of the Body Shop testify.

There is a double danger of overstating 'our' commitment to rationality and New Agers' repudiation of it. Commentators on the New Age recognize this. Heelas (1996: 115) speaks of *humanistic expressivism*, meaning a focus on the interior life, self-exploration and self-development. This is a powerful current in modern culture. What the New Age does is provide a radicalized version of humanistic expressivism, resting on spiritual rather than psychological foundations. We can imagine a spectrum, as Heelas says, moving from the secular to the spiritual, from Freudian psychoanalysis through Jungian analytic psychology and Rogerian therapy to New Age practices. Modern business corporations are not always the secular entities we take them to be. They have been known to employ the services of astrologers and graphologists, which is why they sometimes ask for hand-written letters of application and expect to see date of birth on a curriculum vitae. If it is a short step for the individual from self-development to self-actualization, so it is for the corporation, in which Human Resource Development is not incompatible with Transcendental Meditation.

The future of religion

The themes discussed in this chapter – consumer society, the challenge to religious authority, feminism and New Age religiosity – have often been interpreted as destructive of religion. Cultural fragmentation is seen as the inescapable result of secularization.

Against this, it is possible to see consumerism, feminism and the New Age as harbingers of new modes of religiosity demanding new definitions and frameworks of analysis. In Beckford's terms (1989: 170–2), religion has become not so much a social institution as a cultural resource. It still provides a set of potent symbols and a language through which ideals, emotions, suffering and aspirations can be articulated. Because religion has lost its firm institutional anchorage it is inherently less predictable and more controversial, and likely to be more and more in tension with the state and public policy. Communities of faith are themselves destabilized. Centres of religious authority such as the Vatican have the uncomfortable sense that they are losing their grip over the Catholic faithful despite their firm reassertion of traditional doctrine.

The sociology of religion is engaged in the process of developing the conceptual tools needed to analyse the dynamics of contemporary culture. One influential writer is Danièle Hervieu-Léger. In *La Religion pour Mémoire* she defines religion as: 'An ideological, practical and symbolic mechanism through which the individual and collective consciousness of belonging to a particular lineage of faith is constituted, maintained, developed and controlled' (Hervieu-Léger 1993: 119).

If religion is conceptualized in this way as concerned with the cultivation of memory, what then of the fear that the memory of religion is fading, at least in Europe? This was the point made by the Prayer Book Society in their distress at the erasure from English collective memory of the Book of Common Prayer – a process blamed largely on the clergy and church leaders. Turning to Davie's analysis of the British pattern of religiosity, which she aptly characterizes as 'believing without belonging' (Davie 1994: 93–

116), we may ask whether such a pattern can endure in the longer term. It may be that Britain is living off the cultural capital of its religious past, and failing to preserve anything to hand on to succeeding generations. Hervieu-Léger grapples with the fact that declining church attendance in France together with a strictly secular education system has left students of music, painting and literature ignorant of the fundamentals of Christian symbolism. How then can they begin to appreciate western art? Nothing less is at stake than the potential loss of our cultural heritage. On the other hand, thousands of young people turn out for papal visits, and the community at Taizé has fired the imagination of innumerable pilgrims. Collective amnesia may be a threat but is not yet a reality. The grassroots may rebel against it.

Is consumerism necessarily inimical to religion? Does it inevitably focus attention away from the past toward present gratification, thereby corroding the sense of a collective memory preserved through a lineage of faith? It seems difficult to deny that consumerist approaches have invaded the sacred realm. Contemporary culture does not merely *enable* people to make their own selections from a menu of items of belief (do-it-yourself, *bricolage*). People increasingly regard it as their *right* to pick and choose (Hervieu-Léger 1998: 215–18). Hence the well-documented collapse of Catholic adherence to the officially approved 'rhythm' method of birth control. For growing numbers of Catholic laypeople it has ceased to be a discipline they are willing to accept.

A cultural shift away from a conception of religion as a mandatory set of beliefs and practices incumbent upon all the faithful, towards the conviction that individuals have to choose for themselves their particular path to salvation, has taken place not simply on the periphery (in 'the cults') but in the mainstream of western cultures. Fewer and fewer of the faithful feel an obligation to pass on their faith to their children. Instead, they believe that children should make up their own minds without undue pressure from their parents. The transmission of religion from generation to generation is therefore becoming far more open and fluid.

It follows that people can legitimately choose between a variety of orientations to religious commitment. Hervieu-Léger distinguishes four basic dimensions of this. First, *the communal dimension*. This refers to the social and symbolic badges of belonging to a community, including undergoing an initiation (baptism, circumcision), wearing appropriate clothing (the *hijab*, the turban) and faithfully submitting oneself to the Jewish law or the five pillars of Islam. Second, *the ethical dimension*, which involves accepting the values of a particular tradition – a Christian 'bias to the poor', Quaker pacifism, Buddhist and Jain respect for all life-forms. Third, *the cultural dimension*, which encompasses the heritage of doctrines, texts, rituals, history, legends, art, cuisine and folkways – a community's cultural 'roots'. Fourth, *the emotional dimension*: intense experiences generated in religious assemblies, as emphasized in Durkheim's theory of religion.

The four dimensions interact with one another in dynamic combinations. Hervieu-Léger examines all the possible combinations of two dimensions, which yield six different types of religious identification. She illustrates each of these with specific reference to Christianity.

1 *Emotional Christianity* combines the emotional and communal dimensions. A strong feeling of communal belonging is generated, as in pilgrimages such as the biennial Worldwide Days of Youth involving a mass audience with the Pope.
2 *Patrimonial Christianity* combines the cultural and communal. People identify with the religious tradition as a cultural heritage marking 'us' off from 'them'. In France, this takes the form of linking Catholicism with French identity in an explicit rejection of multiculturalism.
3 *Humanitarian Christianity* combines the emotional and the ethical, in an orientation which seeks to address deprivation and injustice not through political activity but through social action – as in voluntary service overseas.
4 *Political Christianity* combines the communal and the ethical. In contrast to the humanitarian form, political Christianity adopts a militant conception of the role of the church in bringing about socio-political change, as in Catholic Student Youth.
5 *Humanist Christianity* combines the cultural and the ethical. It appeals particularly to intellectuals who possess high levels of cultural capital, which enables them to sit light to the church and to official doctrine while embracing selected aspects of Christianity as a value-system.
6 *Aesthetic Christianity* combines the cultural and the emotional. This involves appreciation of the aesthetic inheritance of Christianity: its music, literature, paintings and architecture. It frequently entails pilgrimage to the great sites of Christian memory.

The relationship between these six modes of identification with Christianity and the mainstream Christian churches is fluid and contestable. They can equally well support organized religion or subvert it. The church can choose to reject some of them. For example, Pope John Paul II has sought to delegitimize the political form of Christianity which emerged in Latin America as Liberation Theology. Similarly, humanistic Christianity is sometimes repudiated as atheism in disguise, a fate that regularly befalls liberal theologians and clerics. As for aesthetic Christianity, it can be dismissed as a form of up-market self-indulgent tourism. A striking feature of the modern condition is that many of those whom the church have sought to discipline or expel have persisted in asserting their right to orient to Christianity in their chosen fashion. This is consumerism, perhaps, but of a deeply serious kind.

European sociologists of religion have tended to join with other intellectuals in lamenting the loss of old cultural forms and in condemning the masses for their addiction to consumerism. None of this will of course make the slightest difference to the course of history. Perhaps it is time, with a new millennium, to abandon the mood of metaphysical pathos and participate in the creation of a new paradigm for the sociological study of religion, one which is more appreciative of the sufferings, aspirations and talents of 'ordinary' citizens.

There is no reason to expect that the twenty-first century will not see the rise of new modes of religiosity, which will demand new styles of analysis and new categories of thought. As a pre-eminently contemporary discipline, sociology has to address the situation in which it finds itself. Social and cultural change is not threatening to the sociology of religion, but a condition of its continued development.

Bibliography

Abercrombie, N., Hill, S. and Turner, B. S. 1980: *The Dominant Ideology Thesis*. London: Allen and Unwin.

Ahmed, A. S. and Donnan, H. (eds) 1994: *Islam, Globalization and Postmodernity*. London: Routledge.

Aldridge, A. E. 1986: Slaves to no sect: the Anglican clergy and liturgical change. *The Sociological Review*, 34 (2), 357–80.

Aldridge, A. E. 1987: In the absence of the minister: structures of subordination in the role of deaconess in the Church of England. *Sociology*, 21 (3), 377–92.

Aldridge, A. E. 1989: Men, women and clergymen: opinion and authority in a sacred organization. *The Sociological Review*, 37 (1), 43–64.

Aldridge, A. E. 1992: Discourse on women in the clerical profession: the diaconate and language-games in the Church of England. *Sociology*, 26 (1), 45–57.

Aldridge, A. E. 1994: The construction of rational consumption in *Which?* magazine: the more blobs the better? *Sociology*, 28 (4), 899–912.

Andreski, S. 1974: *The Essential Comte*. London: Croom Helm.

Anthony, D. and Robbins, T. 1997: Religious totalism, exemplary dualism, and the Waco Tragedy. In T. Robbins and S. J. Palmer (eds), *Millennium, Messiahs, and Mayhem: contemporary apocalyptic movements*. New York: Routledge, 261–84.

Argyle, M. and Beit-Hallahmi, B. 1997: *The Psychology of Religious Behaviour, Belief and Experience*. London: Routledge.

Aron, R. 1968: *Main Currents in Sociological Thought 1*. Harmondsworth: Penguin.

Aron, R. 1970: *Main Currents in Sociological Thought 2*. Harmondsworth: Penguin.

Bainbridge, W. S. 1997: *The Sociology of Social Movements*. New York: Routledge.

Bainbridge, W. S. and Stark, R. 1980: Scientology: to be perfectly clear. *Sociologi-*

cal Analysis, 41 (2), 128–36.

Barker, E. 1984a: *The Making of a Moonie: brainwashing or choice?* Oxford: Blackwell.

Barker, E. 1984b: With enemies like that . . . : some functions of deprogramming as an aid to sectarian membership. In D. G. Bromley and J. A. Richardson (eds), *The Brainwashing/Deprogramming Debate: sociological, psychological, legal and historical perspectives*. New York: Edwin Mellen Press.

Barker, E. 1993: Charismatization: the social production of 'an ethos propitious to the mobilization of sentiments'. In E. Barker, J. A. Beckford and K. Dobbelaere (eds), *Secularization, Rationalism and Sectarianism: essays in honour of Bryan R. Wilson*. Oxford: Clarendon Press, 181–201.

Barker, E. 1995: *New Religious Movements: a practical introduction*. London: HMSO.

Barr, J. 1977: *Fundamentalism*. London: SCM.

Barthes, R. 1972: *Mythologies*. London: Cape.

Beattie, J. 1964: *Other Cultures: aims, methods and achievements in social anthropology*. London: Routledge and Kegan Paul.

Beckford, J. A. 1975: *The Trumpet of Prophecy: a sociological study of Jehovah's Witnesses*. Oxford: Blackwell.

Beckford, J. A. 1978: Accounting for conversion. *British Journal of Sociology*, 29 (2), 249–62.

Beckford, J. A. 1985: *Cult Controversies: the societal response to new religious movements*. London: Tavistock.

Beckford, J. A. 1989: *Religion and Advanced Industrial Society*. London: Unwin Hyman.

Beckford, J. A. 1996: Postmodernity, high modernity and new modernity: three concepts in search of religion. In K. Flanagan and P. C. Jupp (eds), *Postmodernity, Sociology and Religion*. London: Routledge, 30–47.

Bellah, R. N. 1967: Civil religion in America. *Daedalus*, 96 (1), 1–21.

Bellah, R. N. 1990: Religion and legitimation in the American republic. In T. Robbins and D. Anthony (eds), *In Gods We Trust*. New Brunswick: Transaction Publishers, 411–26.

Bellah, R. N., Madsen, R., Sullivan, W. M., Swidler, A. and Tipton, S. M. 1996: *Habits of the Heart: individualism and commitment in American life*. Berkeley: University of California Press.

Bendix, R. and Roth, G. 1971: *Scholarship and Partisanship: essays on Max Weber*. Berkeley: University of California Press.

Berger, P. L. 1967: *The Sacred Canopy: elements of a sociological theory of religion*. New York: Doubleday.

Berger, P. L. 1971: *A Rumour of Angels: modern society and the rediscovery of the supernatural*. Harmondsworth: Penguin.

Berger, P. L. and Luckmann, T. 1966: *The Social Construction of Reality: a treatise in the sociology of knowledge*. New York: Doubleday.

Beyer, P. 1994: *Religion and Globalization*. London: Sage.

Binns, C. A. P. 1979: The changing face of power: revolution and accommodation in the development of the Soviet ceremonial system, Part 1. *Man*, 14, 585–606.

Binns, C. A. P. 1980: The changing face of power: revolution and accommodation in the development of the Soviet ceremonial system, Part 2. *Man*, 15, 170–87.

Blumler, J. G., Brown, J. R., Ewbank, A. J. and Nossiter, T. J. 1971: Attitudes to the monarchy: their structure and development during a ceremonial occasion. *Political Studies*, 19 (2), 149–71.

Bocock, R. 1993: *Consumption*. London: Routledge.

Bourdieu, P. 1984: *Distinction: a social critique of the judgement of taste*. London: Routledge and Kegan Paul.

Boyle, K. and Sheen, J. 1997: *Freedom of Religion and Belief: a world report*. London: Routledge.

Bromley, D. G. and Shupe, A. D. 1979: *'Moonies' in America: cult, church, and crusade*. Beverley Hills: Sage.

Bromley, D. G. and Shupe, A. D. 1980: The Tnevnoc Cult. *Sociological Analysis*, 40 (4), 361–6.

Bromley, D. G. and Shupe, A. D. 1981: *Strange Gods: the great American cult scare*. Boston: Beacon Press.

Bruce, S. 1986: *God Save Ulster: the religion and politics of Paisleyism*. Oxford: Clarendon Press.

Bruce, S. 1988: *The Rise and Fall of the New Christian Right: conservative Protestant politics in America 1978–1988*. Oxford: Clarendon Press.

Bruce, S. (ed.) 1992: *Religion and Modernization: sociologists and historians debate the secularization thesis*. Oxford: Clarendon Press.

Bruce, S. 1995: *Religion in Modern Britain*. Oxford: Oxford University Press.

Bruce, S. 1996: *Religion in the Modern World: from cathedrals to cults*. Oxford: Oxford University Press.

Budd, S. 1973: *Sociologists and Religion*. London: Collier-Macmillan.

Campbell, C. 1972: The cult, the cultic milieu and secularization. In M. Hill (ed.), *A Sociological Yearbook of Religion in Britain, volume 5*. London: SCM, 119–36.

Campbell, C. 1978: The secret religion of the educated classes. *Sociological Analysis*, 39 (2), 146–56.

Cannadine, D. 1983: The content, performance and meaning of ritual: the British monarchy and the 'invention of tradition'. In E. Hobsbawm and T. Ranger (eds), *The Invention of Tradition*. Cambridge: Cambridge University Press, 101–64.

Caporale, R. and Grumelli, A. (eds) 1971: *The Culture of Unbelief*. Berkeley: University of California Press.

Carey, S. 1987: The Indianization of the Hare Krishna movement. In R. Burghart (ed.), *Hinduism in Great Britain*. London: Tavistock, 81–99.

Chaves, M. 1997: *Ordaining Women: culture and conflict in religious organizations*. Cambridge, Mass.: Harvard University Press.

Chidester, D. n.d.: *Scientology: a religion in South Africa*. Los Angeles: Freedom Publishing.

Chryssides, G. 1998: *The Elements of Unitarianism*. Shaftesbury: Element.

Currie, R. 1968: *Methodism Divided: a study in the sociology of ecumenicalism*. London: Faber.

Davie, G. 1994: *Religion in Britain since 1945: believing without belonging*. Oxford: Blackwell.

Davie, G. 1996: Religion and modernity: the work of Danièle Hervieu-Léger. In K. Flanagan and P. C. Jupp (eds), *Postmodernity, Sociology and Religion*. London: Routledge, 101–17.

Davies, C. 1996: Coffee, tea and the ultra-Protestant and Jewish nature of the boundaries of Mormonism. In D. J. Davies (ed.), *Mormon Identities in Transition*. London: Cassell, 35–45.

Douglas, M. 1973: *Natural Symbols: explorations in cosmology*. Harmondsworth: Penguin.

Durkheim, E. 1915: *The Elementary Forms of the Religious Life*. London: Allen and Unwin.

Eldridge, J. E. T. 1980: *Recent British Sociology*. London: Macmillan.

Embry, J. L. 1994: *Black Saints in a White Church: contemporary African American Mormons*. Salt Lake City: Signature Books.

Evans-Pritchard, E. E. 1965: *Theories of Primitive Religion*. Oxford: Clarendon Press.

Festinger, L., Riecken, H. W. and Schachter, S. 1956: *When Prophecy Fails*. Minneapolis: University of Minnesota Press.

Finke, R. 1997: The consequences of religious competition: supply-side explanations for religious change. In L. A. Young (ed.), *Rational Choice Theory and Religion: summary and assessment*. New York: Routledge, 46–65.

Finke, R. and Stark, R. 1992: *The Churching of America 1776–1990: winners and losers in our religious economy*. New Brunswick: Rutgers University Press.

Flanagan, K. and Jupp, P. C. (eds) 1996: *Postmodernity, Sociology and Religion*. London: Routledge.

Geertz, C. 1968: Religion as a cultural system. In M. Banton (ed.), *Anthropological Approaches to the Study of Religion*. London: Tavistock, 1–46.

Gellner, E. 1992: *Postmodernism, Reason and Religion*. London: Routledge.

Giddens, A. 1991: *Modernity and Self-Identity: self and society in the late modern age*. Cambridge: Polity Press.

Gouldner, A. W. 1955: Metaphysical pathos and the theory of bureaucracy. *American Political Science Review*, 49, 496–507.

Gruberger, R. 1991: *A Social History of the Third Reich*. Harmondsworth: Penguin.

Habermas, J. 1973: *Legitimation Crisis*. Boston: Beacon Press.

Hall, J. R. and Schuyler, P. 1997: The mystical apocalypse of the Solar Temple. In T. Robbins and S. J. Palmer (eds), *Millennium, Messiahs, and Mayhem: contemporary apocalyptic movements*. New York: Routledge, 285–311.

Hamilton, M. B. 1995: *The Sociology of Religion: theoretical and comparative perspectives*. London: Routledge.

Hay, D. 1987: *Exploring Inner Space: scientists and religious experience*. London: Mowbray.

Heelas, P. 1994: The limits of consumption and the post-modern 'religion' of the New Age. In R. Keat, N. Whiteley and N. Abercrombie (eds), *The Authority of the Consumer*. London: Routledge, 102–15.

Heelas, P. 1996: *The New Age Movement: the celebration of self and the sacralization of modernity*. Oxford: Blackwell.

Heelas, P. (ed.) 1998: *Religion, Modernity and Postmodernity*. Oxford: Blackwell.

Heeren, J., Lindsey, D. B., Mason, M. 1984: The Mormon concept of Mother in Heaven: a sociological account of its origins and development. *Journal for the Scientific Study of Religion*, 23 (4), 396–411.

Heilman, S. C. and Friedman, M. 1991: Religious fundamentalism and religious Jews: the case of the haredim. In M. E. Marty and R. S. Appleby (eds), *Fundamentalism Observed*. Chicago: University of Chicago Press, 197–264.

Herberg, W. 1983: *Protestant – Catholic – Jew: an essay in American religious sociology*. Chicago: University of Chicago Press.

Hervieu-Léger, D. 1993: *La Religion pour Mémoire*. Paris: Cerf.

Hervieu-Léger, D. 1998: The transmission and formation of socioreligious identities in modernity: an analytical essay. *International Sociology*, 13 (2), 213–28.

Hill, C. 1975: *The World Turned Upside Down: radical ideas during the English Revolution*. Harmondsworth: Penguin.

Hill, M. 1973: *A Sociology of Religion*. London: Heinemann.

Hoover, S. M. and Lundby, K. (eds) 1997: *Rethinking Media, Religion, and Culture*. London: Sage.

Hornsby-Smith, M. P. 1987: *Roman Catholics in England: studies in social structure since the Second World War*. Cambridge: Cambridge University Press.

Hornsby-Smith, M. P. 1991: *Roman Catholic Beliefs in England: customary Catholicism and transformations of religious authority*. Cambridge: Cambridge University Press.

Hornsby-Smith, M. P. 1992: Recent transformations in English Catholicism: evidence of secularization? In S. Bruce (ed.), *Religion and Modernization: sociologists and historians debate the secularization thesis*. Oxford: Clarendon Press, 118–44.

Hutton, W. 1995: *The State We're In*. London: Cape.

Iannaccone, L. R. 1994: Why strict churches are strong. *American Journal of Sociology*, 99 (5), 1180–1211.

Iannaccone, L. R. 1997: Rational choice: framework for the scientific study of religion. In L. A. Young (ed.), *Rational Choice Theory and Religion: summary and assessment*. New York: Routledge, 25–45.

Jarman, N. 1997: *Material Conflicts: parades and visual displays in Northern Ireland*. Oxford: Berg.

Johnson, D. P. 1979: Dilemmas of charismatic leadership: the case of the People's Temple. *Sociological Analysis*, 40 (4), 315–23.

Jung, C. G. 1961: *Modern Man in Search of a Soul*. London: Routledge and Kegan Paul.

Kepel, G. 1994: *The Revenge of God: the resurgence of Islam, Christianity and Judaism in the Modern World*. Cambridge: Polity Press.

Kepel, G. 1997: *Allah in the West: Islamic Movements in America and Europe*. Cambridge: Polity Press.

Kim, A. E. 1993: The absence of pan-Canadian civil religion: plurality, duality, and conflict in symbols of Canadian culture. *Sociology of Religion*, 54 (3), 257–75.

Knott, K. 1998: *Hinduism: a very short introduction*. Oxford: Oxford University Press.

Lane, C. 1981: *The Rites of Rulers: ritual in industrial society – the Soviet case.* Cambridge: Cambridge University Press.

Lanternari, V. 1963: *The Religions of the Oppressed: a study of modern messianic cults.* New York: Alfred A. Knopf.

Lawson, R. 1997: The Apocalyptic fringe groups of Seventh-day Adventism. In T. Robbins and S. J. Palmer (eds), *Millennium, Messiahs, and Mayhem: contemporary apocalyptic movements.* New York: Routledge, 207–28.

Leach, E. R. 1968: Ritual. In D. L. Sills (ed), *International Encyclopedia of the Social Sciences.* New York: Macmillan and Free Press, vol. 13, 520–6.

Leach, E. R. 1969: Virgin Birth. In E. Leach (ed.), *Genesis as Myth and Other Essays.* London: Cape, 85–112.

Leach, E. R. 1982: *Social Anthropology.* London: Fontana.

Lenski, G. 1963: *The Religious Factor.* New York: Doubleday.

Lifton, R. J. 1961: *Thought Reform and the Psychology of Totalism: a study of 'brainwashing' in China.* New York: Norton.

Lofland, J. 1966: *Doomsday Cult.* Englewood Cliffs: Prentice-Hall.

Luckmann, T. 1967: *The Invisible Religion: the problem of religion in modern society.* London: Collier-Macmillan.

Luhrmann, T. 1989: *Persuasions of the Witch's Craft: ritual magic in contemporary England.* Oxford: Blackwell.

Lukes, S. 1973: *Emile Durkheim: his life and work.* London: Allen Lane.

Lukes, S. 1975: Political ritual and social integration. *Sociology,* 9 (2), 289–308.

MacEoin, D. 1997: Baha'ism. In J. R. Hinnells (ed.), *A New Handbook of Living Religions.* Harmondsworth: Penguin, 618–43.

Macfarlane, A. 1970: *Witchcraft in Tudor and Stuart England: a regional and comparative study.* London: Routledge and Kegan Paul.

Marshall, G. 1980: *Presbyteries and Profits: Calvinism and the development of capitalism in Scotland, 1560–1707.* Oxford: Clarendon Press.

Marshall, G. 1982: *In Search of the Spirit of Capitalism: an essay on Max Weber's Protestant Ethic Thesis.* London: Hutchinson.

Martin, D. A. 1965: Towards eliminating the concept of secularization. In J. Gould (ed.), *The Penguin Survey of the Social Sciences, 1965.* Harmondsworth: Penguin.

Martin, D. A. 1978: *A General Theory of Secularization.* Oxford: Blackwell.

Martin, D. A. 1991: The secularization issue: prospect and retrospect. *British Journal of Sociology,* 42 (3), 465–74.

Martin, D. A. and Mullen, P. (eds) 1981: *No Alternative: the Prayer Book controversy.* Oxford: Blackwell.

Mauss, A. L. 1994: Refuge and retrenchment: the Mormon quest for identity. In M. Cornwall and T. B. Heaton (eds), *Contemporary Mormonism: social science perspectives.* Urbana and Chicago: University of Illinois Press, 24–42.

Mauss, A. L. 1996: Identity and boundary maintenance: international prospects for Mormonism at the dawn of the twenty-first century. In D. J. Davies (ed.), *Mormon Identities in Transition.* London: Cassell, 9–19.

McGuire, M. B. 1992: *Religion: the Social Context.* Belmont: Wadsworth.

McLellan, D. 1973: *Karl Marx: his life and thought.* London: Macmillan.

McLellan, D. 1987: *Marxism and Religion: a description and assessment of the Marxist critique of Christianity*. London: Macmillan.

McSweeney, B. 1980: *Roman Catholicism: the search for relevance*. Oxford: Blackwell.

Mellor, P. A. and Shilling, C. 1993: Modernity, self-identity and the sequestration of death. *Sociology*, 27 (3), 411–31.

Melton, J. G. 1992: *Encyclopedic Handbook of Cults in America*. New York: Garland Publishing.

Miller, D. 1998: *A Theory of Shopping*. Cambridge: Polity Press.

Modood, T. (ed.) 1997: *Church, State and Religious Minorities*. London: Policy Studies Institute.

Mullins, M. 1997: Aum Shinrikyo as an apocalyptic movement. In T. Robbins and S. J. Palmer (eds), *Millennium, Messiahs, and Mayhem: contemporary apocalyptic movements*. New York: Routledge, 313–24.

Niebuhr, H. R. 1957: *The Social Sources of Denominationalism*. New York: Meridian.

Nisbet, R. A. 1967: *The Sociological Tradition*. London: Heinemann.

O'Dea, T. F. 1957: *The Mormons*. Chicago: University of Chicago Press.

O'Dea, T. F. 1966: *The Sociology of Religion*. Englewood Cliffs: Prentice-Hall.

Olson, M. 1965: *The Logic of Collective Action*. Cambridge, Mass.: Harvard University Press.

Packard, V. 1957: *The Hidden Persuaders*. London: Longman.

Parkin, F. 1982: *Max Weber*. Chichester: Ellis Horwood. London: Tavistock.

Parkin, F. 1992: *Durkheim*. Oxford: Oxford University Press.

Parsons, T. 1960: Some comments on the pattern of religious organization in the United States. In T. Parsons, *Structure and Process in Modern Societies*, New York: Free Press, 295–321.

Parsons, T. 1967: Christianity and modern industrial society. In T. Parsons, *Sociological Theory and Modern Society*, New York: Free Press, 385–421.

Parsons, T. 1977: *The Evolution of Societies*. Englewood Cliffs: Prentice-Hall.

Parsons, T. 1991: *The Social System*. London: Routledge.

Penton, M. J. 1985: *Apocalypse Delayed: the story of Jehovah's Witnesses*. Toronto: University of Toronto Press.

Perry, N. and Echeverria, L. 1988: *Under the Heel of Mary*. London: Routledge and Kegan Paul.

Pickering, W. S. F. 1989: *Anglo-Catholicism*. London: Routledge and Kegan Paul.

Popper, K. R. 1957: *The Poverty of Historicism*. London: Routledge and Kegan Paul.

Popper, K. R. 1963: *Conjectures and Refutations: the growth of scientific knowledge*. London: Routledge and Kegan Paul.

Punshon, J. 1984: *Portrait in Grey: a short history of the Quakers*. London: Quaker Home Service.

Ranson, S., Bryman, A. and Hinings, B. 1977: *Clergy, Ministers and Priests*. London: Routledge and Kegan Paul.

Rieff, P. 1965: *Freud: the mind of the moralist*. London: Methuen.

Riesman, D. 1969: *The Lonely Crowd: a study of the changing American character*. New Haven: Yale University Press.

Robbins, T. 1988: *Cults, Converts and Charisma: the sociology of new religious movements.* London: New York.

Robbins, T. and Anthony, D. (eds) 1990: *In Gods We Trust.* New Brunswick: Transaction Publishers.

Robbins, T. and Palmer, S. J. 1997: Patterns of contemporary apocalypticism in North America. In T. Robbins and S. J. Palmer (eds), *Millennium, Messiahs, and Mayhem: contemporary apocalyptic movements.* New York: Routledge, 1–27.

Robertson, R. 1970: *The Sociological Interpretation of Religion.* Oxford: Blackwell.

Robertson, R. 1991: The central significance of 'religion' in social theory: Parsons as an epical theorist. In R. Robertson and B. S. Turner (eds), *Talcott Parsons: theorist of modernity.* London: Sage.

Robertson, R. 1993: Community, society, globality, and the category of religion. In E. Barker, J. A. Beckford and K. Dobbelaere (eds), *Secularization, Rationalism and Sectarianism: essays in honour of Bryan R. Wilson.* Oxford: Clarendon Press, 1–17.

Ruane, J. and Todd, J. 1996: *The Dynamics of Conflict in Northern Ireland: power, conflict and emancipation.* Cambridge: Cambridge University Press.

Ruether, R. R. 1979: *Mary – the Feminine Face of the Church.* London: SCM.

Ruthven, M. 1991: *A Satanic Affair: Salman Rushdie and the Wrath of Islam.* London: Hogarth Press.

Ruthven, M. 1997: *Islam: a very short introduction.* Oxford: Oxford University Press.

Said, E. W. 1978: *Orientalism.* London: Routledge and Kegan Paul.

Saks, M. 1998: Beyond the frontiers of science? Religious aspects of alternative medicine. In J. R. Hinnells and R. Porter (eds), *Religion, Health and Suffering.* London: Routledge, 381–98.

Sargant, W. 1957: *Battle for the Mind.* London: Heinemann.

Schama, S. 1989: *Citizens: a chronicle of the French Revolution.* London: Viking.

Scharf, B. R. 1970: *The Sociological Study of Religion.* London: Hutchinson.

Scott, A. 1990: *Ideology and the New Social Movements.* London: Unwin Hyman.

Sharot, S. 1992: Religious fundamentalism: neo-traditionalism in modern societies. In B. R. Wilson (ed.), *Religion: contemporary issues.* London: Bellew, 24–45.

Shils, E. 1965: Charisma, order, and status. *American Sociological Review*, 30 (2), 199–213.

Shils, E. and Young, M. 1953. The meaning of the Coronation. *The Sociological Review*, 1 (2), 63–82.

Shupe, A. D. and Bromley, D. G. 1980: *The New Vigilantes: deprogrammers, anti-cultists, and the new religions.* Beverley Hills: Sage.

Slater, D. 1997: *Consumer Culture and Modernity.* Cambridge: Polity Press.

Smart, N. 1971: *The Religious Experience of Mankind.* London: Fontana.

Smith, P. 1987: *The Babi and Baha'i Religions: from messianic Shi'ism to a world religion.* Cambridge: Cambridge University Press.

Sommerville, C. J. 1992: *The Secularization of Early Modern England: from religious culture to religious faith.* New York: Oxford University Press.

Sorokin, P. A. 1937–41: *Social and Cultural Dynamics.* 4 vols. New York: American Book Company.

Sorokin, P. A. 1947: *Society, Culture and Personality: their structure and dynamics, a system of general sociology.* New York: Harper.

Spiro, M. E. 1966: Religion: problems of definition and explanation. In M. Banton (ed.), *Anthropological Approaches to the Study of Religion.* London: Tavistock, 85–126.

Stark, R. 1990: Modernization, secularization, and Mormon success. In T. Robbins and D. Anthony (eds), *In Gods We Trust.* New Brunswick: Transaction Publishers, 201–18.

Stark, R. 1997: Bringing theory back in. In L. A. Young (ed.), *Rational Choice Theory and Religion: summary and assessment.* New York: Routledge, 3–23.

Stark, R. 1998: The basis of Mormon success: a theoretical application. In J. T. Duke (ed.), *Latter-day Saint Social Life: social research on the LDS Church and its members.* Provo: Brigham Young University, 29–70.

Stark, R. and Bainbridge, W. S. 1985: *The Future of Religion: secularization, revival and cult formation.* Berkeley: University of California Press.

Stark, R. and Bainbridge, W. S. 1987: *A Theory of Religion.* New Brunswick: Rutgers University Press.

Stark, R. and Iannaccone, L. R. 1997: Why the Jehovah's Witnesses grow so rapidly: a theoretical application. *Journal of Contemporary Religion,* 12 (2), 133–57.

Thomas, K. 1971: *Religion and the Decline of Magic: studies in popular beliefs in sixteenth- and seventeenth-century England.* London: Weidenfeld and Nicolson.

Thompson, K. 1976: *Auguste Comte: the foundation of sociology.* London: Nelson.

Thompson, K. 1982: *Emile Durkheim.* London: Routledge.

Tocqueville, A. de 1945: *Democracy in America.* New York: Alfred A. Knopf.

Towler, R. 1974: *Homo Religiosus: sociological problems in the study of religion.* London: Constable.

Towler, R. and Coxon, A. P. M. 1979: *The Fate of the Anglican Clergy.* London: Macmillan.

Troeltsch, E. 1931: *The Social Teaching of the Christian Churches.* 2 vols. London: Allen and Unwin.

Turner, B. S. 1991: *Religion and Social Theory.* London: Sage.

Verba, S. 1965: The Kennedy assassination and the nature of political commitment. In B. S. Greenberg and E. B. Parker (eds), *The Kennedy Assassination and the American Public: social communication in crisis.* Stanford: Stanford University Press, 348–60.

Wach, J. 1944: *The Sociology of Religion.* Chicago: University of Chicago Press.

Wallis, R. (ed.) 1975: *Sectarianism: analyses of religious and non-religious sects.* London: Peter Owen.

Wallis, R. 1976: *The Road to Total Freedom: a sociological analysis of Scientology.* London: Heinemann.

Wallis, R. 1984: *The Elementary Forms of the New Religious Life.* London: Routledge and Kegan Paul.

Wallis, R. and Bruce, S. 1992: Secularization: the orthodox model. In S. Bruce (ed.), *Religion and Modernization: sociologists and historians debate the secularization thesis*. Oxford: Clarendon Press, 8–30.

Warner, M. 1978: *Alone of All Her Sex: the myth and cult of the Virgin Mary*. London: Quartet.

Warner, R. S. 1993: Work in progress toward a new paradigm for the sociological study of religion in the United States. *American Journal of Sociology*, 98 (5), 1044–93.

Warner, W. L. 1959: *The Living and the Dead: a study of the symbolic life of Americans*. Chicago/New Haven: Yale University Press.

Warner, W. L. 1962: *American Life: dream and reality*. Chicago: University of Chicago Press.

Watson, H. 1994: Women and the veil: personal responses to global process. In A. S. Ahmed and H. Donnan (eds), *Islam, Globalization and Postmodernity*. London: Routledge, 141–59.

Weber, M. 1930: *The Protestant Ethic and the Spirit of Capitalism*. London: Allen and Unwin.

Weber, M. 1952: *Ancient Judaism*. New York: Free Press.

Weber, M. 1965: *The Sociology of Religion*. London: Methuen.

Wessinger, C. 1997: Millennialism with and without the mayhem. In T. Robbins and S. J. Palmer (eds), *Millennium, Messiahs, and Mayhem: contemporary apocalyptic movements*. New York: Routledge, 47–59.

Whelehan, I. 1995: *Modern Feminist Thought: from the second wave to 'post-feminism'*. Edinburgh: Edinburgh University Press.

Willaime, J.-P. 1995: *Sociologie des Religions*. Paris: Presses Universitaires de France.

Wilson, B. R. 1966: *Religion in Secular Society: a sociological comment*. London: Watts.

Wilson, B. R. 1970: *Religious Sects: a sociological study*. London: Weidenfeld and Nicolson.

Wilson, B. R. 1975: *The Noble Savages: the primitive origins of charisma and its contemporary survival*. Berkeley: University of California Press.

Wilson, B. R. 1976: *Contemporary Transformations of Religion*. Oxford: Clarendon Press.

Wilson, B. R. 1981: Time, generations, and sectarianism. In B. R. Wilson (ed.), *The Social Impact of New Religious Movements*. New York: Rose of Sharon Press, 217–34.

Wilson B. R. 1982: *Religion in Sociological Perspective*. Oxford: Oxford University Press.

Wilson, B. R. 1990: *The Social Dimensions of Sectarianism*. Oxford: Oxford University Press.

Wilson, B. R. 1992: Reflections on a many sided controversy. In S. Bruce (ed.), *Religion and Modernization: sociologists and historians debate the secularization thesis*. Oxford: Clarendon Press, 195–210.

Wilson, B. R. and Dobbelaere, K. 1994: *A Time to Chant: the Soka Gakkai Buddhists in Britain*. Oxford: Clarendon Press.

Wittgenstein, L. 1958: *Philosophical Investigations*. 2nd edn. Oxford: Blackwell.

Yinger, J. M. 1970: *The Scientific Study of Religion*. London: Routledge.

Young, M. and Willmott, P. 1957: *Family and Kinship in East London*. London: Routledge and Kegan Paul.

Zeitlin, I. M. 1984: *Ancient Judaism: biblical criticism from Max Weber to the present*. Cambridge: Polity Press.

Index